T0179139

Creating Second Lives

Routledge Studies in New Media and Cyberculture

Creating Second Lives

Community, Identity and Spatiality
as Constructions of the Virtual

Edited by Astrid Ensslin
and Eben Muse

Routledge
Taylor & Francis Group
New York   London

First published 2011
by Routledge
711 Third Avenue, New York, NY 10017

Simultaneously published in the UK
by Routledge
2 Park Square, Milton Park, Abingdon, Oxon OX14 4RN

Routledge is an imprint of the Taylor & Francis Group, an informa business

Typeset in Sabon by IBT Global.

Library of Congress Cataloging-in-Publication Data
Creating second lives : community, identity, and spatiality as constructions of the virtual /
    edited by Astrid Ensslin and Eben Muse.
    p. cm. — (Routledge studies in new media and cyberculture ; 8)
    Includes bibliographical references and index.
    1. Human-computer interaction. 2. Virtual reality. 3. Online social networks.
4. Online identities. 5. Second Life (Game)—Social aspects. 6. Avatars (Computer graphics) I. Ensslin, Astrid. II. Muse, Eben J.
    QA76.9.H85C74 2011
    006.8—dc22
    2011011905

ISBN13: 978-0-415-88420-4 (hbk)
ISBN13: 978-0-203-82857-1 (ebk)

Contents

PART III
Creating Second Spaces

Figures and Tables

FIGURES

TABLES

Acknowledgements

The editors would like to thank a number of people, without whose support this book project would not have been possible: not least, Atik Baborie, Eirian Jones Muse, and Stephanie Marriott. We are also especially grateful to Erica Wetter and Liz Levine at Routledge for their consistent help throughout the entire process of planning and production, as well as Eleanor Chan at IBT Global for her meticulous proof reading.

This volume was inspired by the conference, 'Creating Second Lives: Reading and Writing Virtual Communities', held in October 2008 at Bangor University. We are particularly grateful to our sponsors, The Game Creators and Technium CAST, and our tireless conference officers, Simon Holloway, Sonia Fizek, and Jack Green.

Finally, the editors and authors would like to express their gratitude to those individuals and organizations who gave permission to reproduce various items in individual chapters, and to Linden Lab, Blizzard Entertainment, and MindArk, for providing virtual environments within which to research, record, and document 'Second Life' creativity, communities, identities, and spatiality.

Introduction

Astrid Ensslin and Eben Muse

Virtual worlds, ludic and non-ludic alike, have become an indispensable element of mediated reality in digitally enabled societies.[1] Regardless of ethnic and social background, age, or gender, millions of Internet users now inhabit a wide range of online environments.[2] Some of them spend a significant percentage of their work and leisure hours performing 'Second Lives', be those in the roles of creative designers, educators, students, researchers, business people, event organizers, tourists, shoppers, or simply vagrants.[3] Whereas some prefer the 'virtually' limitless behavioral possibilities offered by popular social and creative environments such as *Second Life*™ (Linden Lab 2003–10), others spend much if not most of their waking hours in highly rule-governed massively multiplayer online role-playing games (MMORPGs) such as *World of Warcraft* (Blizzard Entertainment 2004–10). Clearly, however, the social and communicative impact exerted by and through interaction with online environments is such that academic scholarship has finally jumped on the bandwagon. Conferences on *Second Life* (*SL*) and online/offline gaming abound, and both undergraduate and postgraduate curricula have started becoming informed by virtual world and online gaming research. This book is a product of such scholarly engagement in that most of its contributions are based on papers given at 'Creating Second Lives', an interdisciplinary, international conference held at the National Institute for Excellence in the Creative Industries, Bangor University, Wales (UK), in October 2008. 'Most' is not 'all', however, and rather than considering this book as a straightforward proceedings volume, readers are advised to see it as a partly commissioned and hence thematically coherent investigation of the textual and discursive implications of virtual communities.

Digital humanities and social sciences research since the early 1990s has provided fruitful insights into the economic, personal, and social implications of virtual communities as an epiphenomenon of the digital revolution (e.g., Rheingold 1991, 2000; Turkle 1995; Stone 1991; Plant 1995, 1997; Schroeder 1996, 2002; Taylor 2002; Woolley 1992; Massumi 2002; Smith and Kollock 1999). Specific literature on individual blockbuster phenomena such as *Second Life* and *World of Warcraft* has emerged more recently in the wake of the popularization of those highly frequented environments. To begin with, book-length publications on *Second Life* comprised primarily guidebooks, extensive user manuals (e.g., Rymaszewski et al. 2007; Carr and Pond 2007; Tapley 2008; Weber et al. 2008), and autobiographical, quasi-journalistic narratives about personal experiences and media reportage (e.g., Guest 2007; Meadows 2008). More recently, the foundation of dedicated academic journals such as *Journal of Gaming and Virtual Worlds* and *Journal of Virtual Worlds Research* has opened up platforms for systematic, field-defining scholarly and scientific debate. Perhaps the most academic and empirically rigorous exploration of *Second Life* to date is Tom Boellstorff's anthropological study, *Coming of Age in Second Life* (2008), and the present volume places itself in the context and footsteps of his exemplar not least because it appears to pioneer a second wave of critical engagement, which is marked by methodological distinctiveness and commitment. Simultaneously, led by scholars such as Edward Castronova (2005, 2007), Celia Pearce (2006a, 2006b, 2007), and T. L. Taylor (2006a, 2006b), virtual 'communities of *play*' (emphasis ours) have entered academic debate surrounding virtual worlds, and those chapters in this book that take into account the social and discursive features of *ludic* virtual worlds seek to contribute to the ongoing debate surrounding issues of 'digital culture, play and identity' (Corneliussen and Rettberg 2008).

Rather than following either a generalist or an exclusivist route, this book aims to provide an insight into how 'Second Lives' in the sense of virtual identities and communities are constructed textually. In so doing, we adopt Barthes's (1975) comprehensive concept of 'text', which comprises written as well as multimodal and other semiotic artifacts. Although the various contributors to this book are mostly dealing with 3D environments, thus focusing mostly on visual representations, we don't consider 'creating Second Lives' in the context of *graphical* online worlds only. 'Creating' involves variants of 'reading' *and* 'writing' in the sense of decoding and encoding (cf. Hall 1974), using a wide range of representational modes and sensory channels. Thus, reading involves the reception of visual information across various semiotic systems, which includes verbal as well as pictorial modes. Similarly, 'writing' here serves as a hypernym subsuming a multitude of productive communicative activities such as scripting, painting, drafting, encoding, drawing, and composing.

Put in a different way, we accept and embrace the fact that 'visual culture', a contemporary buzz-word that seems to capture J. David Bolter's (2001) concept of 'reverse ekphrasis'[4] in terms of disciplinary dimensions, comprises picto-, photo-, and cinematographic as well as 'written' in the sense of symbolically rather than iconically encoded language (cf. Peirce in Selden 1985). As laid out by reader-response critics (Jauss 1982; Iser 1971, 1978; Fish 1980), text construction is a communicative act and therefore always a joint venture, shared by authors and readers, programmers and user-players. The depersonalizing effect evoked by the agent-free gerund of 'creat-ing' in the title of this book is therefore a deliberate indicator of the debate surrounding agency in discourse formation (cf. Burgess's chapter, this volume). In creative environments such as *Second Life*, such shared creativity surfaces particularly strongly in the observation that residents typically co-create their shared territory by designing and constructing personal habitats from given elementary building blocks, or 'prims', thereby expressing identities as well as providing spaces for avatar interaction. At the same time, however, co-creating always perpetuates and thereby reconfirms ideologies imposed by corporate neo-capitalist structures such as, in the case of *SL*, those followed by Linden Lab.

The plural form 'Second Lives' in the title of this book is not only a reference to Tim Guest's (2007) revealing *Second Life* travelogue. It also hints at the fact that alternative identities and behaviors are enacted and negotiated in a wide range of virtual ontologies (systems of being). Such ontologies include not only online virtual social worlds (OVSW), as Kevin Sherman (this volume) calls web-based, 3D-graphical, non-ludic virtual communities such as *Second Life*, *Entropia Universe* (MindArk 2003–10), *There* (Makena Technologies 2003–10), *Moove online* (Moove 2001–10), *Active Worlds* (Active Worlds, Inc. 1997–2010), and *Kaneva* (Kaneva, Inc. 2004–10), but also ludic environments such as video games and MMORPGs. Indeed, as Isamar Carrillo Masso tells us in her chapter on the verbal and pictorial construction of female characters in computer games,[5] the idea of 'creating' in the sense of 'encoding', or 'writing' identities and communities reaches beyond user-generated avatars. Far more poignant is the mixture between identities and communities inscribed in online gaming interfaces and the corporate ideologies lurking behind them, on the one hand, and the resulting verbal and non-verbal behavior enacted in-world and, paratextually,[6] in online discussion channels, on the other.

The term 'Second Lives' also requires an engagement with the distinctions between the concepts of the virtual, the actual, and the real. Milgram and Calquhoun (1999) posited a continuum of experience between the real and the virtual, and mapped that against how thoroughly the technology had mapped reality; however, as Paul Sermon illustrates in his art installation *Liberate your Avatar* (cf. Sermon and Gould, this volume), reality is now mapping the virtual. Ubiquitous computing in the concrete world (Greenfield and Shute 2009; Bell and Dourish 2006; Weiser 1999) must now compete with ubiquitous reality in the virtual world. 'The distinction between "real" and "virtual"', as Usman Haqu says, 'is becoming as quaint as the 19th century distinction between "mind" and "body"' (quoted in Fong 2008). Discussions of 'imagined communities' (cf. Sherman, this volume), gender identity of avatars (cf. Fizek and Wasilewska, this volume), or even space and geography (cf. Muse, this volume) can be understood only in a phenomenology that avoids reliance on such distinctions as reality, virtual reality, augmented reality, or virtuality (Schnabel et al. 2008) in favor of dynamic relationships between actualizations and virtualities (Deleuze 1981; Lefebvre 1992; Levy 1998), the ideal and the actual, the real and the possible (Shields 2003). After all, the virtual can be considered that element of the real that is not actual (Deleuze 1981). Put differently, what is commonly referred to as 'real' is, in our understanding, a hybrid and fluid mixture of First Life actuality and Second Life virtuality (whereby both 'Lives' are pluralistic concepts).

The contributions to this volume are multi-disciplinary and explore the question of how we as gamers and residents of virtual worlds construct alternative online realities in a variety of ways. The contributors' disciplinary backgrounds include media, communication, cultural, and literary studies, and they examine issues of reception and production, identity, community, gender, spatiality, natural and built environments using a plethora of methodological approaches ranging from theoretical and philosophical contemplation through social semiotics to corpus-based discourse analysis.

The book is divided into three parts. Part I, 'Creating Second Communities', serves as an introduction to essential concepts underlying the idea behind this project. Chapter 1, '*Liberate your Avatar:* The Revolution Will Be Socially Networked' by Paul Sermon and Charlotte Gould, uses mixed-reality installations in the form of encounters between Second Life and First Life to bridge the space between these worlds. Their work extends the technical metaphor which originated in the eighties with installations such as Galloway and Rabinowitz's (1980) *Hole-In-Space* and explores the merging of activity and community within Second Life and First Life social spaces, including parks and shopping malls. Their installations provide visual backdrops and practical examples for an underlying discourse between the disembodied participant and (re-)embodied avatar.

Focusing on the first two aspects of this book's subtitle, Chapter 2, 'An Imagined Community of Avatars?', by Kevin Sherman provides a theoretical investigation of *Second Life* as nation through the lens of Benedict Anderson's *Imagined Communities*. Through the application of Anderson's (1991) construct of nationhood as expressed in his eponymous study on the 'origins and spread of nationalism', Sherman examines aspects of SL in order to interrogate the novel concept of virtual world nationhood from the perspective of the individual. His interrogation relies upon several Andersonian conceptions including nation as imagined community, nation imagined as limited and as sovereign, as well as the historical issues surrounding the notion of actual world nationhood. Ultimately, Sherman argues, such an interrogation offers an analysis of the notion of the virtual world nation while simultaneously casting new light on its actual world counterpart.

Taking creation in the sense of 'reading and writing' as its starting point, Chapter 3, 'Programming Processes: Controlling Second Lives', by Elizabeth Burgess explores essential questions of authorship, control, and agency. Burgess approaches these questions via interdisciplinary debate, particularly theories of reading and theories of play, existing conventions of textual interaction, and a consideration of roles played in the production of interactive texts (such as authors, programmers, designers, and editors).

She argues that these factors contribute to a programming of both the user and the text: a set of rules or codes which determine a user's behavior in, and interaction with, virtual spaces. She brings together a range of cross-disciplinary debates, and begins to identify current and future implications for interactivity, autonomy, and the construction of Second Lives.

Having thus laid the foundations of this book's approach to analyzing virtual communities, its remaining two parts focus on the creation of 'Second Lives' in a dual sense. To 'live' in virtual worlds, users typically create and use digital representations of themselves, also called avatars, or characters. The contributors to Part II, 'Creating Second Identities' (Chapters 4 to 6) explore the gendered and (re-)embodied nature of these avatars across a range of digital platforms, as well as the meta-discourse that contributes to their construction paratextually. By the same token, 'Second Lives' can be created only given certain spatial prerequisites. For this reason, Part III of this book is entitled 'Creating Second Spaces' and deals with the construction of avatar habitats as well as the needs that give rise to them.

Part II begins with Sonia Fizek and Monika Wasilewska's exploration of gender and the body in *Second Life* and *Entropia Universe* against the backdrop of postmodern and post-postmodern feminist theory. Entitled 'Embodiment and Gender Identity in Virtual Worlds: Reconfiguring Our "Volatile Bodies"', this chapter (Chapter 4) starts with the assumption that in cyberspace we are not constrained by actual corporeality. Therefore, we could start the process of identity construction anew, reaching beyond gender constraints. However, despite the flexibility of the Internet as a medium, it seems as if the traditionally defined gender identity based on binary oppositions (male versus female; heterosexual versus homosexual) is still being reinforced online. With this in mind, the authors explore the implications of technology and cyberspace in terms of the way gender identity is or may be constructed in virtual worlds such as *Second Life* and *Entropia Universe*. In so doing, they focus on three main thematic areas revolving around the process of avatar creation, the process of experiencing its body and the phenomenon of gender-restricted regions in *SL*.

Chapter 5 by Denise Doyle leads on by looking in detail at 'the body of the avatar'. In seeking to demonstrate how human presence is constructed in virtual worlds, Doyle addresses a pivotal concern surrounding the recent growth in massively multiplayer online games and virtual worlds: our experience of presence when moving between real and virtual space. Questions she sets out to explore include how we understand our avatar as our represented 'presence' in virtual space; what we are identifying with when we identify with an avatar; and whether or not we have bodily experiences of our avatar. Drawing on Spinoza's theory of the imagination as a form of bodily awareness, Doyle aims to help us understand the phenomenon of embodied experience in virtual worlds. Referring to the Dalai Lama's conception of the mind-body relationship and Bachelard's theory of the material imagination, her chapter tests concepts of the imaginary and the experience of human presence against the backdrop of *Second Life*. It defines these new dimensions of experience that are based on a simultaneity or plurality of presence and absence, and argues that the relationship between the imaginary and the body of the avatar plays a significant role when interacting with virtual worlds.

In the final chapter of Part II (Chapter 6, 'The Grips of Fantasy: Female Characters in Computer Games'), Isamar Carrillo Masso presents an innovative and rigorous methodology for studying the discursive construction of female characters in online and offline gaming environments. She starts from the observation that, due to their immense popularity, computer games are also the didactic means in which a number of social constructs are spread and perpetuated. Carrillo Masso finds this particularly true in the case of *Diablo* and *World of Warcraft*, two role-playing games (offline and online) produced by Blizzard Inc. Her chapter describes a triangulated method to study both games as texts, combining Norman Fairclough's (2003) approach to Critical Discourse Analysis, the use of a raw corpus, and participant questionnaires. The corpus consists of texts dealing with the characters in the two aforementioned computer games and their accompanying visual representations from official Blizzard websites and user-edited websites and forums. The devised methodology makes a strong emphasis in the correlation of linguistic and visual data. Based on this correlation and analysis, Carrillo Masso identifies a strong discourse of gender difference operating within the two selected gaming environments.

Part III, finally, approaches the issue of 'second spaces' from three focal angles: nature, architecture, and landscapes. In Chapter 7, 'Second Chances', Joseph S. Clark explores 'the natural world in the multi-user environment *Second Life*'. Clark takes the literature on virtual reality and on the way nature is represented, constructed, and experienced in museums, theme parks, and tourism as his starting point, as it reveals a complex interconnection between the actual and the virtual, with effects that are potentially both revelatory and damaging. Arguing further that *Second Life* is a visually rich 3-D virtual space comprising user-built content in a world with physics much like our own, Clark explains that objects, places, and activities from real in the sense of actual life can be replicated there, as well as utopian (and dystopian) fantasies and alternative realities. With this in mind, he explores representations of 'nature' and natural areas found in *Second Life*. He identifies several environmental islands ('sims') in *SL* as expressions of popular culture, in that they replicate or indeed challenge dominant hegemonic discourses about relationships between humanity and its natural environment. Focusing particularly on depictions of aquatic environments as key components of the endangered human biosphere, Clark explores the question as to whether these representations replicate and enact a hegemonic industrial/consumerist orientation; or indeed whether they suggest alternatives and possibilities for environmental awareness and social change.

Shifting from natural to built environments, Chapter 8 by Astrid Ens-slin looks at 'avatar needs and the remediation of architecture in *Second Life*'. She discusses the role of First Life (FL) architecture as social space in general and, more specifically, its relationship to and rootedness in human spatial needs such as stimulation, identity, and security. In seeking to explore the main differences between First Life and *Second Life* architectural requirements, Ensslin revisits Abraham Maslow's (1943) basic needs hierarchy in the light of empirical evidence revealing the prepotent needs of *SL* avatars in contrast to human beings. Inspired by social semioticians' applications of Michael Halliday's (1978) three communicative metafunctions to built spaces, she examines the social semiotics of *SL* architecture, particularly in the context of its physical and physiological idiosyncracies. Drawing on Bolter and Grusin (1999), she argues, finally, that FL and SL architectures remediate each other and concludes that, although offering a seemingly ideal experimentation platform for pioneering architects, *SL* developers are lagging behind the affordances yielded by contemporary digital technology.

In the final chapter (Chapter 9), Eben Muse explores issues relating to landscape, space, and place, which he considers fundamental to the experience of interactive fiction, virtual realities, and computer games. Muse contends that, for many, the pleasure of these texts comes from the opportunity to explore the virtual world that has been created, much the same way that Tolkien or Austen fans enjoy exploring the literary world those authors create. His chapter proposes a model for a discourse around virtual landscapes and the spaces and places created by these digital locations. After establishing a concept of space and place taken from social geography (e.g., Tuan 2001), it reviews alternative, older technologies that have been used for the creation of three-dimensional space, particularly geometric perspective and architectural design. Virtual space and place, argues Muse, transcend both these technologies of expression as they are both illustrated places and lived-in spaces. A different semantics is required for the virtual landscape, a three-dimensional space that, while insisting on bringing its subject in through Alberti's framing window, continues to insist on that window's presence and power. Finally, Muse explores the possibility of applying R. Murray Schafer's (1993) soundscape model for aural (not visual) space and proposes one possible discursive model, which he then applies to several digital places.

The volume closes with an afterword by *Second Life* anthropologist, Tom Boellstorff. Boellstorff discusses the state of virtual worlds research in light of the chapters included in this volume. He attends particularly to the issue of defining research questions in the context of a nascent and rapidly shifting field of inquiry. Issues discussed include relationships between virtual worlds and the physical world; dynamics of creation, collaboration, and control; and interactions between textual and graphical socialities.

In conclusion, it is precisely the combination of animate, or animat*ed*, embodiment and spatiality that lies at the heart of this book's trajectory of exploring the textual nature of 'Second Lives'. As such, the contributors offer explorations of textual encoding and decoding; of the reception, production, and interaction of and with virtual worlds; of the similarities and differences between the virtual, the real, and the actual; of embodiment, disembodiment, and re-embodiment and their complex interrelationships with selfhood and otherness; and the intricate ways in which community, social interaction, and communication are afforded, facilitated, and constructed by interfaces, 3D design, in-world creativity, and paratext.

NOTES

1. The term 'ludic' refers to the distinctly playful, rule-governed characteristics of (computer) games. Online virtual communities such as *Second Life* are, by contrast, essentially non-ludic as their users create their own rules and norms in the social groups they establish online.
2. Note that no conceptual distinction is made here between virtual worlds and virtual/online environments. The various contributors to this book differ in their uses of specific terminology. As we do not wish to impose any theoretical dictates, we have left the explanation of terminological idiosyncracies to the discretion of individual authors.
3. The term 'Second Life/Lives' is used to denote a continuum with First (actual) Life as an overarching paradigm of 'real life'. When the term '*Second Life*™' (or short: *Second Life*, in italics) is used it refers directly to Linden Lab's online virtual world.
4. Bolter defines reverse ekphrasis in terms of 'images [being] given the task of explaining words', which runs counter to ancient and Renaissance rhetoric, where 'the spoken word controlled the image' (2001: 56). Ekphrasis (without 'reverse') was seen as a rhetorical skill: the ability to make an object (of art) come to life by means of verbal paraphrase (cf. Ensslin 2007: 164).
5. The terms 'video game' and 'computer game' are used interchangeably in this volume.
6. The Genettian term 'paratext' (Genette 1997) refers to texts surrounding other, primary texts, thus including, for instance, blurbs, titles, epigraphs, and annotations, but also epi-phenomena such as gaming magazines, reviews, and commentary such as can be found in online discussion groups.

REFERENCES

Active Worlds, Inc. (1997–2010) *Active Worlds*. Las Vegas, NV. Online. Available HTTP: http://www.activeworlds.com (accessed 17 July 2009).

Anderson, B (2001) *Imagined communities: Reflections on the origin and spread of nationalism*, 2nd ed. London: Verso.

Barthes, R (1975) *The pleasure of the text*, trans. R Miller. New York: Hill and Wang.

Bell, G and P Dourish (2006) Yesterday's tomorrows: Notes on ubiquitous computing's dominant vision. *Personal and Ubiquitous Computing* 11, no. 2: 133–43.

Blizzard Entertainment (2004–10) *World of Warcraft*. Irvine, CA. Online. Available HTTP: http://www.worldofwarcraft.com (accessed 17 July 2009).

Boellstorff, T (2008) *Coming of age in Second Life: An anthropologist explores the virtually human*. Princeton and Oxford: Princeton University Press.

Bolter, JD (2001) *Writing space: Computers, hypertext, and the remediation of print*. Mahwah, NJ: Lawrence Erlbaum Associates.

Bolter, JD and RA Grusin (1999) *Remediation: Understanding new media*. Cambridge, MA: MIT Press.

Carr, P and G Pond (2007) *The unofficial tourist's guide to Second Life*. London: Boxtree.

Castronova, E (2005) *Synthetic worlds: The business and culture of online games*. Chicago: University of Chicago Press.

———. (2007) *Exodus to the virtual world: How online fun is changing reality*. Basingstoke: Palgrave Macmillan.

Corneliussen, HG and JW Rettberg (eds) (2008) *Digital culture, play and identity: A World of Warcraft® reader*. Cambridge, MA: MIT Press.

Deleuze, G (1981) *Difference and repetition*. New York: Columbia University Press.

Ensslin, A (2007) *Canonizing hypertext: Explorations and constructions*. London: Continuum.

Fairclough, N (2003) *Analysing discourse: Textual analysis for social research*. London: Routledge.

Fish, S (1980) *Is there a text in this class? The authority of interpretive communities*. Cambridge, MA: Harvard University Press.

Fong, C (2008) Internetting every thing, everywhere, all the time. CNN.Com/Technology. Online. Available HTTP: http://edition.cnn.com/2008/TECH/11/02/digitalbiz.rfid/ (accessed 16 July 2010).

Galloway, K and S Rabinowitz (1980) Hole-In-Space. Online. Available HTTP: http://www.ecafe.com/getty/HIS/index.html (accessed 20 June 2010).

Genette, G (1997) *Paratexts: Thresholds of interpretation*. Cambridge: Cambridge University Press.

Greenfield, A and T Shute (2009) FEATURE at the end of the world, plant a tree: Six questions for Adam Greenfield. *interactions* 16, no. 4: 16–20.

Guest, T (2007) *Second lives: A journey through virtual worlds*. London: Hutchinson.

Hall, S (1974) The television discourse—encoding and decoding. *Education and Culture* 25: 8–14.

Halliday, MAK (1978) *Language as a social semiotic: The social interpretation of language and meaning*. London: Edward Arnold.

Iser, W (1971) Indeterminacy and the reader's response in prose fiction. In *Aspects of narrative: Selected papers from the English Institute*, ed JH Miller, 1–45. New York: Columbia University Press.

———. (1978) *The act of reading: A theory of aesthetic response*, trans. W Iser. Baltimore: Johns Hopkins University Press.

Jauss, HR (1982) *Theory and history of literature, Vol. 2: Toward an aesthetic of reception*, trans. T Bahti. Minneapolis: University of Minnesota Press.

Kaneva, Inc. (2004–10) *Kaneva*. Atlanta, GA. Online. Available HTTP: http://www.kaneva.com (accessed 17 July 2009).

Lefebvre, H (1992) *The production of space*. New York: Wiley-Blackwell.

Levy, P (1998) *Becoming virtual: Reality in the digital age*, trans. R Bononno. New York: Plenum Press.

Linden Lab (2003–10) *Second Life*. San Francisco, CA. Online. Available HTTP: http://www.secondlife.com (accessed 15 July 2009).

Makena Technologies (2003–10) *There*. San Mateo, CA. Online. Available HTTP: http://www.there.com (accessed 17 July 2009).

Maslow, A (1943) A theory of human motivation. *Psychological Review* 50, no. 4: 370–96.

Massumi, B (2002) *Parables for the virtual: Movement, affect, sensation*. Durham, NC: Duke University Press.

Meadows, MS (2008) *I, avatar: The culture and consequences of having a second life*. Berkeley, CA: New Riders.

Milgram, P and H Colquhoun (1999) A taxonomy of real and virtual world display integration. In *Mixed Reality, Merging Real and Virtual Worlds*, ed. Y Ohta and H Tamura, 5–30. Berlin and Heidelberg: Springer-Verlag.

MindArk (2003–10) *Entropia Universe*. Gothenburg, Sweden. Online. Available HTTP: http://www.entropiauniverse.com (accessed 17 July 2009).

Moove (2001–10) *Moove online*. Cologne, Germany. Online. Available HTTP: http://www.moove.com (accessed 17 July 2009).

Pearce, C (2006a) *Playing ethnography: A study of emergent behaviour in online games and virtual worlds*. Ph.D. Thesis: SMARTlab Centre, Central Saint Martins College of Art and Design, University of the Arts, London.

———. (2006b) Productive play: Game culture from the bottom up. *Games and Culture* 1, no. 1: 17–24.

———. (2007) Communities of play: The social construction of identity in persistent online game worlds. In *Second person: Role-playing and story in games and playable media*, ed. P Harrigan amd N Wardrip-Fruin, 311–17. Cambridge, MA: MIT Press.

Plant, S (1995) The future looms: Weaving women and cybernetics. In *Cyberspace/cyberbodies/cyberpunk: Cultures of technological embodiment*, ed. M Featherstone and R Burrows, 45–64. London: Sage.

———. (1997) *Zeros + ones: Digital women + the new technoculture*. London: Fourth Estate.

Rheingold, H (1991) *Virtual reality*. New York: Simon and Schuster.

———. (2000) *The virtual community: Homesteading on the electronic frontier*, Rev. ed. Cambridge, MA: MIT Press.

Rymaszewski, M, WJ Au, M Wallace, C Winters, C Ondrejka, B Batstone-Cunningham, and Second Life residents from around the world (2007) *Second Life®: The official guide*. Indianapolis, IN: Wiley.

Schafer, RM (1993) *The soundscape: Our sonic environment and the tuning of the world*. Rochester, VT: Destiny Books.

Schroeder, R (1996) *Possible worlds: The social dynamic of virtual reality technology*. Boulder, CO: Westview Press.

———. (2002) Social interaction in virtual environments: Key issues, common themes, and a framework for research. In *The social life of avatars: Presence and interaction in shared virtual environments*, ed. R Schroeder, 1–18. London: Springer.

Schnabel, MA, X Wang, H Seichter, and T Kvan (2008) Touching the untouchables: Virtual-, augmented- and reality. In *Proceedings of the 13th International Conference on Computer Aided Architectural Design Research in Asia (CAADRIA)*, Department of Architecture, U of Chiang Mai, Thailand, 293–99.

Selden, R. (1985) *A reader's guide to contemporary literary theory*. Brighton: Harvester.

Shields, R (2003) *The Virtual*. London: Routledge.

Smith, MA and P Kollock (eds) (1999) *Communities in cyberspace*. London: Routledge.

Stone, AR (1991) Will the real body please stand up? Boundary stories about virtual cultures. In *Cyberspace: First steps*, ed. M Benedikt, 81–118. Cambridge, MA: MIT Press.

Tapley, R (2008) *Designing your second life: Techniques and inspiration for you to design your ideal parallel universe within the online community, Second Life.* Berkeley, CA: New Riders.

Taylor, TL (2002) Living digitally: Embodiment in virtual worlds. In *The social life of avatars: Presence and interaction in shared virtual environments*, ed. R Schroeder, 40–62. London: Springer.

———. (2006a) Beyond management: Considering participatory design and governance in player culture. *First Monday*, special issue 7. Online. Available HTTP: http://firstmonday.org/htbin/cgiwrap/bin/ojs/index.php/fm/article/view/1611/1526 (accessed 17 July 2009).

———. (2006b) *Play between worlds: Exploring online game culture.* Cambridge, MA: MIT Press.

Tuan, Y-F (2001) *Space and place: The perspective of experience.* Minneapolis: University of Minnesota Press.

Turkle, S (1995) *Life on the screen: Identity in the age of the Internet.* New York: Simon and Schuster.

Weber, A, K Rufer-Bach, and R Platel (2008) *Creating your world: The official guide to advanced content creation for Second Life®.* Indianapolis, IN: Wiley.

Weiser, M (1999) The computer for the 21st century. *SIGMOBILE Mobile Computing and Communications Review* 3, no. 3: 3–11.

Woolley, B (1992) *Virtual worlds: A journey in hype and hyperreality.* Oxford: Blackwell.

Part I
Creating Second Communities

1   *Liberate your Avatar*
The Revolution Will Be
Socially Networked

Paul Sermon and Charlotte Gould

INTRODUCTION: NEW FORMS OF SOCIAL NARRATIVE

This opening chapter provides a creative-practical perspective on Second Life through a survey of our work as visual artists, set against a theoretical and philosophical backdrop that combines poststructuralism and semiotics. Our practical examples of merged and created Second Lives draw on our mixed-reality installations in the form of encounters between Second Life and First Life. Starting from created communities in *Second Life*™ (cf. Sherman's social encounters, and Fizek and Wasilewska's creation of second bodies, both this volume), our aim is to provide a visual backdrop and practical examples to this underlying theoretical and philosophical discourse, where the disembodied participant and (re)-embodied avatar in our installations find themselves in an increasingly social and political Second Life context.

Whereas the underlying theoretical framework of this chapter clearly identifies a number of critical and philosophical standpoints ranging from a poststructuralist position that follows the linguistic and semiotic guiding principles of de Saussure (1998) to the formation of the ego in relation to the body image in Lacan's mirror stage (2007), it is the artistic outcomes of our own practiced-based research that identifies and pronounces these theoretical stances within our art installations. Through the development of these artistic works since the early 1990s a philosophical discourse has emerged through experience and practice rather than initiated by theory alone, but one that is now completely entwined where we as artists feel both the theory and practice are at the forefront of our work.

In what follows, we shall outline our respective practice-based creative research, culminating in a collaborative interactive installation that investigates new forms of social and political narrative in multi-user virtual environments. Our artistic projects deal with the ironies and stereotypes that are found within *Second Life* in particular. Paul Sermon's current creative practice looks specifically at the concepts of presence and performance within Second Life and First Life, and attempts to bridge these two spaces through mixed-reality techniques and interfaces. Charlotte Gould's *Ludic*

Second Life Narrative radically questions the way that users embody themselves in online virtual environments and identifies a counter-aesthetic that challenges the conventions of digital realism and consumerism.

Through practical accounts of recent projects we shall explore issues of virtual embodiment and identity in relation to presence and social change as experienced and performed in telematic and virtual environments. The concept of the 'telematic' artwork is rooted in the discourse that Roy Ascott, Robert Adrian X, and others proclaimed in the early 1980s as collaborative arts practice on a global scale (Ascott 2003). Aided by the proliferation of private computer networks and telecommunications devices as a hybrid of existing *(tele)*communication systems and infor*(matics)* of the time, the creative potential for collaborative interactive network art through 'distributed authorship' (Ascott 2003) was born. Initially through text exchange between globally remote participants, most notably in Roy Ascott's seminal telematic artwork *La Plissure du Texte* from 1983, telematic arts have continued to embrace image and video exchange and collaboration that have paved the way for the Internet and World Wide Web and identified the fundamental collaborative principles and theories that form the conceptual framework of *social networking* today.

Our current collaborative practice asks at what point the participant is embodying the virtual performer in front of them, and whether they have become disembodied in doing so. In what follows, a number of interactive *Second Life* artworks are looked at in detail, to provide answers to these questions, ranging from Paul Sermon's telematic experiments in the early 1990s to current collaborative site-specific, user-generated presence and performance in *Second Life* that polarizes fundamental existential questions concerning identity, the self, the ego, and the embodied avatar.

These research activities and outcomes come together within a collaborative site-specific public installation entitled *Urban Intersections* for ISEA09, focusing on contested virtual spaces that mirror the social and political history of Belfast. Our current collaborative practice critically investigates social, cultural, and creative interactions in *Second Life*. Through these practice-based experiments we argue that an enhanced social and cultural discourse within multi-user virtual environments will inevitably lead to creative growth, cultural cohesion, and public empowerment and, like all social networking platforms, contribute to greater social and political change in First Life. In January 2009, for instance, Labour Party MP Peter Mandelson launched his *Second Life* avatar as part of Labour's strategy to beat the Conservatives in using new technologies for political trajectories. Labour's decisive embrace of social networking was reaffirmed by Mandelson's statement to the online electorate: 'When it comes to new media we have to recognize that the days of command and control are over. Instead we need to embrace and engage' (Mandelson in Keegan 2009).

Although rather obvious to the active online community, this is a clear indication of the political significance social networking environments such as *Second Life* have to play in governmental party politics. The publicity stunt aimed to introduce an 'independent' blog, *LabourList.org*, simultaneously launched in *Second Life* and First Life, but ironically Peter Mandelson was not controlling his own avatar at the time of the launch, suggesting perhaps that the need to fully engage has not yet been embraced (Keegan 2009).

Throughout the 1990s media art was dominated by interactivity and interface design. However, through the increasing importance of user-generated content via public networks in both online and offline contexts the contemporary media art discourse now finds itself in an ever-increasing socially networked environment. In what follows, we investigate how the experience of tactility and physicality, as explored in our own creative practices, makes both the participants/performers and the artists/directors more susceptible to new forms of social narrative,[1] yet also offers altered ways of generating effective responsive experiences. Our artistic projects deal with the ironies and stereotypes in multi-user virtual environments such as cultural identity, gender roles, digital consumption, and the virtual desire to fly, teleport, construct, design, and code the world around us. Our work aims to utilize alternative interactive functionality and techniques in multi-user virtual environments, techniques which allow the participants to embody performer roles to interact and direct new socially networked creative narratives by their communication, presence, and movements.

Our collaborative practice aims to examine the notion of telepresence in Second Life and First Life spaces through a blurring between 'online' and 'offline' identities, and the signifiers and conditions that make us feel present in this world. This artistic practice questions how subjectivity is articulated in relation to embodiment and disembodiment.[2] It explores the avatar in relation to its activating First Life agent, focusing on the avatar's multiple identifications, such as gender roles, human/animal hybrids, and other archetypes, identifiable through visible codes and body forms in *Second Life*.

These works seek to question the trend in visualizations of environments and avatars that incontrovertibly conform to the conventions of ultra-realism and 'super-humanism' in multi-user virtual environments, looking for an unconventional aesthetical paradigm counter to the stereotypes that prevail in *Second Life*. These alternative avatars possess a hand-made, imperfect, puppet-like quality as opposed to the formulaic Barbie and Ken 'body-beautiful' archetypes that abound. In 1995 Sherry Turkle argued that the experience of inhabiting a virtual world can be liberating, as the user is unbound from the shackles of their own body, gender, or image and can be whoever they choose. However, since the introduction of multi-user virtual environments it would appear that the majority of Second Life users have chosen to accentuate the sexual signifiers of the 'perfect body'. Turkle went on to say that, when inhabiting an avatar of a different gender to the First Life user, stereotypical choices are often made (Turkle 1995), which affirms that heteronormative gender politics as well as aesthetics are very much still at play.

Whereas the majority of users appear to be journeying unknowingly towards the 'uncanny-valley'[3] (Mori 1970) on a quest for super-human aesthetics, and the buildings and landscapes they create similarly strive to replicate our First Life environment (see also Heilesen 2009; Ensslin, this volume), there is an implicit irony when we build virtual roads we do not use because we can fly or even teleport, and fit roofs and windows in a landscape where it never rains. Moreover, this landscape is not so dissimilar from our current First Life hyper-reality that Umberto Eco described in the mid 1980s as a culture obsessed with fabricating environments and experiences in an effort to create a space that is better than real (Eco 1986)— think of Venice Las Vegas, urban beaches, or the proliferation of celebrity plastic surgery, and the discourses of First and Second Life become increasingly blurred.

This reality crisis and apparent decay of the real is polarized in the recent project *AVATARIUM—A Consumer Paradox* (Sermon 2008), inspired by Slavoj Zizek's semiotic account of John Carpenter's 1988 sci-fi classic *They Live* (Zizek 2009). Sermon combines Istanbul's premier shopping mall 'City's Nişantaşı' with a deconstructed derelict shopping mall in the virtual world of *Second Life*. Through a live video link between First and Second Life, the installation allows both real- and virtual-life visitors/customers to converse, interact, and confront the consumption-driven aesthetic and architecture of contemporary shopping spaces.

The installation in *Second Life* depicts a shopping mall in ruin that reflects the current global economic credit crunch, as the last bastion of the consumer-driven Western economy. Instead of shops, logos, and brands of consumption, the shoppers of the virtual world are presented with semiotic instructions such as 'buy', 'pay', and 'desire' that evade the subliminal messages we are presented with in today's shopping centers. By placing large format public video screens in both the Second and the First Life shopping centers, Paul Sermon created a portal between these two parallel worlds through which the shopping-driven world of *Second Life* meets our consumer-obsessed society of First Life. Whereas the online consumers in *Second Life* wander the escalators of the crumbling mall in search of answers to our economic future, the offline consumers in City's Nişantaşı have the opportunity to question their own existence and desire to consume an imposed identity.

THE CONVERGENCE OF TELEMATIC PRACTICE AND SECOND LIFE NARRATIVES

Since the early 1990s Paul Sermon's work has explored the emergence of user-determined narrative by bringing remote participants together in shared telepresent environments. Through the use of live chroma-keying and videoconferencing technology,[4] two public rooms or installations and their audiences are joined in a virtual duplicate that turns into a mutual space of activity. This work locates itself in a telematic arts discourse defined by Roy Ascott, who advocated collaborative cybernetic and telematic arts practice and networked consciousness on a global scale as early as the late 1970s (Ascott 2003). A pioneering work implementing this idea is the east-coast to west-coast public communication sculpture *Hole-In-Space* by Kit Galloway and Sherrie Rabinowitz (1980), which allowed public audiences on pedestrian zones outside the Lincoln Center for the Performing Arts in New York and the Broadway Department Store in Los Angeles to communicate live, over three evenings in November of 1980, via a satellite up-link. The event was purposely unannounced in the press, aiming to attract an unexpected audience of passers-by.

> Suddenly head-to-toe, life-sized, television images of the people on the opposite coast appeared. They could now see, hear, and speak with each other as if encountering each other on the same sidewalk. Hole-In-Space suddenly severed the distance between both cities and created an outrageous pedestrian intersection. There was the evening of discovery, followed by the evening of intentional word-of-mouth rendez-vous, followed by a mass migration of families and trans-continental loved ones, some of which had not seen each other for over twenty years. (Galloway and Rabinowitz 1980)

Other examples of telematic practice include the global fax and text exchange happening *The World in 24 Hours* by Robert Adrian X (1982), a world-wide 24 hour telecommunications project for the 1982 Ars Electronica Linz, and virtual presence experiment *VIDEOPLACE* by Myron Krueger (1983). *VIDEOPLACE* is based on a system that composited live silhouetted images of participants in separate rooms and allowed them to collaboratively control and play with overlaid graphic creatures and images (Krueger1983)—research which led to the development of the artificial reality lab at the University of Connecticut. The theoretical position and telematic experiments of Paul Sermon's work such as *Telematic Dreaming* (1992) have drawn upon this telematic discourse, continually pertaining to concepts of user-generated content and socially networked communication.

In Sermon's work the audiences form an integral part within these telematic experiments, which simply wouldn't function without their presence and participation. Initially the viewers seem to enter a passive space, but they are instantly thrown into the performer role by discovering their own body-double in communication with another physically remote user on video monitors in front of them. They usually adapt to the situation quickly and start controlling and choreographing their human avatar as puppeteer controllers of their own telepresent body, absorbed by the performing role. However, the episodes that unfold are determined not only by the participants, but also by the given dramatic context. As artistic creator, Paul Sermon is then designer of the environment and, consequently, 'instigator' of the narrative, which is determined through the social and political milieu that he chooses to play out in the telepresent encounter. These experiments have been explored through simulated public and private settings, such as Paul Sermon's *Peace Talks* (2003) installation for Worcester City Art Gallery, where two remote users witness themselves existing together within a computer game environment that simulates a United Nations negotiations room. Whereas this installation context provokes a critique of the 'peace talks process' and its methods through its game-like aesthetics, it also seriously offers a viable and practical alternative to it when placed in front of this politically charged backdrop.

Our more recent collaborative practice looks specifically at the concepts of presence and performance within *Second Life* and First Life, and attempts to bridge these two spaces through telematic mixed-reality techniques and interfaces. Since 2007 Charlotte Gould has developed a number of site-specific works using *Second Life*, which enter into a discourse on the identity politics of online virtual environment aesthetics. These works aim to respond and enhance a First Life experience through a counter-culture landscape in *Second Life*, relying on alternative hand-drawn textures and low-tech handmade objects such as props, costumes, and body parts. Working with XML-based feeds from avatar to controller, these experiments make use of motion tracking to develop a link between First Life participant and avatar, where the position of the person in First Life triggers the movement of the avatar in *Second Life*. The user's body controls the puppet-like avatar that appears to intuitively wander the virtual landscape in response to the First Life puppeteer.

UNDERPINNING CONCEPTS OF THE
COLLABORATIVE PRACTICE

Whereas there is an apparent shift of emphasis from Paul Sermon's previous telematic projects here, there are significant parallels between the earlier networked video experiments, particularly that of *Telematic Dreaming* (Sermon 1992), and the presence and absence experiments he is developing in collaboration with Charlotte Gould using *Second Life*. *Telematic Dreaming* is a work consisting of two double beds in different locations. One bed is within a blue-screen environment; the other in a darkened space. Both beds have cameras above them and are surrounded by monitors; each bed has one person lying in it. The darkened bed has a digital projector above it that projects onto it a live video image of the person on the blue-screen bed. Thus, the camera above the darkened bed captures the image of both people on one bed, sending the image to the monitors in the blue-screen room. A further surreal twist is added by the addition of pre-recorded video mixed into the live projections, for example, when the bed surface is blended with an image of water in a swimming pool. *Telematic Dreaming*, with its connotations of intimacy and dream states, extends telepresence beyond the screen to spatialize the site of interaction and transform it into a live theatrical event in which visitors are key performers, exploring presence, absence, and the psychology of human interaction within technologically mediated communications. Just as the combined visuals of remote participants on the projected bed surface in *Telematic Dreaming* (Sermon 1992) allowed them to interact by 'touching with their eyes', the same sensory-shift occurs in the embodied relationship between the *Second Life* avatar and its puppeteer controller. This shift of senses occurs through the exchange of sight with the sense of touch, reaching the equivalent cognitive experience of closeness through the visual stimulation of the body at a distance—as if extending their finger nerve endings through a telepresent body. The same is said of Myron Krueger's initial *Metaplay* experiments in the late '70s that identified a consistent shared telepresence experience that later became *VIDEOPLACE* in 1983.

> On Metaplay [. . .] I was struck with the thought that he was uncomfortable about the image of my hand touching the image of his [. . .] The inescapable conclusion was that the same etiquette of personal space and avoidance of touching that exists in the real world was operating at that moment in this purely visual experience. (Krueger 1991: 125–27)

This is an analogy that Tom Boellstorff identifies as one of the principal origins of *Second Life* when we consider Myron Krueger's *VIDEOPLACE* experiments that identified a third shared space he termed 'artificial reality' accessed by two remote participants as an alternative to the sender/receiver telecommunication model. Krueger later termed it the 'megaenvironment' in 1991, when speculating on the idea of multi-dyadic *VIDEOPLACE* environment of multiple participants—what is today referred to as *massively multiplayer* environment (Boellstorff 2008).

   The aim of our current collaborative practice is to critically investigate how online participants in three-dimensional worlds, *Second Life* in particular, socially interact within innovative creative environments and appropriate these cultural experiences as part of their everyday lives—questioning what is 'real' in this relationship. Our work brings together ethnographic and creative practice-based research that identifies and develops innovative interactive applications, interface design, and new cultural and sociological experience. This creative practice aims to help shape and define the emerging online 'metaverse' (Stephenson 2000) society by significantly contributing to the quality of both First and Second Life equally. Together these aspects of telepresence and the merger of First and Second Life aim to question fundamental assumptions of the Second Life/First Life phenomenon.

The ontological questions associated with identity in virtual reality, be it online or offline, have been at the centre of the contemporary media arts and science debate for the past three decades, and this discourse continues to dominate the annual conference themes of Ars Electronica Linz, the Transmediale Berlin, and SIGGRAPH USA. At the height of rapid increase in users of multi-user virtual environments (Stocker and Schopf 2007) they were brought under this microscope, noticeably by inclusion at Ars Electronic 2007 in 'Second City', a festival strand that paralleled First and Second Life in mixed-reality artworks, scientific experiments, and theoretical critique. This creative practice and debate is firmly rooted in the discourse of semiotics, reflecting a poststructuralist debate from the linguistic origins of Ferdinand de Saussure's notion of reality as a construct of language (Saussure 1998) to Jacques Lacan's construction of identity through the mirror image of the self (Lacan 2007), and Jean Baudrillard's concept of reality as 'Simulacra' or simulations of it (Baudrillard 1995).

So as to explore this emerging relationship between First and Second Life, we have developed interfaces that focus on the interaction and exchange between online and offline identities through social practices, such as performance, narrative, embodiment, activism, place, and identity construction. Our collaborative experiments seek to question whether *Second Life* is a platform for potential social and cultural change—appropriated as a mirror image of First Life. By consciously deciding to refer to this image that is mirrored as 'First' rather than 'real' life, our central question poses a paradox in Second Life when we consider Jacques Lacan's proposition that the 'self' (or ego) is a formulation of our own body image reflected in the 'mirror stage' (Lacan 1949). However, there is no 'mirror stage' in Second Life, which would suggest that the computer screen itself is the very mirror we are looking for, one that allows users to formulate their 'second self' according to their visual and social preferences. Although an 'alter ego', this is nonetheless a self that can have an engaged social identity, or, as Deleuze would see it, a single identity with a difference between first and second self (Deleuze 1994).

In *Second Life* you create an avatar that lives out an online existence. There are no set objectives for that existence; you can buy property, clothing, or accessories, furnish your home, modify your identity, and interact in a myriad of ways with other users. This online community has grown to 17 million residents since launching in 2003, generating a thriving economy. However, whereas the virtual shopping malls, nightclubs, bars, and beaches often reach their user capacity, there is a noticeable lack of creative and sociological modes of attraction. Consequently, in 2006 the growing media attention around *Second Life* (Keegan 2006) warned that this expanding community had become ambivalent and numbed by their virtual consumption, and there was an increasing need to identify new forms of interaction, creativity, cultural production, and sociability. The growth in *Second Life* users has leveled out since the media hype, and this has allowed for a period of more focused observation and reflection by educators and artists alike.

However, when the 'Front National', the far right French political party of Jean-Marie Le Pen, opened its *Second Life* headquarters in January 2007, residents reacted in a way that would suggest they are far from complacent avatars wandering around a virtual landscape; suggesting rather that they possess a far greater degree of social conscience than the consumerist aesthetics of *Second Life* may suggest. Through prolonged mass virtual protest the centre was razed to the ground in the space of a week and has not returned since. The reaction to the Le Pen *Second Life* office suggests that *Second Life* is indeed a platform for potential social and cultural change (Burkeman 2007), and there is a hidden desire and ambition to interact and engage with this online community at an intellectual and creative level that transcends the collective 'I shop therefore I am'[5] apparentness of its community. Moreover, *Second Life* could then influence our First Lives. As the landmass and population of *Second Life* expands at an ever-increasing rate, it is clear that essential research into the intersection and interplay between First and Second Life, and both new and old patterns of consumption, cultural production, and sociability are urgently needed.

CROSSING THE SOCIAL DIVIDE THROUGH COLLABORATIVE CREATIVE PRACTICE

Due to the urban setting of the aforementioned installations, the augmented *Second Life* interfaces are designed for large format public video screens. The designated public space opened up by these experiments further explores innovative and creative ways of engaging with the public in an urban environment. Through the mixing of realities of the virtual and the actual, users can then explore alternative networked spaces and develop unique narrative events. The work aims to encourage ludic urban interaction for people of all ages and explores how enjoyment and social interaction can be enhanced in this context.

The creative and cultural potential that large format urban screens offer is becoming increasingly evident as more screens appear in the urban landscape. These emerging technologies and networked infrastructures impact on the way that the public interacts within the urban environment, both with each other and with the space—potentially allowing the user to engage in an active role rather than passively consume this new digital content. Through our artistic work we look to rediscover and reclaim the urban screen as a space for critical discourse and political debate. Using action research, documentation, and observation of these urban media spaces, we use everyday practices to inform further research (see de Certeau 2002). The creative opportunities that digital and pervasive media offer for the public to actively engage and contribute content to the urban screen extends beyond the notion of the 'user-generated'. As Matt Adams (2009) from Blast Theory argues, instead we should talk about public-created content, where accessibility of new technologies opens up the potential for new creative content, in line with Barthes's conclusion that the public completes the work through the creation of their unique narrative (Barthes 1993).

Sermon's first telepresence performance experiment, *Liberate your Avatar* (Sermon 2007), incorporating *Second Life* users in a real-life environment was located on All Saints Gardens, Oxford Road, Manchester, for the Urban Screens Festival in October 2007. This installation merged the realities of All Saints Gardens with its online three-dimensional counterpart in *Second Life*, and for the first time allowed First Life visitors and *Second Life* avatars to coexist and share the same park bench in a live interactive public video installation (see Figure 1.1).

This *Second Life* presence experiment, commissioned by 'Lets Go Global Manchester', brought a public telematic video installation to online avatars through a live video streaming encounter in *Second Life*. The project investigated the notion of demonstration and how it has been transposed from the actual into the virtual and back again, including a First Life demonstration on the streets of Manchester, provoking debate around both online identity and rounding up a public audience. *Liberate your Avatar* exposed the history of All Saints Gardens, relocating Mancunian Suffragette Emmeline Pankhurst as an avatar within *Second Life*, where she remained locked to the railings of the park, just as she did 100 years ago, reminding us of

Figure 1.1   Liberate your Avatar, a merged-reality demonstration, Manchester, 2007.

the need to continually evaluate our role in this new online digital society. The installation examined this new crisis whilst drawing upon the history of the site, creating a rich, provoking, and entirely innovative, interactive experience.

The project consisted of three specific spaces, two of which were located in the virtual world of *Second Life* and the other one in the actual All Saints Gardens on Oxford Road, Manchester. The two virtual environments included a blue box studio and a three-dimensional replica of All Saints Gardens, and were located adjacent to each other, allowing the *Second Life* avatars to move freely between the two spaces. When an avatar entered the blue box space their image became chroma-keyed with a live video image from the real 'All Saints Gardens'. This combined live video image of the avatar in the actual square was then streamed back onto the Internet and presented on a virtual screen in both Second Life spaces. An image of the *Second Life* version of All Saints Gardens with its virtual 'big screen' was then presented on the actual public video screen in the First Life All Saints Gardens (see Figure 1.2).

The research activities and outcomes of *Liberate your Avatar* and other previous experiments in *Second Life* have recently come together within a collaborative site-specific public installation entitled *Urban Intersections* focused on contested virtual spaces that mirror the social and political history of Belfast as a divided city, presented at ISEA09 (International Symposium of Electronic Arts 2009) (see Figure 1.3). This collaborative project specifically reflected on the ironies of contested spaces, and stereotypes in multi-user virtual environments, exposing an absurd online world that consists of perimeter fences, public surveillance, and national identity. These futile efforts to divide and deny movement and social interaction were an uncanny reflection of the First Life urban and social landscape of Belfast. So whereas it is possible to defy and transcend these restrictions in *Second Life* where we can fly, teleport, and communicate without political constraint and national identity, we can question the need for such social and political boundaries enforced in First Life and consider the opportunity to initiate social change in First Life through our Second Life experience (see Figure 1.3).

The installation was located on the regenerated landscape of the Waterfront Plaza Belfast, directly outside the newly developed Concert Hall building. This utilitarian environment was used as a stage set to represent an augmented garden that explored the concept of boundaries and territories, a virtual plaza encapsulated by the ironies, contradictions, and obscurities of a divided city, and a metaphor of Belfast's social history. As the participants walked through this urban landscape, both First and Second Life inhabitants came 'face-to-face' on screen, in the form of a live digital mural projected on the façade of the Waterfront building. This mural formed the central focus of the installation and immediately spoke of the infamous painted murals on houses across West Belfast. Those depict a

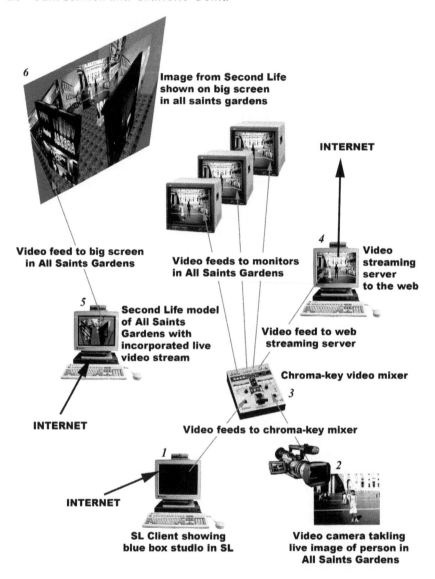

Figure 1.2   Liberate your Avatar, live video streaming flow diagram, Manchester, 2007.

deep political divide, but post-conflict society now refers to them as a stark reminder of recent troubles, thereby maintaining the peace that now prevails. In a city such as Belfast it would be impossible to evade such references when projecting images onto a building, as though the project itself were projected onto the gable end wall of a house on the Falls Road or the Shankill Estate.

Figure 1.3   Urban Intersections: Sermon and Gould at ISEA Belfast, August 2009.

Figure 1.4   Motion tracking movement of avatar, Charlotte Gould, ISEA, August 2009.

The local audience formed an integral part of this installation that relied on user interaction and aimed to transcend boundaries through user-generated storytelling and memory building in a post-conflict society. The complete installation utilized three interface techniques. Charlotte Gould's motion tracking interface allowed visitors in Belfast to wear a large puppet-like copy of Charlotte's unique avatar head. Covered in an array of LED lights that were tracked (see Figure 1.4), participants could then control the movements of the *Second Life* avatar as a means of alternative navigation through a maze of chain-link garden fences. Paul Sermon's interface combined First Life visitors and *Second Life* avatars within the same live video stream. By constructing a blue chroma-key studio in *Second Life*, it was possible to mix live video images of online avatars with the audience in Belfast, enabling these participants to play and converse on a collaborative video stream simultaneously displayed in both First and Second Life situations. The third interface was developed by sound and media artist Peter Appleton, whose contribution included a barbecue on the Waterfront plaza that simultaneously controlled the conditions of an identical *Second Life* barbecue (see Figure 1.5). Through a series of light and heat sensors it was possible to relay commands to the online situation, so that when the First Life barbecue was lit so too was the *Second Life* barbecue, and as food started to cook and brown so did its online duplicate. All these interfaces referred to the domestic garden and the infamous Belfast perimeter fences. The aim was to break down these boundaries through social interaction that prevailed, be it through a video portal, through a didactic maze, or over a grilled sausage.

CONCLUSION

Audience participation is the key component to the success of all recent merged-reality *Second Life* experiments described in this chapter. Whereas they are still crude attempts to bring these audiences closer together, there is always an increasing level of excitement and ludic engagement in the participants who take part. When public audiences first encounter these spaces, as with *Liberate your Avatar* in Manchester (2007) and *Urban Intersections* in Belfast (2009), a sense of play is immediately evoked, followed by mimicry and role-paying games, laughter, and moreover a desire to achieve a level of communication that is both fun and meaningful. These public reactions are not dissimilar from those in 1980 when audiences in Los Angeles and New York confronted each other via a satellite link in Kit Galloway and Sherrie Rabinowitz's *Hole-In-Space*. Exclamations of wonder and disbelief as well as games, jokes, and songs prevail. By situating these ludic interfaces in the context of political demonstration or social conflicts, we aim to unite audiences and add an objective viewpoint to the encounters and experiences we can share between First and Second Life,

Figure 1.5 Barbecue in First Life controlling *Second Life* barbecue, ISEA09 Belfast, August 2009.

thereby evoking notions of a mirror-like extension of the human (McLuhan 1994) and inducing a collective conscious effect. These attempts to communicate between Lives, and the consequent humorous interactions that result, break through the tension between Second and First Life or, as Lacan would see it, the tension between the immediacy of sensations and its objectification in the ego (Lacan 2007).

Our collaborative work will continue to explore the wider social consequence of multi-user virtual environments, be that on *Second Life* or the platform that supersedes it. Whichever is the case, it is essential that multi-user virtual environments such as *Second Life* move away from the imbedded linden dollar economy that intrinsically defines its capitalist principles and growth. The *Urban Intersections* project has already contributed to this paradigm shift by alternatively locating itself on an OpenSim, currently available as a derivative open-source beta version of *Second Life* that locates its island sims on geographically distributed servers. Following a similar model to the WWW, this fundamental network architecture shift moves away from the centralized San Francisco Linden Lab monopoly to an open-source networked model, and is in many ways reminiscent of the VRML architecture of the mid 1990s and its collective ideology. This distributed content and ownership will inevitably lead to social growth,

cohesion, and public empowerment and, like all social networking platforms, contribute to greater social and political change.

NOTES

1. The term 'social narrative' is used to identify public engagement and interaction that determines the narrative outcome of the installations' content and
   theme.
2. The term 'telepresence' in the context of this telematic arts practice is used
   to identify the corporeal presence of the participant within the artwork as an
   interactive performer within a shared space.
3. The term 'Uncanny Valley' was coined by roboticist Masahiro Mori (1970)
   to explain the uncomfortable repulsive response to near perfect simulated
   replicas of the human form, particularly the face. The valley represents a dip
   in a proposed graph of the human reaction to the simulated life form, being
   most repulsive at its lowest point.
4. Chroma-keying refers to a video technique that combines two video images
   in a video mixer and extracts the blue or green colour in one image and
   replaces it with the other image. This is often used when an actor is placed in
   front of a blue screen to reveal another image behind them, such as television
   weather reports.
5. Barbara Kruger, a prominent American artist, coined the term 'I shop therefore I am' in 1987, as a pun on consumerism and René Descartes's statement
   'I think therefore I am'.

REFERENCES

Adams, M (2009) Visiting lecture. The Salford School of Art & Design Visiting
   Lecture Programme, Salford. 13 March 2009.
Ascott, R (2003) *Telematic embrace.* Berkeley: University of California Press,
   232–46.
Barthes, R (1993) *Image-music-text: The death of the author.* London: Fontana
   Press. Originally published 1977.
Baudrillard, J (1995) *Simulacra and simulation (The body, in theory: Histories
   of cultural materialism),* trans. SF Glaser. Ann Arbor: University of Michigan
   Press. Originally published 1981.
Boellstorff, T (2008) *Coming of age in Second Life: An anthropologist explores
   the virtually human.* Princeton: Princeton University Press.
Burkeman, O (2007) Exploding pigs and volleys of gunfire as Le Pen opens HQ in
   virtual world. Guardian.co.uk. Online. Available HTTP: http://www.guardian.
   co.uk/technology/2007/jan/20/news.france (accessed 28 May 2010).
de Certeau, M (2002) *The practice of everyday life.* Berkeley: University of California Press. Originally published 1980.
Deleuze, G (1994) *Difference and repetition.* London: Athlone Press. Originally
   published in Great Britain 1994.
de Saussure, F (1998) *Course in general linguistics,* trans. R Harris. Peru, IL: Open
   Court Classics. Originally published 1964.
Eco, U (1986) *Travels in hyperreality.* London: Picador.
Galloway, K and S Rabinowitz (1980) Hole-In-Space. Online. Available HTTP:
   <http://www.ecafe.com/getty/HIS/index.html> (accessed 20 June 2010).

Heilesen, S (2009) Teleporting the library. *Journal of Gaming and Virtual Worlds* 1, no. 2: 117–30.

Keegan, V (2006) The profits of virtual insanity. Guardian.co.uk. Online. Available HTTP: <http://www.guardian.co.uk/technology/2006/dec/08/comment.business> (accessed 28 May 2010).

———. (2009) Peter Mandelson ushers in a virtual New Labour revolution. Guardian.co.uk. Online. Available HTTP: http://www.guardian.co.uk/politics/blog/2009/jan/12/labour-media (accessed 20 June 2010).

Krueger, MW (1991) *Artificial reality II*, 2nd ed. Reading, MA: Addison-Wesley Professional.

Lacan, J (2007) *Ecrits: The first complete edition in English*. NewYork: W. W. Norton. Originally published 1966.

McLuhan, M (1994) *Understanding media: The extension of man*. Cambridge, MA: MIT Press.

Mori, M (1970) Bukimi no tani (the uncanny valley). *Energy* 7: 33–35. (In Japanese).

Sermon, P (1992–2010) Paul Sermon official homepage. Online. Available HTTP: http://www.paulsermon.org/ (accessed 18 May 2010).

Stephenson, N (2000) *Snow crash*. Crockett, CA: Spectra Paperback. Originally published 1992.

Stocker, G and C Schopf (eds) (2007) *Ars Electronica 2007: Goodbye privacy—welcome to the brave new world*. Ostfildern, Germany: Hatje Cantz.

Turkle, S (1995) *Life on the screen: Identity in the age of the Internet*. London: Simon and Schuster.

Zizek, S (2009) *First as tragedy, then as farce*. London: Verso Books.

2 An Imagined Community of Avatars?

A Theoretical Interrogation of *Second Life*™ as Nation through the Lens of Benedict Anderson's Imagined Communities

Kevin Miguel Sherman

INTRODUCTION

> [...] VWs (Virtual Worlds) offer something that is perhaps a bit more than a mere entertainment to which the players have become addicted. Rather, they offer an alternative reality, a different country in which one can live most of one's life if one so chooses [...]
>
> —Edward Castronova (2001: 10)

As more and more people spend more and more of their waking hours participating in online virtual worlds (OVWs) of one type or another, we are left to consider the simple question of how to explain this. As Castronova suggests, OVW usage is often associated with addiction (see, for example, Charlton and Danforth 2004; Chiu, Lee, and Huang 2004; Clarke and Duimering 2006; Fisher 1994; Whang and Chang 2004; Yee 2006). This is not surprising considering its very essence, that is, its virtual reality, could be taken to imply an escape from actual reality.[1] Yet, besides pathological explanations, what else could account for a robust attachment or sense of belonging that individuals may experience with regards to an OVW?

First of all, we might wish to consider any combination of the following theoretical constructs: brand loyalty (Knox and Walker 2001), product attachment (Desmet and Hekkert 2007)—although both of these reduce (rightly or wrongly) an OVW to a mere product such as a box of cereal—or social identity theory (Tajfel and Turner 1979); i.e., people may derive a sense of themselves through the social relationships they form in an OVW. At a more basic level, an OVW may simply fill the need for companionship (see Mennecke et al. 2007) (for a counter-argument, see Ducheneaut et al. 2006). On the other hand, perhaps there are individuals who are able to enjoy OVWs in ways they are unable to enjoy actual-world (AW) societies. (For example, for a discussion of the benefits of OVWs to children with cancer, see Loving 2006.) We might also consider that individuals use OVWs to make money, either through the sale of virtual objects or through the provision of virtual services (e.g., virtual prostitution, virtual housing construction, virtual plastic surgery, etc.) (see the economic report on

Second Life provided by Linden Lab 2008; and for a discussion of avatar as commodity, see Manninen 2007). And I am sure there are countless other explanations as to why individuals might commit a significant portion of their time to an OVW—the most straightforward being that OVWs offer an entertaining way to pass some time; i.e., people participate in such sites because they are fun (Ardévol et al. 2006; Meikle 2006).

ACTUAL-WORLD NATIONAL IDENTITY

But are these merely 'fun places to hang out in' or do they mean more than that to at least some inhabitants? For example, do some virtual-world members approach OVWs in the way that individuals approach AW nations? In other words, could something akin to national identity exist within an online virtual world? As others have noted, there are many competing notions about the meaning of national identity (Huddy and Khatib 2007; Luedtke 2005; Paasi 1997). For my objectives, I use national identity in the broadest of senses, to refer to that feeling one has of belonging to or being a part of a nation (Billig 1995; Huddy and Khatib 2007; Luedtke 2005) (e.g., New Zealand national identity might be defined as feeling or being a New Zealander).

Furthermore, I contend that the importance of national identity cannot be overstated. For example, national identity scholar, Anthony Smith (1991), claims that national identity exerts 'a more potent and durable influence than other collective cultural identities . . . and this type of collective identity is likely to continue to command humanity's allegiances for a long time to come' (175–76). The question is this—does the word 'humanity' consist only of the flesh and blood type of humans? Or is it flexible enough to include the virtual type as well? And make no mistake, although some might dismiss OVWs as being just silly games (for such a discussion, see Boellstorff 2006), this is no trivial matter. For as more and more people migrate from actual world to virtual world and back again, it becomes increasingly legitimate to query as to which entity holds greater sway over the individual: an actual-world nation or an online virtual world.

What follows, then, is an interrogation into the nature of the relationship that exists between individuals and online virtual worlds through a theoretical discussion of AW nationhood. In so doing, it is first necessary to describe and define some of the key components of this interrogation, including online virtual worlds, the concept of virtuality, and AW nationhood. Using these definitions, I next offer a rationale for drawing the comparison to nationhood in the first place. With a rationale in place, I then interrogate this notion of virtual world as nation from the perspective of the individual, examining both the theoretical and practical implications of such a comparison. The chapter ends with a few concluding remarks about individual perception and the plausibility of virtual-world nationhood.

WHAT IS AN ONLINE VIRTUAL WORLD?

An Internet-enabled phenomenon, online virtual worlds (OVWs) often employ computer generated imaging (CGI) to simulate three-dimensional environments populated by user-created avatars, which Yee (2006) succinctly defines as 'customizable characters'. An OVW can take a number of different forms (Klastrup 2003), but here the focus is primarily directed at one type in particular: online virtual social worlds (OVSWs) and specifically at the OVSW known as *Second Life*. An OVSW, for the most part, does not involve the character skill development (e.g., improving one's swordplay) or strategy objectives (e.g., defeating an opposing army) more typically associated with online virtual-world games (e.g., massively multiplayer online role-playing games or MMORPGs) (Klastrup 2003). Rather, the purpose or point of OVSWs is much more open to interpretation. For example, *Second Life* allows users (through their avatars) to buy and sell virtual property (and other virtual items), explore the world as they choose (although some areas are often private and access to them, therefore, is blocked to some users), build and create items (e.g., vehicles, houses, clothing, etc.), and interact with other avatars through avatar gestures (Thoma et al. 1999) (e.g., waving, thumbs up, smiling, frowning, laughing), virtual physical contact (e.g., virtual hugging, kissing, etc.), various text-based communication options (e.g., instant messaging that is either private or public), and a speech-based option as well. In addition, *Second Life* has its own currency known as Linden dollars; users are even able to exchange Linden dollars for AW currencies and vice versa. That said, unlike MMORPGs, in *SL* avatars cannot be killed (unless their owners choose to end their lives by discontinuing the use of them) nor do they progress to higher levels as they gain experience in-world. On the other hand, such clear distinctions obscure the fuzzy overlap that exists among the various forms of OVWs. For example, *Second Life* members are able to play any of a number of multiplayer games within *SL*, including but not limited to combat/war games, urban crime games, and fantasy/adventure games. For that matter, members of MMORPGs spend considerable in-game time just hanging out with friends, socializing (for example, see Taylor 2006).

Thus, OVSWs are a multifaceted phenomenon: there are economic aspects, social aspects, interpersonal aspects, community aspects, and cultural aspects. But are they nations? And specifically, can we conceive of *Second Life* as nation, or in this case, as *virtual* nation? Which leads to the question of how to define such a novel concept as virtual-world nationhood in the first place.

ACTUAL-WORLD VS. VIRTUAL-WORLD NATIONHOOD

Some might claim that it would be a mistake to define virtual nationhood via an understanding of AW nations. In other words, virtual worlds, the argument goes, should be studied 'in situ, as a form of human behavior with its own characteristics worthy of study' (Boellstorff 2008; Clarke and Duimering 2006: 2; see also MacKinnon 1998). Whereas I readily acknowledge that for some individuals online virtual worlds are as real and as important as anything in the actual world (Castronova 2001; Taylor 1999; Turkle 1997; Yee 2006), I tend to support the notion advanced by such scholars as T. L. Taylor (2006) that OVWs are mutually constitutive of the real and the virtual. For example, OVW virtual inhabitants (i.e., avatars) are unavoidably imbued with the real-life experiences of their creators. Thus, from my perspective, a theoretical interrogation of virtual-world nationhood should begin with an understanding of what we mean by AW nationhood.

There is little agreement as to what is meant by the term nation (Luedtke 2005; A. D. Smith 2002) and as such, a thorough interrogation of the term falls beyond the scope of this chapter. That said, a nation, according to the online *Compact Oxford English Dictionary for Students*, is: 'a large body of people united by common descent, culture, or language, inhabiting a particular state or territory'. Although such a definition may raise as many questions as it answers (e.g., what is meant by culture?), it is instructive in that it clearly delineates some of the characteristics of nationhood: nations are entities comprised of masses of people who share certain traits, who make claims to certain, specific territory, and who are often organized and governed via states, hence the term nation-states.

Yet, such specific features aside, another perspective deals less directly with defining the precise characteristics of nationhood and focuses more upon the nature of the relationship between a nation and its members. Benedict Anderson (1991), in his influential book, *Imagined Communities: Reflections on the Origin and Spread of Nationalism*, defines a nation as an imagined community comprised of individual members who, despite the fact that most will never meet nor even hear of one another, envision '[. . .] a deep horizontal comradeship' (7). Thus, '[. . .] in the minds of each (fellow-national) lives the image of their communion' (6). Moreover, according to Anderson a nation is also imagined as being limited—in other words, it is imagined to possess bounded territory beyond which presumably lie other nations. Lastly, a nation is imagined to be sovereign, i.e., self-governing and independent. Thus, as is implied by the use of the word 'imagined', a nation, then, is a mental construct—other than some lines on a map there is nothing concrete to which a person could point and say, 'There. That is a nation.'

That said, it is a bit of an overstatement to claim that there is *nothing* about nationhood that is tangible. For instance, you can sift your fingers through the dirt of a nation and you can literally touch at least some of the people who make up a nation. Nevertheless, we have no choice but to imagine (as Anderson suggests) the entirety of the land and the people—thus, the issue of tangibility (or intangibility, as the case may be) is related to the sheer scale of a nation. It should also be noted that this notion of tangibility is an important one for it is central to an understanding of virtuality, a concept that factors prominently throughout this discussion.

WHAT DOES IT MEAN TO BE VIRTUAL?

> The key idea here is not that VR (virtual reality) worlds have the final claim on reality, so much as that the RW (real world) has overstated its claim on reality. Maybe RW isn't the final arbiter of what's real after all. (Peter Ludlow 2001: 4)

I use the term virtual in the way that Rob Shields (2000, 2003) describes it, as something real but not actualized, as a threshold between the abstract and the material (also known as a liminal state). In other words, the 'virtual is not merely an incomplete imitation of the real but another register or manifestation of the real' (2003: 46). Thus, with regards to a digital virtual world, the world is real, the experiences real but '[. . .] everything is representational, a convenient fiction by which participants "meet" but only figuratively; elements interact "in essence" but not physically' (Shields 2000, sec. 3, para. 6). To illustrate these points, consider an entity like *Second Life* which mimics many of the characteristics of nationhood, from territory to (masses of) people (Sherman 2010). And yet, the software which enables *SL* does not possess any actual, tangible territory and is not comprised of any actual, tangible people. In other words, the liminal nature of *SL* is one of the characteristic which makes it an excellent candidate for the entity that I will later describe as virtual-world nation—real but not actual. In the meantime, consider what others have written about this notion of virtual-world nationhood.

WHAT DOES THE LITERATURE TELL US ABOUT VIRTUAL-WORLD NATIONHOOD?

Jerry Everard (2000), writing in *Virtual States: The Internet and the Boundaries of the Nation-State*, poses the question thusly, 'Can there be a state purely based in cyberspace?' (151).[2] Initially, Everard responds to his own question by offering some of the perceived problems with the notion of a virtual state:

> Traditionalists might want to deny the possibility on the grounds that people live in geographical space, and Internet servers are based within sovereign territories—subject already to the vagaries of state-based legislation. The people within such a notional cyberspatial state are also already subject to state-based legislation and so cannot secede into cyberspace. (151)

On the other hand, he does not necessarily view these objections as insurmountable or even, for that matter, as problems as such:

> [. . .] another way to look at this [. . .] is that we are already living in virtual states. That is to say that the state is nothing more or less than a legal fiction [. . .] . [C]onstantly shifting map boundaries remind us that the state is historically contingent and essentially contested. The state [. . .] is like an email discussion list—an identity to which we subscribe, and thereby derive the benefits and responsibilities of a co-operative society. The problem then is not whether a fictive [. . .] state can exist in cyberspace as opposed to 'real' states, but rather whether there can be a fiction within a fiction. (152)

Although Everard does oversimplify things (e.g., surely the process of 'unsubscribing' from a state is exponentially more complex than clicking 'unsubscribe' on an email discussion list), he raises an important point about the nature of AW nation-states: like cyberspace, they too are in many ways intangible, virtual. And whereas Anderson (1991), for his part, considers the territory which a nation occupies as imagined as limited (i.e., having finite boundaries), it is clear that he did not conceive the nation itself to be '"imaginary" as in "unicorn"' (226). Thus, although broadly speaking Anderson and Everard offer complimentary analyses, Anderson would likely part company with Everard over his use of the term 'fictive state'. For in Anderson's view the nation-state, although it may be imagined and it may even be virtual, is, after all, real. In other words, just because the nation-state is an entity that we must imagine does not suggest that it is therefore somehow fictitious. Nevertheless, in describing a nation as an *imagined* community, Anderson is a clear advocate of the abstract nature of nationhood.

Others have more directly confronted such abstraction via an interrogation of the potentially problematic relationship between nationhood and territory. In the process, such scholars edge, however unwittingly, towards what I would call virtual nationhood. For instance, Roberts (2003) offers examples of AW nations that do not possess internationally recognized borders as such and thus could be classified as virtual nations, existing, as it were, within the land of other nations, their own claims to territory unrecognized by the powers that be. His examples include: the Uyghurs, the Palestinians, the Kurds, and various Native American nations. For such groups, a homeland is a purely historical concept, one that lives solely within the hearts and minds and texts of a nation of people, but not one that is actualized in the actual world. The liminal nature of these particular nations, i.e., their threshold status of existence between no place and a fully territorialized nation, exhibits the very essence of virtuality. Others (including Everard) make the related point that the physical borders of actual-world nation-states are increasingly challenged by the globalizing forces of transnational entities and corporations, cultural flows and movements of people (Castells 2004; Cerwonka

1997; Paasi 1997). As Cerwonka puts it, 'Globalization [. . .] diminishes the significance of national borders. [As a result], nation-states are being imagined in new ways in the present era' (1997: 2).

Coincidentally, if we were to take this notion of the diminishing significance of actual-world national territory to its logical conclusion, we might end up with an entity like *Second Life*. But perhaps this is not coincidence. Perhaps the diminishing significance of actual-world national borders is associated in some way with the popularity of *Second Life* and other online virtual worlds. For example, it could be argued that the uncertain nature of AW nations has driven some to seek comfort in OVWs, their territory (albeit virtual) contained within the tidy rectangular borders of our friendly[3] computer screens. Nevertheless, despite the seeming plausibility of virtual-world nationhood, the rationale for applying such a construct to *SL* in the first place remains to be discussed.

ASPECTS OF *SL* THAT EVOKE
NATIONAL-TYPE COMPARISONS

Ultimately, such rationale is tied to the notion of virtuality and the degree to which virtual characteristics of nationhood are able to inspire perceptions of the actual thing. Specifically, at issue is whether there are aspects of *SL* that might lead an individual to feel for it in the way he or she feels for an actual-world nation (what Guibernau 2004 refers to as the psychological dimension of national identity; see also Tajfel and Turner's 1979 discussion of social identity theory).

From a purely visual perspective, much of *SL* looks and feels like a country (or series of countries), or in other words, *SL* possesses the territorial and societal trappings which define many if not all nations. Scattered across more than 1,100 square kilometers of virtual land (Linden Lab 2008) are three-dimensional representations of familiar settings, including virtual villages, towns, and cities. Such settings contain a wide array of virtual objects and life forms, including trees, roads, cars, houses, buildings, animals, and, of course, people.

Further, such virtual representations are not merely there to be looked at, they are there to be interacted with and in some cases 'inhabited,' and as a result, have the potential to create the illusion (at least for some individuals) of actually being there (what virtual reality researchers refer to as presence [Slater et al. 1994]). Hypothetically, the immersive potential of *SL* might work to encourage the sort of emotional responses individuals feel when visiting AW places (e.g., national landmarks) (see Williams and Vaske 2003). There is certainly research on virtual environments to support such a claim (Biocca and Harms 2002; Garau et al. 2005; McMahan and Tortell 2004). That said, *Second Life* offers its members something beyond just virtual habitation; members are also able to create, design, and build

SL from the 'ground up' (what the *SL* website refers to as 'user-created' ([2009]). This level of 'people power' is something most actual-world fellow nationals could only dream of achieving.

On a related note, there are many groups in *SL* which seem closely related to what could be termed AW civic groups. By civic groups I mean those groups which encourage civic engagement and thereby attempt to address specific concerns of society, or in this case, of *Second Life*. These *SL* groups include those that are humanitarian (e.g., those who help AW disabled people learn to use *SL*), educational (e.g., groups which teach members how to build and design in *SL*), political (e.g., groups which discuss AW or *SL*-specific political issues), business-related (e.g., groups which promote and encourage business activity in *SL*), etc. If research into the benefits of AW civic involvement is any indication (Huddy and Khatib 2007), virtual-world civic-type groups may also facilitate the sort of involvement which might lead to a more deeply felt emotional response to *SL*, generating, for example, the sort of patriotic love more typically associated with AW nations.

Furthermore, the sheer size of *SL*—more than 1,000 virtual islands and a total population of some 13 million members[4] (Linden Lab 2008)—suggests that other categories such as the particularistic notion of community are inadequate descriptors of *SL*, at least when considered in its entirety. *SL* is certainly populous and vast enough to meet Anderson's (1991) threshold of nationhood, i.e., that it be populous enough that members do not know most of their fellow members, have never met one another, or even heard of one another.

Lastly, the economy of *SL* is similar, in terms of both its mechanics and scale, to that of AW nations. For example, insofar as the mechanism is concerned, as with most actual-world economies, the *SL* system involves the buying and selling of goods and services using a single, virtual-world currency known as Linden dollars (for more on the *SL* economy see Ondrejka 2005, and for analysis of the economies of various MMORPGs, see Castronova 2001, 2006). In terms of its economic scale, by April 2008, nearly 22 million US dollars were in circulation in *SL* (Linden Lab 2008). In 2006, at least one commentator placed the *SL* gross domestic product at around 150 million dollars US (Delderfield 2006), which, at the time, would have made it the 166th largest economy in the world, falling just behind the Marshall Islands (NationMaster.com 2006). Thus, the suggestion here is that such a large and mechanically familiar economy might encourage a sense of belonging comparable to that engendered by actual-world national economies (A. D. Smith 1991).

For some, the actual-world mimicry can be a disappointment: In a virtual world where anything is possible, why do most things look and feel so familiar? Yet, it is precisely this banality (see Billig 1995), this reproduction of mundane actual-world objects and settings, which encourages me to ask the question of whether we can conceive of *SL* as a nation in the first place. And if such a comparison seems reasonable, how might we take it one analytical step further? Specifically, in what ways might an individual member perceive *SL* to be a nation as framed within AW theory of nationhood and in particular Anderson's notion of the imagined community?

THROUGH THE LENS OF ANDERSON'S IMAGINED COMMUNITIES: IN WHAT WAYS MIGHT AN ONLINE VIRTUAL WORLD BE PERCEIVED TO BE A NATION?

An Imagined Community of Avatars

Let us begin this discussion with Anderson's notion that a nation is an imagined community. As Anderson implies, whereas such a community is imagined at the level of the individual, it is an imagining borne of the collective. In other words, to suggest that an individual imagines a national community signifies that such an individual is deeply connected not to some disembodied abstraction (e.g., the idea of nationhood) but to the collection of people who comprise this abstraction, who breathe meaning into it. It follows then that to achieve such identification requires a general sense of what defines this collective—who are these fellow nationals, what are their hopes, fears, and aspirations, in what do they believe, how do they communicate with one another, what are their cultural practices, etc. Thus, whereas a nation may be imagined, such imagining does not occur in a vacuum, without some type of input, some type of mass distributed information. Put another way, the people of a nation are able to develop 'a deep horizontal comradeship' (Anderson 1991: 7) for one another only via an understanding of the qualities they share; an understanding achieved through mass communication. In Anderson's view, such national information was disseminated within the earliest nations (e.g., in the Americas in the late 18th and early 19th centuries) through what he termed 'print-capitalism' or the process of mass producing and distributing newspapers and books, a phenomenon made possible by the invention of the printing press.

As the term print-capitalism suggests, such a phenomenon was arguably able to achieve the widespread reach necessary to foster a national-type consciousness due to the economic capital it produced. In other words, it was a self-sustaining phenomenon. However, contrary to the notion that such reach was inspired by people-led movements for national recognition, print-capitalism engendered nations by assisting governments in legitimizing and maintaining their hegemonic dominance over their people (see Castells 2004). Yet such issues of consumption, profit, and power maintenance/legitimization aside, the mass media (initially newspapers and books, followed by radio, film, television, and the Internet) play a key role, even today, in the development and maintenance of a national consciousness (Billig 1995; Edensor 2002; see also Eriksen 2007 for a discussion of the degree to which the Internet may strengthen national identity).

The important question raised by the phenomenon of print capitalism is whether or not such a mechanism exists in *Second Life*. In other words, is an informed collective consciousness even possible in *SL*?[5] In *Second Life*, we find virtual counterparts to many, if not all, of the forms of mass media prevalent in actual-world nations, including *SL*-specific radio stations, television programs, films, magazines, and newspapers. In much the same way that such technologies have enabled the spread of a national consciousness in the actual world, it is conceivable that such media are enabling a similar phenomenon to occur in the virtual world. On any given day, an individual avatar is able to read an online *SL*-specific newspaper article, listen to an online *SL*-specific radio news program, and watch an online *SL*-specific television program. In addition, many *SL* residents blog about their SL experiences, sometimes documenting these experiences via the inclusion of word-for-word in-world conversations (for example, see Sputnik 2007)—one might even be inclined to classify such activities as the virtual-world equivalent of (actual-world) citizen journalism (Hirst forthcoming). On the other hand, such blogging activities also indicate the important role that word of mouth can play in the formation of collective virtual consciousnesses—a single conversation amplified via the Internet can now become part of the collective conversation, so to speak, no matter how small a part. Of course, the same can also be said of actual national consciousnesses, with the Internet enabling the ideas of some individuals to spread relatively quickly to the masses (Castells 2008).

Such forms of (mass) communication raise a number of questions about the relationship of *Second Life*rs to *SL*. For example, are these various mass media spreading an understanding of what it means to be a *Second Life*r? Are they conveying a sense of the shared cultural practices, common beliefs, and shared language(s) of *Second Life*rs? Might these media be contributing to the construction of a *Second Life* virtual-world consciousness similar to that found in actual-world nations?

In lieu of any known relevant empirical research that might assist in answering these questions, let us assume that *SL* does possess the capacity, at least, for a shared, collective consciousness, or what Anderson terms an imagined political community. Using an Andersonian framework, how might we describe this notion of the imagined community insofar as a virtual world is concerned? Like its actual-world counterpart, the imagined community of a virtual-world nation would be comprised of members who envision a deeply-felt solidarity with one another. However, in this case, membership would be vested in avatars rather than actual people. But avatars are owned and operated, so to speak, by actual people who live in actual nations. Thus, a mental image of the communion of avatars would ultimately occur within the mind of an actual person, although the manifestation of such virtual national identity would most likely occur through the words, deeds, and actions of that actual person's avatar. Therefore, to a large degree, the act of imagining such a community would be substantively similar in both an actual nation and a virtual one. In other words, regardless of whether there exists a virtual placeholder for an actual person (i.e., an avatar), the ability to perceive the imagined community of a nation (be it virtual or actual) still resides within a flesh and blood human. That said, I do recognize that the digital human placeholder and the virtual environment more generally may be capable in some way of shaping or affecting the perceptions of the individual behind the avatar. Thus, whereas the act of imagining the community may be similar in both an actual nation and a virtual one, there may be qualitative differences in terms of the content of such imaginings from one world to the next. This view is not as technologically deterministic as it may at first sound. Rather, such a perspective is much more influenced by the role that social and cultural context plays in shaping our beliefs and values (see, for example, Mann and Stewart 2000; Marshall and Rossman 2006) than it is by any specific technology per se. That is to say that just as I would expect different levels of attachment to exist from one actual nation to the next (see, for example, T. W. Smith and Kim 2006) and that immigrants would have a different relationship to their host nation than to their homeland nation (see, for example, Biswas 2005; Wald and Williams 2005), so too might I speculate that the manifestation of virtual-world national identity, for example, would be qualitatively different from its actual-world counterpart.

Thus, the notion of the imagined community is intrinsically related to the *people* of a nation and the way in which individuals imagine a deeply felt attachment to those people. Yet, Anderson's conception of nationhood includes other imaginings, beyond just those related to one's co-nationals.

Imagined as Limited

Next, let us consider Anderson's contention that a nation is imagined as having a limited, finite territory. In contrast, the territory of a virtual world is not only imagined, it is also, in this case, imaginary; i.e., you *cannot* sift the dirt of a virtual world through your fingertips. Moreover, it is plausible to assume that an individual member of *Second Life* might imagine its virtual territory to be limitless (as opposed to limited) in the sense that, all things being equal (particularly the computing power on which OVWs depend), the virtual territory of *SL* can always be expanded (and reduced) at the whim of Linden Lab, the company that owns *SL*. On the other hand, an individual might argue that beyond the seemingly limitless borders of *SL* do lie other OVWs, a notion which perhaps suggests that although the *SL* territory can go on and on indefinitely, there are practical restrictions as to *where* this territory can go—e.g., it quite literally is incapable of intruding upon the territory of other OVWs.[6] Practically speaking then, *SL* members are presented with a paradox: Although in one sense *SL*'s territorial boundaries may be limitless, in another they are much more limited and restricted than those of actual-world nations whose 'shifting map boundaries' (152) encroach upon one another with relative frequency (Everard 2000; see also Billig 1995 for a discussion of the nation-state's obsession with borders and the dire consequences which can result from one nation infringing on the territory of another).

Yet due to the territorial limitlessness of *SL*, it would not be unreasonable to suggest that an individual *SL*er might find the word 'nation' inadequate to the task of describing *SL* and might prefer a word that better reflects its vastness. For example, in describing *SL* many, including myself, refer to it as an online virtual world, which might suggest that the question of what *SL* is has already been answered—in other words, it is, for all intents and purposes, a world. And although we might be inclined to try to argue for or against such an assessment, a perception should not be viewed in such value-laden terms—that is to say that it is neither right nor wrong to perceive *SL* as a world; rather, perception simply *is*. However, that is not to say that there is nothing problematic about comparing *SL* to a world (see also Aarseth 2008). The issue with making such a comparison is not based on the perception being right or wrong; the issue arises from the word itself. Namely, the word 'world' lacks the specificity necessary to distinguish *SL* from other entities; i.e., what exactly does it mean to be a world? Like the academic whose reflexive use of the word 'society' tends to conceal the actual world of nations in which we live (Billig 1995), the use of the word 'world' has similar repercussions to the virtual realm: Its indistinctness is unhelpful in delimiting the true nature of *SL*. Is a world, as Boellstorff (2008) suggests, a borderless, naturally created (i.e., non-human built) planet? Whereas *SL* may be borderless, it certainly is not a *natural* phenomenon. But could it be perceived to be a planet? Perhaps, but then the question becomes—well then what is *on* this planet, how is this planet organized?

There is nothing inherently incompatible about 'planet-hood' and nation-hood. Theoretically, a planet could consist of a single nation or it could consist of many nations—as our planet earth does—or it could be nation-less. Unquestionably, *SL* is organized into regions or what are known as sims. It certainly would not be unreasonable for someone to perceive each region or consortium of regions as single nations. Yet even this scenario would not disqualify *SL* as a whole from being perceived as a nation. Consider the United States of America—a conglomeration of individual states which form a single nation-state; or consider the European Union—what A. D. Smith (1991) might classify as pan-nation, i.e., an overarching entity consisting of individual nation-states; in both cases we have single nations consisting of smaller regions. That said, it could be that *SL* regions do not factor prominently enough into the experience of *Second Life*rs to shape perceptions in the first place and therefore we return again to the possibility that individuals might perceive *SL* as a single nation, irrespective of the significance of regions.

Imagined as Sovereign

As with the previous discussion, the related notion of virtual-world sovereignty raises a number of problematic issues. Briefly stated, the main issue that arises when contemplating virtual-world sovereignty has to do with the fact that ultimately an online virtual world falls under the legal jurisdiction and governance of the actual-world country in which its computer servers reside (Everard 2000). That said, such an issue does not in my mind disqualify an OVW inhabitant from perceiving their OVW homeland as being a sovereign entity, i.e., self-governing and independent from any actual-world jurisdiction. As John Perry Barlow (1996) famously declared in *A Declaration of the Independence of Cyberspace:* 'Governments of the Industrial World, you weary giants of flesh and steel, I come from Cyberspace, the new home of Mind. On behalf of the future, I ask you of the past to leave us alone. You are not welcome among us. You have no sovereignty where we gather [. . .].' Yet, ignoring for a moment the issue of actual-world governance, an individual could certainly be said to imagine an OVW like *SL* as sovereign, particularly if we discuss such sovereignty solely in terms of the virtual realm. In other words, a company which owns an OVW will maintain complete independence from other OVWs if for no other reason than to help differentiate their virtual-world brand. That said, just as actual-world immigrants often possess ties to two or more nations, individuals can and do engage with multiple OVWs. In fact, Pearce (2006a, 2006b) provides a fascinating account of what she calls '[. . .] the Uru Diaspora: a group of online game players who were rendered refugees when their MMOG (massively multiplayer online game) Uru: Ages Beyond Myst [. . .] closed after nine months of operation' (8). Through extensive virtual ethnographic research, she has documented the migration of the Uru diaspora into new online virtual worlds (including *Second Life*), resulting in both creative and disruptive effects upon the existing virtual residents and the migrants themselves.

The issues of sovereignty and territory point to another feature often associated with actual-world national identity, namely that of 'the other.' Many scholars highlight the role of 'othering' in developing one's sense of national identity (Billig 1995; Brockmeier 2001; Edensor 2002). By this, I mean to suggest that we carve out our own national identity by comparing and contrasting our nation with that of others—in other words, we define ourselves by who we are not. What might individuals perceive to be the 'other' nations in the case of an online virtual world such as *Second Life*? The obvious answer would be other online virtual worlds. There likely is a rivalry that develops among those who prefer one OVW to another. A *World of Warcraft* user might belittle a *Star Wars Galaxy* user and a member of *Second Life* might scoff at a member of *There* and through these (in this case negative) comparisons users might come to better understand their own OVW.

Yet perhaps a less obvious answer to the question of what might an individual perceive to be the 'other' insofar as a virtual-world nation is concerned is an AW nation. For instance, there are some researchers who offer examples of users who do not understand why actual-world experiences are privileged over virtual-world ones (Taylor 1999; Turkle 1997). Turkle puts it thusly: 'As more people spend more time in these virtual spaces, some go so far as to challenge the idea of giving any priority to RL [real life] at all' (Turkle 1997: 14). In fact, some people have gotten very upset over what they consider to be the intrusion of actual-world entities (such as actual-world corporations) and other non-VW phenomena into *Second Life*. Angered over the constant influx of corporations into *Second Life* (vis-à-vis corporate storefronts and other marketing elements), the Second Life Liberation Army '[. . .] staged a number of protests in *Second Life* to publicize its position. Three gun-toting members shot customers outside American Apparel—bullet wounds in *Second Life* are not fatal but merely disrupt a user's experience—and Reebok stores [. . .] Then they stepped up the campaign, exploding nukes, which manifested themselves in swirling fireballs that thrust users at the scene into motionless limbo' (Alana Semuels, *Los Angeles Times*, 22 February 2007). Thus, there are individuals who see the actual world as the other, i.e., as the entity against which they come to understand and appreciate their own virtual world.

Historical Issues

Whereas the preceding discussion may help us to understand the theoretical and practical implications of applying Anderson's dimensions of nationhood to an online virtual world, there still is something not quite right about making such a comparison in the first place. I believe that something is captured succinctly by this statement from Anderson: 'If nation-states are widely conceded to be "new" and "historical," the nations to which they give political expression always loom out of an immemorial past [. . .]' (11). In A. D. Smith's (1991) complementary analysis, he claims that the components of a nation include 'an historic territory, common myths and historical memories' (14), all of which can be traced back over several generations. So whereas both of these scholars consider nationhood and national identity to be a modern invention, it is nevertheless an invention built, as it were, upon the rubble of history, generations of history, sometimes even ancient history (see also Thompson 2001).

And therein lies one of the seemingly problematic aspects of the notion of virtual-world nationhood. Considering the fact that online virtual worlds have been in existence only since the early 1990s (Taylor 2006), how can there be generations of history in an online virtual world? The short answer is that there cannot be generations of history in an online virtual world. Furthermore, some might even argue that the rich history intrinsic to AW nationhood invalidates such a comparison be made in the first place. In other words, the insurmountable difference between nation-hood and virtual worldhood may well be the momentous role that the nation-state has played (and continues to play) in the lives of people past and present. For example, A. D. Smith (1991) summarizes the rich, his-torical significance of the homeland of a nation as 'a repository of historic memories and associations, the place where "our" sages, saints and heroes lived, worked, prayed and fought' (9). An online virtual world seems to pale in comparison.

The preceding objections raise two interrelated issues with respect to the plausibility of virtual-world nationhood: First, is virtual-world history a reasonable enough concept, and second, could a virtual world ever claim (even remotely) the level of societal significance reserved for AW nations? In addressing these questions, it is, first of all, worth noting that to ascribe some reverential immutability to the history which precedes most nations, ignores the creative, some would say inventive (see Anderson 1991), aspects of nationhood and national identity. For although most scholars agree that nations and national identities are in some way linked to historical pasts, those histories are, as Anderson puts it, imagined (1991). It is a mytholo-gized history (A. D. Smith 1991), one invented and handed down from generation to generation and/or through state-based educational programs (see Bourdieu 1994; Castells 2004), yet one decidedly indifferent to notions of accuracy or truth (Anderson 1991; Guibernau 2004). That is not to suggest that such history is necessarily fabricated or falsified (as Gelner claims according to Anderson 1991), but that it is imagined and created. As Brockmeier (2001) puts it, '[. . .] conceptions of national identity . . . are invented as a [political] function of the present and then re-projected into the past' (220). Anderson even goes so far as to provide examples of nations that have adopted historical events for their own, such as the Turks who, according to Anderson (1991: 11–12), may seriously consider the Hittites and Sumerians as their forebears, although this is easily disputed.

All of this helps to support the prospect that virtual-world history could exist, could be constructed, as it were, out of histories relating to other times, other places; narratives told from one generation to the next and borrowed, perhaps, by those who inhabit, for example, online virtual worlds. That is to say, that a present-day online virtual-world nation could not possibly be formed solely from online virtual-world history—simply put, there is not yet enough of the stuff. However, just as other nations have creatively borrowed and invented their own histories, so too could such a process be found to exist within a VW nation, perhaps even formalized by the educational systems that exist in at least some OVWs (as we similarly find in actual-world nations [see Bourdieu 1994; Guibernau 2004]).

On the other hand, we should not so quickly dismiss the possibility of virtual-world history, that is, history directly tied to virtual places, people, and events or put another way, non-actual-world history. From my perspec-tive, there are two possible sources of VW history, both of which I believe are interrelated. One would be fictional narratives, mediated via literature, film, television, console games, or the Internet, and the other would be the milieu of events which constitutes the everyday experience of OVWs themselves.

Many of today's online virtual worlds surround themselves in, or at least hint at, back-stories (which we might call history) borrowed from popular and perhaps not-so-popular narratives, oftentimes in the fantasy genre (see Taylor 2006). Sometimes this back-story is self-contained without reference to other narratives; other times it makes homage to existing narratives. For example, *Star Wars Galaxies* unambiguously draws its back-story from the *Star Wars* films and books created by George Lucas (Lucasfilm Entertainment Company 2007).

Such narratives alone, however, do not constitute the entirety of what I would term virtual-world history. Rather, they are inexorably intertwined with the history-making stuff, for lack of a better term, that occurs within the online virtual worlds themselves, a process much more comparable to the process found in actual-world nation-building as documented by scholars such as Anderson and Smith. That virtual stuff would include the interactions of avatars, places, and events which combine to form, over time, what we might call virtual-world history. However, I believe it important to again remind ourselves that such history, to be legitimate and not ludicrous, must involve a considerable passage of time (multiple generations, as A. D. Smith 1991 puts it), and therefore it is quite premature to conclude that the history now being formed in many online virtual worlds is rich enough (i.e., historical enough) to contemporaneously support virtual-world nationhood. Rather, it is better, in my opinion, to view the current online virtual-world inhabitants, places, and events together with their OVW back-stories as the potential building blocks in the formation of future virtual nations—in other words, what we may be currently witnessing with online virtual worlds is the forming of virtual-world nations rather than the already-formed.

However, whereas such a trend will require rigorous research to confirm or deny, the truth may not be revealed until such time has passed as to legitimately support the notion of VW nationhood, a time period for which there are no hard and fast rules. If AW nations offer any guidance, then perhaps as many as a few centuries (see Anderson 1991: 7) would need to pass before we could judge whether online virtual-world nations had formed. On the other hand, it is just as likely that the history of an online virtual-world nation might include an intricate combination of actual-world histories borrowed and invented and virtual history which includes the fictional narrative OVW back-stories and the ongoing OVW everyday life.

Yet even if VW history is a possibility, that says nothing of the importance of such history, whether, in other words, a VW could ever claim a societal role of a magnitude comparable to that of AW nations. Is such salience possible? Perhaps. Is it likely to occur? Who can say? As one researcher of virtual worlds puts it, 'What I have found is that virtual worlds are as real as the physical world. They are filled with real people interacting with each other evoking real emotions and leading to real consequences' (Jakobsson 2006: abstract). It is certainly conceivable that such emotions and consequences could contribute, ever-so-gradually, to the formation of virtual-world history and subsequent virtual-world nations, and that such entities might begin to develop more weighty significance in the lives of at least some members. However, whether such significance rises to a level comparable to that enjoyed by AW nation-states, whether, to paraphrase Anthony Smith, we begin to hear tell of virtual-world heroes, sages, and saints, this is something that can be sorted only with the passage of time.

CONCLUSION

The preceding discussion is meant to offer a theoretical exploration of the notion of online virtual-world nationhood with an emphasis upon the perceptions of those who inhabit such virtual spaces. In applying Anderson's and others' theories of nationhood to the phenomenon of online virtual worlds, I have attempted to work through some of the issues that arise from such an application. Based upon the preceding, it seems to me that an individual could perceive *SL* to be a nation and that therefore the phenomenon of an online virtual-world nation is at least within the realm of possibility. However, a more thorough understanding of the reasons that some users spend significant portions of their waking hours within such OVWs as *Second Life* can be accomplished, in my view, only through diligent research. As noted national identity scholar, Montserrat Guibernau (2004), suggests, '[. . .] what matters is whether [the components of national identity] are felt as real by those sharing a common identity' (135). Thus, determining the degree to which the inhabitants of *Second Life* (for example) perceive it to be a nation will go a long way to uncovering (or not) the presence of online virtual-world nationhood and national identity and the degree to which an OVW nation might hold greater sway over the individual than its AW counterpart. For as Jenkins (2004) suggests, '[g]roup members, in recognizing themselves as [intersubjectively "real"], effectively constitute that to which they believe they belong' (83).

NOTES

1. An oft cited reason for actual-world addictions (such as substance abuse, compulsive gambling, etc.) is that they provide the addict with an escape from everyday problems (for example, see Kausch 2003).

2. It is important to note here that a question about the state is fundamentally different from a question about the nation. Nations are associated with cultures, ethnicities, histories, etc., whereas a state is the entity that governs and structures a nation. Yet despite their being separate and distinct entities, these terms are closely related. For instance, the role of a unifying government (or state) in developing a sense of nationhood is well documented (see, for example, Smith 1991, 26–27).
3. See Turkle (1997) for a discussion of the ways in which we humanize computers.
4. A healthy degree of skepticism should be applied when considering these Linden Lab statistics. For example, in terms of total population, Linden Lab readily admits there is a churn rate of 90%—i.e., after three months, only 10% of new residents remain (see Wagner 2007). Thus, a more meaningful population figure might be closer to 1 million, although such a claim is purely speculative as Linden Lab does not provide statistics on the number of members who remain after three months' time.
5. In terms of the range of media available, the answer is yes, however the reach of such media has been questioned by at least one commentator (see Llewelyn 2009).
6. For technical, practical, and legal reasons, OVWs do not allow an inhabitant to move freely from one competing OVW to another (see Frelik 2008)—e.g., when a person is in *Second Life*, he or she cannot teleport outside of *Second Life* and into another OVW.

REFERENCES

Aarseth, E (2008) Virtual geo-poetics: Towards a critical understanding of ludic landscapes. Paper presented at the *Creating Second Lives: Reading and Writing Virtual Communities Conference*, Bangor, Wales.

Anderson, B (1991) *Imagined communities: Reflections on the origin and spread of nationalism*, 2nd ed. London: Verso.

Ardévol, E, A Roig, GS Cornelio, R Pagès, and P Alsina (2006) Game pleasures and media practices. Paper presented at the *9th Bi-Annual Conference (Europe and the World)*, Bristol, UK.

Barlow, JP (1996). A declaration of the independence of cyberspace. Online. Available HTTP: http://homes.eff.org/~barlow/Declaration-Final.html (accessed 23 January 2007).

Billig, M (1995) *Banal nationalism*. London: Sage.

Biocca, F and C Harms (2002) Defining and measuring social presence: Contribution to the networked minds theory and measure. Paper presented at the *Fifth Annual International Workshop: Presence 2002*, University Fernando Pessoa, Portugal.

Biswas, S (2005) Globalization and the nation beyond: The Indian-American Diaspora and the rethinking of territory, citizenship and democracy. *New Political Science* 27, no.1: 43–67.

Boellstorff, T (2006) A ludicrous discipline? Ethnography and game studies. *Games and Culture* 1, no. 1: 29–35.

———. (2008) *Coming of age in Second Life: An anthropologist explores the virtually human*. Princeton: Princeton University Press.

Bourdieu, P (1994) Rethinking the state: Genesis and structure of the bureaucratic field. *Sociological Theory* 12, no. 1: 1–18.

Brockmeier, J (2001) Texts and other symbolic spaces. *Mind, Culture, and Activity* 8, no. 3: 215–30.

Castells, M (2004) *The power of identity*, 2nd ed., Vol. 2. Cambridge, MA: Blackwell.

———. (2008) Communication power in the network society. Paper presented at the *Oxford Internet Institute*, Oxford, UK.

Castronova, E (2001) Virtual worlds: A first-hand account of market and society on the cyberian frontier. CESifo Working Paper No. 618. Online. Available HTTP: http://ssrn.com/paper=294828 (accessed 15 January 2008).

———. (2006) *Synthetic worlds: The business and culture of online games.* Chicago: University of Chicago Press.

Cerwonka, A (1997) *Space and nation in a global era: In search of Australia.* Unpublished Ph.D. Dissertation: University of California, Irvine.

Charlton, JP and DW Danforth (2004) Differentiating computer-related addictions and high engagement. Paper presented at the *First International Conference on Human Perspectives in the Internet Society: Culture, Psychology and Gender*, Southampton, UK.

Chiu, S-I, J-Z Lee, and D-H Huang (2004) Video game addiction in children and teenagers in Taiwan. *CyberPsychology and Behavior* 7, no. 5: 571–81.

Clarke, D and PR Duimering (2006) How computer gamers experience the game situation: A behavioral study. *ACM Computers in Entertainment* 4, no. 3: 1–23.

Delderfield, JB (2006) 'Second Life' 3-D digital world grows. *Jake's Journal*. Blog posting. Online. Available HTTP: http://jake.qaix.com/0–53-second-life-3-d-digital-world-grows.zhtml (accessed 23 April 2008).

Desmet, P and P Hekkert (2007) Framework of product experience. *International Journal of Design* 1, no. 1: 57–66.

Ducheneaut, N, N Yee, E Nickell, and RJ Moore (2006). "Alone together?": Exploring the social dynamics of massively multiplayer online games. Paper presented at the *SIGCHI Conference on Human Factors in Computing Systems*, Montreal, Quebec, Canada.

Edensor, T (2002) *National identity, popular culture and everyday life.* New York: Berg.

Eriksen, TH (2007) Nationalism and the Internet. *Nations and Nationalism* 13, no. 1: 1–17.

Everard, J (2000). *Virtual states: The Internet and the boundaries of the nation-state.* London: Routledge.

Fisher, S (1994) Identifying video game addiction in children and adolescents. *Addictive Behaviors* 19, no. 5: 545–53.

Frelik, P (2008) When virtual worlds (don't) collide. Paper presented at the *Creating Second Lives Conference: Reading and Writing Virtual Communities*, Bangor, Wales.

Garau, M, M Slater, D-P Pertaub, and S Razzaque (2005) The responses of people to virtual humans in an immersive virtual environment. *Presence* 14, no. 1: 104–16.

Guibernau, M (2004). Anthony D. Smith on nations and national identity: A critical assessment. *Nations and Nationalism* 10, no. 1/2: 125–41.

Hirst, M (forthcoming) *News 2.0: Can journalism survive.* Sydney: Allen and Unwin.

Huddy, L and N Khatib (2007) American patriotism, national identity and political involvement. *American Journal of Political Science* 51, no. 1: 63–77.

Jakobsson, M (2006) *Virtual worlds and social interaction design.* Unpublished Ph.D. Dissertation: Umea University, Umea, Sweden.

Jenkins, R (2004) *Social Identity,* 2nd ed. London: Routledge.

Kausch, O (2003) Patterns of substance abuse among treatment-seeking pathological gamblers. *Journal of Substance Abuse Treatment* 25, no. 4: 263–70.

Klastrup, L (2003) A poetics of virtual worlds. Paper presented at the *5th International Digital Arts and Culture Conference,* Melbourne, Australia.

Knox, S and D Walker (2001) Measuring and managing brand loyalty. *Journal of Strategic Marketing* 9, no. 2: 111–28.

Linden Lab (2008) Second Life virtual economy key metrics (BETA) through April 2008. Online. Available HTTP: http://static.secondlife.com/economy/stats_200804.xls (accessed 6 June 2008).

Llewelyn, G (2009) Second Life's most read blogs. *Gwyn's Home.* Blog posting. Online. Available HTTP: http://gwynethllewelyn.net/2009/03/22/second-lifes-most-read-blogs/ (accessed 23March 2009).

Loving, M (2006) *Elves and fairies in the hospital: Virtual worlds to influence the quality of life among child oncology patients.* Unpublished undergraduate term paper: Trinity University, San Antonio, TX.

Lucasfilm Entertainment Company (2007) Star Wars Galaxies home page. Online. Available HTTP: http://starwarsgalaxies.station.sony.com/ (accessed 1 August 2007).

Ludlow, P (2001) New foundations: On the emergence of sovereign cyberstates and their governance structures. In *Crypto anarchy, cyberstates, and pirate utopias,* ed. P Ludlow, 1–24. Cambridge, MA: MIT Press.

Luedtke, A (2005) European integration, public opinion and immigration policy: Testing the impact of national identity. *European Union Politics* 6, no. 1: 83–112.

MacKinnon, RC (1998) The social construction of rape in virtual reality. In *Network and netplay: Virtual groups on the Internet,* ed. F Sudweeks, M McLaughlin, and S Rafaeli, 148–172. Menlo Park, CA: AAAI/MIT Press.

Mann, C and F Stewart (2000) *Internet communication and qualitative research: A handbook for researching online.* London: Sage.

Manninen, T (2007) The value of virtual assets—the role of game characters in MMOGs. *International Journal of Business Science and Applied Management* 2, no. 1: 22–33.

Marshall, C and GB Rossman (2006) *Designing qualitative research,* 4th ed. Thousand Oaks, CA: Sage.

McMahan, A and R Tortell (2004) Virtual reality and the internal experience. Paper presented at the *IEEE VR04,* Chicago, IL.

Meikle, G (2006) The uses of satire in online activism. Paper presented at the *IR 7.0: Internet Convergences,* Brisbane, Australia.

Mennecke, B, EM Roche, DA. Bray, B Konsynski, J Lester, M Rowe, and AM Townsend (2007) Second Life and other virtual worlds: A roadmap for research. Paper presented at the *28th International Conference on Information Systems (ICIS).* Online. Available HTTP: http://ssrn.com/abstract=1021441 (accessed 11 December 2007).

NationMaster.com (2006) Economy statistics > GDP (2006) by country. Online. Available HTTP: http://www.nationmaster.com/graph/eco_gdp-economy-gdp-nominal&date=2006 (accessed 10 March 2008).

Ondrejka, CR (2005) Aviators, moguls, fashionistas and barons: Economics and ownership in Second Life. Online. Available HTTP: http://ssrn.com/abstract=614663 (accessed 10 April 2007).

Paasi, A (1997) Geographical perspectives on Finnish national identity. *GeoJournal* 43: 41–50.

Pearce, C (2006a) *Playing ethnography: A study of emergent behaviour in online games and virtual worlds*. Unpublished Ph.D. Dissertation: University of the Arts, London.
———. (2006b) Productive play: Game culture from the bottom up. *Games and Culture* 1, no. 1: 17–24.
Roberts, SR (2003) *Uyghur neighborhoods and nationalisms in the former Sino-Soviet borderland: An historical ethnography of a stateless nation on the margins of modernity*. Unpublished Ph.D. Dissertation: University of Southern California, Los Angeles.
Second Life (2009) Second Life home page. Online. Available HTTP: http://secondlife.com/ (accessed 30 March 2009).
Sherman, K (2010) Imitating the nation-state. *Information, Communication and Society* 13(6): 844–69.
Shields, R (2000) Performing virtualities: Liminality on and off the 'Net'. Paper presented at the *Performing Virtualities Workshop*, Middlesex, England. Online. Available HTTP: http://virtualsociety.sbs.ox.ac.uk/events/pvshields.htm (accessed 14 August 2007).
———. (2003) *The virtual*. London: Routledge.
Slater, M, M Usoh, and A Steed (1994) Depth of presence in virtual environments. *Presence: Teleoperators and Virtual Environments* 3, no. 2: 130–44.
Smith, AD (1991) *National identity*. London: Penguin.
Smith, AD (2002) When is a nation? *Geopolitics* 7, no. 2: 5–32.
Smith, TW and S Kim (2006) World opinion. National pride in comparative perspective: 1995/96 and 2003/04. *International Journal of Public Opinion Research* 18, no. 1: 127–36.
Sputnik, O (2007) Visiting the relatives. *500 year diary*. Blog posting. Online. Available HTTP: http://oolonsputnik.blogspot.com/2007/07/visiting-relatives.html (accessed 19 January 2008).
Tajfel, H and JC Turner (1979) An integrative theory of intergroup conflict. In *The social psychology of intergroup relations*, ed. WG Austin and S Worchel, 33–47. Monterey, CA: Brooks/Cole.
Taylor, TL (1999) Life in virtual worlds: Plural existence, multimodalities, and other online research challenges. *The American Behavioral Scientist* 43, no. 3: 436–49.
———. (2006) *Play between Worlds: Exploring online game culture*. Cambridge, MA: MIT Press.
Thoma, V, A Haf, and A Hitzges (1999). Communicating with avatars in virtual 3D worlds. Online. Available HTTP: http://www.visualize.uk.com/conf/activeweb/proceed/pap9/ (accessed 11 January 2007).
Thompson, A (2001) Nations, national identities and human agency: Putting people back into nations. *The Sociological Review* 49, no. 1: 18–32.
Turkle, S (1997) *Life on the screen: Identity in the age of the Internet*, Reprint ed. New York: Simon and Schuster.
Wagner, M (2007) Why is Linden Lab still publicizing misleading usage stats? *The Information Week*. Online. Available HTTP: http://www.informationweek.com/blog/main/archives/2007/05/why_is_linden_l.html (accessed 2 January 2007).
Wald, KD and B Williams (2005) Diaspora political consciousness: Variation in the transnational ethnic alliance of American Jews. Paper presented at the *annual meeting of the American Political Science Association*, Washington, DC. Online. Available HTTP: http://www.allacademic.com//meta/p_mla_apa_research_citation/0/4/1/3/4/pages41345/p41345-1.php (accessed 8 January 2007).

Whang, LS-M. and G Chang (2004) Lifestyles of virtual world residents: Living in the on-line game 'Lineage'. *CyberPsychology and Behavior* 7, no. 5: 592–600.

Williams, DR and JJ Vaske (2003). The measurement of place attachment: Validity and generalizability of a psychometric approach. *Forest Science* 49, no. 6: 830–40.

Yee, N (2006) The demographics, motivations and derived expectations of users of massively multi-user online graphical environments. *Presence: Teleoperators and Virtual Environments* 15: 309–29.

3 Programming Processes
Controlling Second Lives

Elizabeth Burgess

INTRODUCTION: TEXTUAL PROGRAMMING

Taking the creation of 'Second Lives' as its starting point, this chapter will explore the essential question: Who or what is in control? The term 'Second Lives' is loaded with meanings; in this case I take Second Lives to be those experiences, both physical and abstract, gained through participatory texts. Exploring this question necessarily takes into account theories of reading and theories of play; how a reader or participant interacts with a text; and the agencies involved in the creation of such texts (such as authors, publishers, programmers, designers, or editors). This chapter considers different types of text, including printed materials and virtual environments, to discuss the role of the participant in interacting with texts on screen and on page. It debates the relationship between participant, creator, and text, and considers the agencies which play a role in this relationship.

In pursuing questions of control and agency within texts, there are several key issues and definitions to clarify before close analysis of specific texts can begin. Firstly, what is a text? A text is definable in a number of ways. For instance, consider the layers that go into the object which we call a book. A book has a material interface: the physical aspects of the book, the surface through which a reader engages with it. A book has a graphic surface: its letters, its font—the features that 'relate to the face of any page of printed text' (White 2005: 5). A book also has a narrative within it, whether that is an invented narrative (fiction), a person's life story (autobiography/biography), a textbook (instructional), or any other form of literature.[1]

I do not intend to provide an in-depth study of content; in addition to the (most probably invariable) printed marks on a page, a text has different meanings which emerge from the many layers that exist within that text (which include distinctions between form and associations), but it should be noted for the purposes of this chapter that a text is something to which readers respond and which responds to readers. As readers, we engage with a text through its interface, we create interpretations of that text, and, in this, we program it through our engagement. The other side of this is that, as readers, we are also programmed by the text, and by reading. This is apparent in the way in which we interact with texts, and when considering issues of agency. On a material level there are recognizable conventions employed in reading what is thought of as traditional literature. These conventions are usually learnt at an early age, and as readers we are programmed to follow them throughout our reading lives. In the majority of Western adult fiction these conventions fall into two areas. The textual: such things as left-to-right, top-to-bottom reading with entire words arranged into sentences and paragraphs. The material: whole pages bound together on the left-hand side, and encased with a cardboard paperback cover, or a sturdier hardback cover on the front, the back, and the spine. I wish to be careful not to gloss over the many varied forms of books, but taking these types of features as conventions of traditional Western literature, experimental fiction is thus that which appears to subvert these conventions in order to distinguish itself formally or narratologically. It is unlikely that a reader will read a book backwards, or by rearranging the chapters, unless told that that is how he or she is supposed to read; experimental fiction often does tell the reader to interact with the text in a different way than his or her interactions with more traditional literature.

The second question to be raised is: What is an author? Within the scope of this chapter, I could not begin to summarise responses to this question, but will instead define the author as the named creator of a text.[2] Despite theories of the diminishment of the author and a growing awareness of the participatory origins of the text, there is still a special authority and distinguished originality attributed to the author figure. The author is not the only creator; consider the production of a book. The finished product is a result of the combined efforts of the named author, the publisher, the designers, the editors, and a host of other people. Anybody who has had any hand in the product becomes, in part, a creator or author. In his or her interpretative activity the reader too becomes part of this process.

The third question which must be raised is: What is a reader? The reader is no less complex a figure than the author. A key issue here is that, in talking about the reader, who exactly do we mean? Each reader is an individual with his or her own historical situation: How can we discuss the figure that is called 'the reader', when this figure does not exist?[3] What it means to be a reader, or an author, of a text, is not straightforward and cannot be simply written off as a case of author writes text, reader reads text. Who, or what, is in control when a reader reads a text? What controls our understanding and our response? What rules and controls exist in our interaction with texts and are we able to interact with a text without complying with rules external to individual agency?

PROGRAMMING FREEDOM/RESTRICTION

At the 2008 Austin Game Developers Conference, Chris Crawford gave a lecture entitled '14 Conceptual Shifts: Moving from Games to Interactive Storytelling', in which he argued that graphics are proving to be an obstruction to interactivity in gaming. After telling a room full of game developers to 'screw graphics' in favour of a primacy of interactivity, he argued that it is ridiculous that the average graphical user interface recognizes 100 verbs, whereas his 24-page introduction-to-reading book *The Little Mermaid* has, by his count, 122 different verbs. Crawford traces this back to the command-line prompt, through text-based gaming and as a limit that remains in contemporary graphics-based games. In accepting the estimation that the average game has only 100 verbs, say 100 actions that a user can take and see represented in their avatar's physical movement, questions are raised about both the way in which participation is signaled in a text, and the different agencies involved in participation. In the case of a game that ostensibly restricts choice because of its inability to recognize a wider variety of verbs, it is not that the designers have set intentional limits on recognition, and nor is it that the game is not capable of allowing a broader diversity. It is rather something that exists in the nature of the game program itself, a factor within the game-as-text that restricts user agency and exists because, historically, it always has (Crawford 2008).

The obvious response to this apparent lack of space for the participant to act freely is that it would be unnecessary to create a program which recognizes any verb in (to take one market) the English speaking world. This may be true: In usual circumstances a gamer would not require such a vast amount of choice to progress through the game story. Crawford's observation may be accurate, but it is problematic. Does the official recognition of more verbs make for a more interactive gaming experience? A gamer is able to communicate any verb, and thus any additional actions desired, via the text communication boxes included in many MMORPGs. To take one example for the sake of clarity, ArenaNet's *Guild Wars* includes a range of actions a player can take by typing into the chat box, for instance '/wave' would result in the avatar waving their hand; other actions include '/jump' and '/clap'. The '/dance' command is arguably the most pervasive of these actions. On '/dance', an avatar will perform a looped dance, the specific movements of which are decided by character class. Arguably, the inclusion of a visual representation of the 'dance' verb does not increase interactivity within game play: As a YouTube search confirms, players spend time within the game world, quite separately to any activity intended to advance progression through the game, organizing flashmobs of avatars to converge in one area, then synchronizing their '/dance' commands, thus performing a looped dance *en masse*. These performances are usually set to music from outside of the game world before being broadcast on the Internet. In doing this, the players exhibit themselves as a community (which is both virtual and, in games which require co-operative play such as *Guild Wars* or *World of Warcraft*, present in the real world: a community comprised of a group of people working together to achieve certain goals) in both physical world and virtual world spaces. The virtual community interactions are made possible by organized group interactions in the physical world; organized group activity in the physical world commands keyboard strokes, creating virtual group movement: Physical real-world actions both program the performance of movements in virtual spaces and enable the existence of mirrored virtual-world/real-world community organization.

Whereas this raises some interesting questions about the divide between reality and virtuality, it also posits the idea that verbs could amplify interactivity as erroneous. It may be true that games do not recognize and attribute action to a vast number of verbs, but it is also true that a larger list of verbs would not move game design in the direction of heightened interactivity, and gamer agency would be affected only marginally. A wide variety of pathways are not necessary, but Crawford's observation does indirectly raise a question about the extent to which regulations are made clear within a text.

REGULATIONS OF READING

In the form of learnt reading conventions, regulations are not always explicit when reading a novel. As discussed at the beginning of this chapter, experimental fiction is distinguished by the way in which the reader interacts with it. Julio Cortázar's novel *Rayuela*, originally published in 1963 and translated into English as *Hopscotch*, has been labeled as experimental by virtue of the changes it makes to the standard act of reading a novel—its interactive design encourages its readers to engage with it in a physical sense. All literature is interactive—reading would not be possible without a level of interaction—but some literature, such as *Hopscotch*, draws attention to its interactivity in a deliberate manner; as a metafictional novel,[4] it draws attention to the process of reading, the creation of writing, and the artifice of fiction.[5] *Hopscotch* is by no means the only text with an experimental structure but, in addition to explicit instructions and a requirement for the reader to physically traverse the text by flipping between chapters, unlike other examples of experimental fiction,[6] *Hopscotch* retains its conventional binding. With this in mind, the novel enables a discussion of agency and notions of programming within literature, without the need to digress too far into matters of binding and material structure.

Hopscotch consists of 155 chapters, organized into three sections, and is separated into 'two books' (Cortázar 1966: Table of Instructions) by means of two explicit choices of interaction method for readers. Chapters 1–36 (titled 'From the Other Side') and 37–56 (titled 'From This Side') comprise one book; a second emerges by reading according to the chapter map provided, which interweaves the first books with chapters 57–155 (titled 'From Diverse Sides: Expendable Chapters'), beginning the book at chapter 73. The novel opens with instructions on how to proceed:

> In its own way, this book consists of many books, but two books above all. The reader is invited to choose between these two possibilities:
>
> The first can be read in a normal fashion and it ends with Chapter 56, at the close of which there are three garish little stars which stand for the words The End. Consequently, the reader may ignore what follows with a clean conscience.
>
> The second should be read by beginning with Chapter 73 and then following the sequence indicated at the end of each chapter. In case of confusion or forgetfulness, one need only consult the following list:
>
> 73—1—2 -116—3—84—4—71 [. . .]—131—58—131 -
>
> Each chapter has its number at the top of every right-hand page to facilitate the search.

This functions as a manual on how to read the text; following the second method provides a code through the text, interweaving the 'first book' with the expendable passages. A reader left to his or her own devices is unlikely to read a conventionally structured novel in any order other than that in which it came; in *Hopscotch*, the existence of instructions (a manual on how to read) presents the reader with an explicit choice between two methods of approaching the text. The reader can read as one would read a conventionally structured novel by using the first method: In doing this, the reader is told that he or she may ignore the rest of *Hopscotch* 'with a clean conscience'; in following the second option (the map) it is then suggested that the reader's conscience may be sullied in some way. This posits the reader as a figure with a certain ethics, a responsibility of reading: If he or she chooses to read according to the chapter map then this allows for a clean conscience; if choosing the seemingly darker path—to go against the actions prescribed—his or her conscience is no longer 'clean'. When reading by the second method, it is easy in the physical movement between chapters to become lost in the labyrinthine spaces of the narrative; the map requires the reader physically to traverse the text to follow the story and, once lost, it is not easy to backtrack and rediscover the path. If the reader can make such mistakes, there is a potential for his or her engagement with the narrative to go awry, or even the possibility of failing at reading due to an inability to engage successfully (that is, as stated in the rules) with the formally experimental aspects of the text. Readers are not usually accused of cheating or hacking a literary interface, yet considering reading in the context of these terms begins to open up productive discussions in the study of what it means to be a reader or user of a text.

ETHICAL READING AND SUBVERSIVE READING

To describe two relationships between subject and action—between reader and reading—I wish to draw comparisons with Graeme Kirkpatrick's discussion of computational temperaments. In *Critical Technology* (2004), Kirkpatrick presents two opposing temperaments which are most clearly expressed in the figures of the computer gamer and the computer hacker. The gamer is a 'conformist, who finds the world provided for her at the interface quite seamless and satisfactory'; the hacker has an 'intense, focused engagement [. . .] at levels that are deliberately obscured by [the] interface' (2004: xi). There is much scope for discussion of what falls between these two temperaments, but this discussion is deserving of more space than it can be given here. For the purposes of this chapter, consider the description of the gamer—happy with playing via the seamless interface—as linked with that of the reader: the ethical figure acting as he or she has been told, whether through explicit instructions such as those found in *Hopscotch*, or more implicit instructions derived from reading conventions learnt in early life.[7]

As in Kirkpatrick's juxtaposition, in contrast to the ethical reader who is happy with the available actions, the figure of the hacker, who 'demands transparency' (2004: xi) yields ideas about a subversive reader, a figure who may (attempt to) choose to disregard these available actions and reprogram the reading process, intentionally or otherwise. Taking further the comparison, Kirkpatrick describes the gamer as a 'good user' (2004: xi), happy with the interface provided; the notion that a reader can stop reading *Hopscotch* at chapter 56 with 'a clean conscience' raises a question regarding the reader: Is a 'good' reader one who follows this instruction, reading the novel without delving into the expendable chapters and thus carrying out an ethical responsibility, rather than risking dirtying his or her conscience?

Put a different way, if the reader does give up his or her 'clean conscience' and reads the expendable chapters, is that then an act of rebellion against convention? In reading the book in a different order to a front-to-back conventional text, is the reader actually doing anything subversive? The answer to this is no: Although the text, in its metafictionality, is preventing the suspension of disbelief, and drawing attention to its own artifice and the reader's investment in causality and chronology, what the reader is doing is simply adding the author's instructions onto his or her learnt reading conventions: reading top-to-bottom, left-to-right, and still beginning at the start and ending at the end—it is just that, in this case, the rules state that chapter 73 *is* the start. In following the instructions, a reader is not delving past the interface (the surface through which he or she interacts with the text—both the graphic surface and the actions carried out in reading), but has simply substituted one method of interaction for another: The navigational interface of *Hopscotch* replaces the standard interface of a novel that requires reading from page 1 to the end. The reader is only following instructions; Cortázar's offer of a 'clean conscience' functions more as a device of temptation, seeming to grant readers a greater (illusory) agency than they actually possess and present them with a sinful look deeper into the narrative, an opportunity to delve past the literary interface. In truth, it does nothing of the sort; in substituting Cortázar's instructions for standard reading conventions, the reader is certainly not reading subversively.

MacCallum-Stewart and Parsler describe the false sense of agency created in the reader as 'Illusory Agency':

> The process of 'tricking' a reader into believing they have greater impact on and import within the game [. . .] a facet of the game design which appears to allow the player free reign [sic] and personal choice, but in fact guides them along rigid lines through a relatively linear narrative. (2007: para. 3)

Investigating Illusory Agency through a reading of *Vampire: The Masquerade—Bloodlines*, MacCallum-Stewart and Parsler suggest that the illusion of free choice creates a feeling of empowerment in users. The example given describes the way in which the *VtM* game plot works towards this:

> *Vampire: The Masquerade* [allows the player] mild subversion within the game. The focus of the main story arc concerns the vampire prince, but the player is allowed to ally with his rebellious enemies. This alliance makes no difference until the very end of the game: the enemies tell the player to stick close to the prince and spy on him and, essentially, follow the same story arc as they would have anyway. These choices allow the player to feel subversive: an authority figure is set up and then the player is allowed to rebel against them. [. . .] Once again the illusion of free choice is produced to satisfy the player's need for a sense of empowerment within the game.

The character of the vampire prince in *VtM* is a fictional authority figure against which the player can appear to rebel. In reading *Hopscotch*, a reader is faced with two primary figures of authority: Cortázar's instructions, and the regulations of reading learnt by the reader. As Cortázar's instructions serve as a replacement for standard reading conventions, neither the authority of the instructions, nor of the conventions, is rebelled against successfully: The reader can read only using a set of rules comprised of a formal layer of instructions (the order in which to read), and a cognitive layer (the learnt ability of making meaning from written text). What, then, would be a truly subversive reader, a reader that genuinely reprograms the literary interface? One way of reprogramming the reading process—hacking into the literary interface and subverting it—would be to read the end first or read pages at random, but this would destroy much of the pleasure associated with the act of reading; there is nothing to be gained by this, other than the act of subversion itself. In fact, readers do skip ahead in novels: Even this, then, is not subversive. The way in which the literary interface is hacked is in extending the boundaries of texts—by taking something central to the work and reprogramming it in a different context.

FAN FICTION AND USER-GENERATED CONTENT

Notions of pleasure within the text extend beyond the act of reading when looking at reprogramming texts in different contexts.[8] Thomas (2007) highlights that fan fiction 'precisely aims to extend the fictional world of the source text and to even go beyond it to create alternate universes [. . .] the concept of an individual piece of fiction as a fixed entity gives way to a more fluid conception of "text"'. Fan fiction is a method of both extending, and reclaiming, the text for the reader; Henry Jenkins refers to writers of fan fiction as 'textual poachers' (Jenkins 1992: 24) and observes that '[f]an fiction is a way of the culture repairing the damage done in a system where contemporary myths are owned by corporations instead of owned by the folk' (Katyal 2006: 482). Particularly prevalent examples of the folk taking back the narrative from the corporations exist within what has been labeled on Internet shopping sites such as Amazon.com as 'Pro Fanfiction': fan fiction that has been published professionally and is now available on general sale in print format (as opposed to only over the Internet).[9] The evolution of this is apparent in the media in which the books are published. Tor, an imprint of Tor-Forge which is part of Macmillan, publish several printed fan fiction books, written by different authors, based on the *Halo* (Bungie 2001) videogame series. Tor.com provides a virtual forum for those fans aspiring to publication to get their work displayed online, to then be read and commented on by other fans.

The *Halo* series of fan fiction tends to focus on the playing out of scenarios that did not exist in the original games, as does much fan fiction. Thomas (2007) refers to material created as 'an addition or supplement to the canon' (the original source text) as the 'fanon': material which is accepted by the fan fiction community as a valid variation on the source text, and as a result is often included in the work of other fan fiction writers. As Thomas notes, the fanon is 'something that is collaboratively achieved and subject to constant revision and updating' (2007). The acting out of fanonical scenarios, and thus the fulfilling of different narratives that could emerge from the basics of the text, satisfies unfulfilled potential for which the games simply would not have the space (nor, perhaps, the inclination).

The significance of pleasure is more apparent when looking at slash fiction, a variant of fan fiction that concentrates on erotic fantasy, usually between characters that have no such explicit connection in the original text (or, indeed, did not exist in the original text). Concerned explicitly with sex, slash fiction displays elements of subversion, as the author(s) write the desires of their readers into the text. Readers already project their desires and fantasies onto a text, and slash fiction is an explicit way of putting the self into the text and engaging directly with those fantasies. Writing slash fiction reprograms the desires and relationships of the characters and, as it is designed to provoke a response from the reader, it also programs the readers' responses to the text, tapping into those desire-based narratives that were never fulfilled in the original story. This raises a question about rules: If the original text is the interface through which the new text operates, what happens to the controlling forces within the text? It is accepted that certain rules should be observed—for instance, the characters must retain characteristics of the original characters in order for it to work. One writer on website *deviantART* explains the rules as follows: [10]

> For characters, always use the main ones. Everyone knows who Fred and George are; the audience isn't going to be interested in ol' Jor-something. There is an added bonus to using characters that everybody knows already. You don't have to waste precious time that could be spent on the plot with characterization. Why bother with those deep and meaningful moments that define the psyche of a character, or even the minute ones that give insights into their personality? That's the job of the original author, not yours. All you do is put them into a new and insightful plot that no one has done before [. . .] Remember, fanfictions exist to fulfill [sic] your own dreams and fantasies. (child-dragon [pseudo.] 2008)

The extension of textual boundaries is expressed in a different form in user-generated content (UGC) in gaming. Creating UGC, like fan fiction, enables users to put something of themselves into the game. A simple expression of this is the ability to design objects in programs external to the game world and import them: very simply, a photograph of your real self in a house in *The Sims* (Maxis 2000). More complexly, larger virtual environments are created by users in *Second Life*™ (Linden Lab 2003). Differently, and no less complexly, the premise of *LittleBigPlanet* (Media Molecule 2008) is UGC: It was reported that, as of 13 November 2008, more than 84,000 individual user-created levels had been published online (Sony Computer Entertainment Europe 2008).

Going further into the realm of reclaiming texts is UGC that hacks into hardware which is not intended to be user-programmable. For instance, a group known on the Internet as 'Team Twiizers' created and made available software that allow users to play, or read, DVDs on the Nintendo Wii console: This was not something users were able to do prior to this intervention. Adaptation in this way is a very literal reprogramming, but ties back to Jenkins's idea of 'repairing the damage done in a system where contemporary myths are owned by corporations instead of owned by the folk': In this respect, we see the users taking back the hardware and literally reprogramming it to suit their own objectives. Taylor looks at the 'ways people innovate play, whether through strategies or extending the games' bounds through collectively produced sites' (2006: 131–32) and Mulligan and Patrovsky observe that:

> Developers spend years focused on making a game. If they're not careful, this will breed certain assumptions, such as the world they created will remain their world and the players will play the game the way the creators want it played. That will not happen. Players have their own motivations and objectives. (2003: 217)

This is true: Participants involved in making meaning and interacting with a program-based text (which I would argue that a literary text is) do have their own objectives in their interpretative and virtual or material interactions with the text. It has been widely acknowledged (Taylor 2006: 136) that online games are 'co-constructed by a variety of agents', and that despite this, there is 'a thread of authorial control [remaining] that at times expresses itself with statements about players "not playing right", "causing trouble", or "ruining gameplay".' This links back to the notion of failing at the reading or interpreting of a text. Players who cause trouble can be accused of ruining the game for other players, but there is also a sense that they are ruining the game simply by going against the wishes of the designers. Differently to obvious methods of 'cheating' (such as cheat codes), in MMORPGS, participants may build highly specialized characters in order to achieve a certain aim in gameplay; for instance rather than acting within a guild, players choose to farm large amounts of gold on solo outings. The game's designers may then nerf the build, rendering ineffective that character's superior abilities.[11] In the light of such actions, Mulligan and Patrovsky's advice to designers that '[i]t isn't your game; it's the players['] game' seems to attribute more creative agency to the players than actually exists. Player interaction is also restricted spatially. Maps, whereas often appearing visually limitless, inevitably reach an end. This is often signaled with a virtual wall or, in more open landscapes, a hill that the player cannot walk across, and places a finite limit on what movement the player can perform within that space. The issue of interpretation poses similar questions. In many ways, the game as a textual object appears to be less malleable in its potential meanings, less open to interpretation than the book object (particularly fiction). It is accepted that readers interpret fiction in different ways, and that different meanings can emerge from the literary text. It is less accepted, and perhaps less obvious, that game texts are open to different types of user interaction and emergent meanings. One of the most interesting ways in which game texts are being interpreted is in the work of digital artists JODI (Joan Heemskerk and Dirk

Paesmans), whose modifications of game texts provide new contexts for the interpretation of those texts.

Linked into these ideas are issues of ownership. Foucault observes (1977: 124–27) that the emergence of modern conceptions of authorship goes hand in hand with issues of copyright, highlighting the impact of material or economic factors on both literary and non-literary texts. As Taylor points out (2006: 134), '[W]hile the owners of a game provide the raw materials through which users can participate in a space, it is in large part *only through the labor of the players* that dynamic identities and characters are created that culture and community come to grow, and that the game is made animate.' (Italics in original.) Evidence of the labor of the players is saved within the game, is visible in the sense that the progress made can actually be seen on screen—for instance the advancement of a character to a high level, or the procuring of a particularly powerful weapon—and is also of actual economic value in the real world.[12]

Thinking about the different levels of interaction with labor and possessions in virtual worlds invokes ideas about the existence of those interactions—or the products of those interactions—in the physical world. Georges Poulet argues that a (literary) text gains life only when it is read; it becomes animated through the process of readerly participation (1980: 43). A text therefore, once participated in, has a life that exists outside of the boundaries of its creation, both materially and authorially speaking.[13] This implies that, prior to the arrival of the reader's participation, the text is inanimate—the text comes to life only once it is read by a reader. This further pushes an understanding of ownership in relation to the text. If ownership of a game is dubious because of the effort put in by players, does ownership of a book then become dubious? Although it is through the reader's intervention that the book becomes alive, it is not the case that copyright boundaries are blurred. Copyright lies firmly with the named author of a book, and so it should—whereas players can put hundreds or thousands of hours' worth of play into developing a character, a character whose items can bring increased enjoyment or superiority in play (and thus the items become of fiscal value in a real sense), it cannot be said that a reader develops a novel in a way that has such clear economic value. The reader may have a collaborative hand in shaping the narrative, but this does not alter the real economic worth of the narrative, the characters, or the book itself; the reader's participation may create a different version or order of narrative, but this new text is transient and, unlike the '*labor of the players*', the labor of the readers is not visible. The game player can 'own' his or her avatar, items, and choices in a more real—and specifically economic—sense, whereas the reader can 'own' the choices he or she makes in reading but this is of no real value. The only way a reader can make something of economic value is to write *about* the text—for instance in a 'Pro Fanfiction' or academic context—and in this he or she makes something of value linked to the text, but very much external to it, whereas the gamer makes something of economic value internal to the text.

THE I-SUBJECT AND THE AVATAR

In her statement that the 'game is made animate' through the labor of the players, Taylor makes a similar observation to Poulet, that a text gains life only when it is read:

> When I am absorbed in reading, a second self takes over, a self which thinks and feels for me. Withdrawn in some recess of myself, do I then silently witness this dispossession? Do I derive from it some comfort, or, on the contrary, a kind of anguish? However that may be, someone else holds the centre of the stage, and the question which imposes itself, which I am absolutely obliged to ask myself, is this: 'Who is the usurper who occupies the forefront? Who is this mind who alone all by himself fills my consciousness and who, when I say I, is indeed that I?' (Poulet 1980: 45)

That 'I' is not the 'I' of the reader, nor of the author, but what Poulet terms the 'I-subject', a second self which is given life during the reading process, placing the reader in the background. Poulet argues that, rather than concentrating on the text itself, we need to concentrate on the I-subject, the textual entity responsible for the reader 'thinking another's thoughts'.

Indeed, the actions taking place within the text are complex, but cannot be concretized into that of any one contributing agency that could be labeled (for instance) an 'I-subject'. They are instead part of a network of intentional and unintentional actions, learnt codes, and power struggles— this is highlighted in this chapter through discussion of players ruining gameplay by 'not playing right'; authorial instructions as a manual on how to read; fan fiction; and ownership. Rethinking the I-subject in the light of online gaming provides elucidation and concretization of this intangible figure. Poulet makes two statements which open this exploration:

> I often have the impression, whilst reading, of simply witnessing an action which at the same time both concerns and yet does not concern me. This provokes a certain feeling of surprise within me. I am a consciousness astonished by an existence which is not mine, but which I experience as though it were mine. (1980: 48)

> What is this subject left standing in isolation after every examination of a literary work? [. . .] Whatever it may be, I am constrained to acknowledge that all subjective activity present in a literary work is not entirely explained by its relationship with forms and objects within the work. There is in the work a mental activity profoundly

engaged in objective forms; and there is, at another level, forsaking all forms, a subject which reveals itself to itself (and to me) in its transcendence relative to all which is reflected in it. At this point, no object can any longer express it; no structure can any longer define it; it is exposed in its ineffability and in its fundamental interdeterminancy. (1980: 48–49)

I propose that the I-subject—this figure who is 'left standing in isolation' at the end of an examination of the text, at the end of the process of participation—is a figure akin to the avatar created by participants in virtual environments. Different forms of avatar exist in different contexts: Three of the most noticeable are avatars used in a discussion forum, in MMORPGs (and other gaming genres), and in virtual environments such as *Second Life*. The necessarily limited scope of this chapter does not permit a full examination of these figures, so I will gesture towards a discussion with the intention of reviewing it later in time.

An avatar is a (not necessarily true-to-life, and often fantastic) visual representation of its user. In designing the visual characteristics of the avatar, the user programs his or her personal appearance within the text, but—as the decisions made by the user are inevitably affected by the choices available, the choices of other users, stereotypes of fantasy or other genre, or other extra-textual references—it is also the case that the user is programmed by the text itself, and by extra-textual material. The avatar is the figure through which the reader experiences the virtual world; Poulet's 'impression, whilst reading, of simply witnessing an action which at the same time both concerns and yet does not concern [. . .] an existence which is not mine, but which I experience as though it were mine', suggests the I-subject to be an avatar of the reader: a figure which is separate to the reader, but also *is* the reader; a figure through which the reader experiences the fictional world. The modes of operation for the figures of the avatar and of the I-subject are similar: The way in which the avatar acts within virtual environments is controlled by the user's actions and choices, and the agency of the user is limited by the designers of the virtual world (authors) and the game world itself (the form of the text).

This is also true in fiction: Here, the reader's responses to a text and his or her personal history will shape the experience of the I-subject, and of reading, and his or her agency is limited by textual form and learnt (or imposed) rules of reading. Poulet's 'second self' which 'fills [the participant's] consciousness' is a figure the essence of which exists not only in reading, but also in interaction with virtual environments. I am not suggesting that the avatar is a figure which is directly interchangeable with the I-subject—that would be far too simplistic; I do believe that studying the abstract figures through which participants interact with texts will prove valuable in discerning an answer to Poulet's question, 'who, when I say I, is indeed that I?'.

CONCLUSION: THE VALUE OF TEXTUAL INTERACTIVITY

What is means to be a reader is changing dramatically. Is it now easier for readers to appropriate a text and reprogram it to suit their own objectives, their own desires? While literary theory has been considering the relationship between readers and authors for decades, experimental and electronic texts situate reader-author collaboration as an increasingly key feature of the process of reading. Crawford's calling for primacy of interactivity in gaming reflects wider responses to interactive texts: Interactivity is put forward as a textual feature with intrinsic value. The question that must be asked is what is the *real* value of interactivity between reader and text? Specifically for our purposes, if interactivity should allow for complete reader-author collaboration, would the reading population actually value the texts created? I suspect the answer is no. Burke asks,

> If interactivity allows the reader to become the co-author of, say, Paradise Lost, are we to expect that this 'new' text—reconfigured and replete with readerly interpolations—will be a document of widespread cultural interest? (1998: 195)

The text will be of little, if any, cultural interest and is likely to be of no economic value. The original text of *Paradise Lost* will lose none of its validity in the process; in essence, the reader's version of the text would be as worthless as his or her transient readings of *Hopscotch*. One reason for this is captured in *The Death and Return of the Author*: '[T]he active reader necessarily collaborate[s] with the author in producing a text by the choices he or she makes. If this is the case, however, then the number of texts produced by readers are innumerable' (Burke 1998: 195).

The 'innumerable' transient readings of texts acknowledged by Burke are accompanied by the innumerable and visible collaborative efforts published on the Internet by aspiring writers, for instance in fan fiction, and supposedly more interactive versions of texts reprogrammed for the Internet.[14] I would not wish to imply that collaboration and interactivity are of no worth, as that is by no means the case. What is the case is that interactivity does not necessarily provide a reader with more agency, but rather that ostensibly 'more interactive' texts come with a set of rules or codes not dissimilar to that of conventional literature; as the text is programmed by the reader, so too is the reader programmed by the text.

NOTES

1. These forms are not divided from one another: For instance, true-life aspects can spill into fictional narratives, and fiction can spill into biography.

2. For a discussion of the function of the author see Michel Foucault (1977). A further key text on the subject is Roland Barthes's 'Death of the Author' (1977).

3. For further reading on the topic, see Iser (1978), Fish (1980), and, for a good introduction to the field in general, Bennett (1995).

4. Self-conscious fiction. Patricia Waugh observes that '[t]he metacommentary provided by self-conscious fiction carries the more or less explicit message: "this is make-believe" or "this is play"' (Waugh 1984, 35). Although a detailed discussion of metafiction here would be interesting, the limits on space lead me to instead provide three examples of metafictional writing, with clarifications:

     1. You are about to begin reading Italo Calvino's new novel, If on a winter's night a traveler. Relax. Concentrate. Dispel every other thought. Let the world around you fade. Best to close the door; the TV is always on in the next room. Tell the others right away, 'No, I don't want to watch TV!' Raise your voice—they won't hear you otherwise—'I'm reading! I don't want to be disturbed!' Maybe they haven't heard you, with all that racket; speak louder, yell: 'I'm beginning to read Italo Calvino's new novel!' Or if you prefer, don't say anything; just hope they'll leave you alone (Calvino 1998, 3).

     2. 'Fuck all this lying look what I'm really trying to write about is writing not all this stuff' (Johnson 1964, 163).

     3. 'Oh Jamesy let me up out of this Pooh' (Joyce 1969, 691)

5. The novel's clearest points of metafictionality, narratively speaking, tend to occur in the pages of 'Morelliana' situated in the expendable chapters. For instance, Morelli comments that '[he is] revising a story that [he] wanted to be the least literary possible' (Cortázar 1966, 474) and 'Reading the book, one had the impression for a while that Morelli had hoped that the accumulation of fragments would quickly crystallize into a total reality' (1966, 169), remind the reader that they are reading, and reading a piece of fiction.

6. For instance, B. S. Johnson's *The Unfortunates* (1969) (which consists of 27 separately bound chapters, with the 'First' and 'Last' labeled; the reader is instructed to shuffle the remaining 25 chapters and read the novel in whatever order emerges) and Marc Saporta's *Composition No. 1* (1963) (a novel consisting of 150 loose sheets of type in a box; the reader is instructed to shuffle the pack 'like a deck of cards').

7. Metafictional devices appear to complicate this picture. In drawing attention to the fictional status of a text, metafictional elements make explicit the artifice of both the act of reading and the text itself: The interface, arguably, does not provide a seamless experience. Thus, in *Hopscotch*, it could be argued that the reader may not encounter a seamless experience to the same degree that he or she would in a conventionally structured novel. However, in reading *Hopscotch* according to the instructions provided, the reader is interacting with the interface through unchangeable rules and so, whilst reading in this way, the interface continues to provide a seamless experience.

8. For further reading on notions of pleasure in reading, see Barthes (1976), described in Richard Howard's introduction to the text as 'for the first time in the history of criticism [. . .] not only a poetics of reading [. . .] but a much more difficult (because supposedly inexpressible, apparently ineffable) achievement, an *erotics of reading*' (Italics in original) (Barthes 1975, vii–viii).

9. The term 'profic' has been used to refer specifically to fiction created by professional writers. Thomas's (2007) 'Canons and Fanons: Literary Fanfiction Online' cites Pugh (2005) to highlight that the use of the term is 'not intended to suggest some kind of hierarchy based on quality or success, but

to distinguish between commercially produced fictions and those made freely available on the web and elsewhere.'

10. The CEO of *deviantART* states that the aims of website are explicitly fan-based: 'It is our intention to create the most powerful outlet in the world for known and unknown artists alike. [. . .] For the first time in history there is connection and communication between artists and fans on a massive scale' (Sotira 2008).

11. The use of the term 'nerf' spread quickly through online gaming communities, and although definitions and etymologies of 'a nerf' or 'nerfing' are not identical, the variations are so slight that the meaning of the term is standard across online games. A 'nerf' is defined in the *Guild Wars* community as 'a game mechanic change made by ArenaNet which lessens the effectiveness of anything within the game, this includes skills and extends to builds, or tactics', the term 'originat[ing] in various internet gaming from the NERF line of toys. To "nerf", in essence, is to make something powerful and alter it into something basic or harmless, in the same way that the Nerf company does with weapons, and various balls' (Guild Wars Wiki 2008). The *World of Warcraft* community defines the term as a verb, meaning 'To downgrade, to be made softer, or make less effective. "X has been nerfed"' (World of Warcraft Community Site 2008).

12. The economic value of virtual items is an increasingly debated area. An early consideration asserts that 'there is no descriptive disconnection between our real-world property system and virtual assets. From both descriptive and normative positions, owners of virtual assets do, or should, possess property rights' (Lastowka and Hunter 2004: 20). A news article in *Gamespot UK* (Thorsen 2007) noted that, as of January 2007, online auction site eBay would remove all listings advertising virtual items, with the exception of *Second Life* items; controversially, the rationale given was that virtual environments like *World of Warcraft* are games, but *Second Life* is not.

13. It should be noted that in Poulet's discussion, interaction with the text is explored as an abstract interaction, rather than with a material interface such as I define at the beginning of the chapter. According to different models of interactivity, notions of interface shift between the concrete and the abstract.

14. For instance, Borges's short story 'The Book of Sand' (1977) has been digitized as a 'hypertext/puzzle' at http://artificeeternity.com/bookofsand/.

REFERENCES

ArenaNet (2005) *Guild wars: Prophecies.* Texas and California: NCsoft.
Barthes, R (1975) *The pleasure of the text*, trans. R Miller. New York: Hill and Wang.
———. (1977) Death of the author. In *Image music text*, trans. Stephen Heath, 142–48. London: Fontana Press. Originally published 1967.
Bennett, A, ed (1995) *Readers and reading.* Harlow: Longman.
Borges, JL (1977). The book of sand. In *The book of sand*, trans. Norman Thomas di Giovanni, 87–91. London: Penguin.
Bungie (2001) *Halo: Combat evolved.* [CD-ROM]. Redmond, WA: Microsoft.
Burke, Sean (1988) *The Death and Return of the Author: Criticism and Subjectivity in Barthes, Foucault and Derrida.* Edinburgh: Edinburgh University Press.
Calvino, Italo (1998) If on a winter's night a traveller, trans. William Weaver. New York: Vintage.
child-dragon [pseudo] (2004) The rules of fan fiction. Online. Available HTTP: <http://child-dragon.deviantart.com> (accessed 14 December 2008).

Crawford, C (2008) 14 conceptual shifts: Moving from games to interactive storytelling. Paper presented at the *Austin Game Developers Conference*, Texas.

Cortázar, J (1966) *Hopscotch*, trans. G Rabassa. London: Random House.

Fish, S (1980) *Is there a text in this class? The authority of interpretative communities*. Cambridge, MA, and London: Harvard University Press.

Foucault, M (1977) What is an author? In *Language, counter-memory, practice: Selected essays and interviews*, ed. DF Bouchard, trans. DF Bouchard and S Simon, 113–38. Oxford: Blackwell. Originally published 1969.

Guild Wars Wiki (2008) Nerf. Online. Available HTTP: <http://wiki.guildwars.com/wiki/Nerf> (accessed 13 December 2008).

Iser, W (1978) *The act of reading: A theory of aesthetic response*. London and Henley: Routledge and Kegan Paul.

Jenkins, H (1992) *Textual poachers: Television fans and participatory culture*. London: Routledge.

Johnson, BS (1964) *Albert Angelo*. London: Constable.

———. (1969) *The unfortunates*. London: Panther.

Joyce, J (1969) *Ulysses*. Harmondsworth: Penguin. Originally published 1922.

Katyal, SK (2006) Performance, property, and the slashing of gender in fan fiction. *Journal of Gender, Social Policy and the Law* 14, no. 3: 461–518.

Kirkpatrick, G (2004) *Critical technology: A social theory of personal computing*. Aldershot: Ashgate.

Lastowka, FG and D Hunter (2004) The laws of the virtual worlds. *California Law Review* 92, no. 1:18–26.

Linden Lab (2003) *Second Life*. California: Linden Research Inc.

MacCallum-Stewart, E and J Parsler (2007) Illusory agency in *Vampire: The Masquerade—Bloodlines*. *dichtung-digital* 37, no. 1. Online. Available HTTP: <http://www.dichtung-digital.org> (accessed 17 March 2009).

Maxis (2000) *The Sims*. Redwood City, CA: Electronic Arts.

Media Molecule (2008) *LittleBigPlanet*. London: Sony Computer Entertainment Europe.

Mulligan, J and B Patrovsky (2003) *Developing online games: An insider's guide*. Boston: New Riders.

Poulet, G (1980) Criticism and the experience of interiority. In *Reader-response criticism*, ed. JP Tompkins, 41–49. Baltimore and London: Johns Hopkins University Press.

Pugh, S (2005) *The democratic genre: Fan fiction in a literary context*. Bridgend: Seren Books.

Saporta, M (1963) *Composition no. 1*, trans. R Howard. New York: Simon and Schuster.

Sony Computer Entertainment Europe (2008) LittleBigPlanet community content update. Online. Available HTTP: <http://threespeech.com> (accessed 13 November 2008).

Sotira, A (2008) deviantART: About deviantART's core staff. Online. Available HTTP: <http://about.deviantart.com> (accessed 16 December 2008).

Taylor, TL (2006) *Play between worlds: Exploring online game culture*. Cambridge, MA, and London: MIT Press.

Thomas, B (2007) Canons and fanons: Literary fanfiction online. *dichtung-digital* 37, no. 1. Online. Available HTTP: <http://www.dichtung-digital.org> (accessed 10 March 2009).

Thorsen, T (2007) Ebay delisting most virtual items. *Gamespot UK*. Online. Available HTTP: <http://uk.gamespot.com/news> (accessed 13 December 2008).

Waugh, P (1984) *Metafiction: The theory and practice of self-conscious fiction.* London and New York: Routledge.

White, G (2005) *Reading the graphic surface: The presence of the book in prose fiction.* Manchester and New York: Manchester University Press.

World of Warcraft Community Site (2008). Online. Available HTTP: <http://www.worldofwarcraft.com> (accessed 13 December 2008).

Part II
Creating Second Identities

4 Embodiment and Gender Identity in Virtual Worlds

Reconfiguring Our 'Volatile Bodies'[1]

Sonia Fizek and Monika Wasilewska

INTRODUCTION

Since the emergence of graphical virtual worlds, such as *Second Life*™ (Linden Lab 2003) and *Entropia Universe*™ (MindArk 2003), the creation of our Second Lives in cyberspace no longer relies predominantly on text-based means, as it was in the case of MUDs (Multi-User Dungeons) or MOOs (object oriented MUDs). The focus of the online existence in VWs (virtual worlds) shifted from text-based descriptions to graphical representations of ourselves as avatars and of the virtual reality surrounding us. The customization of our virtual personas (choosing the name, adjusting body parts, and selecting clothes) entails above all gender specification. As it turns out, coexisting in virtual communities as avatars, the majority of us seem to project an equivalent of reality onto our cyber bodies. Despite the fact that the Internet itself constitutes a flexible tool, which could be used to implement revolutionary ideas contradicting stable and fixed gender boundaries, the traditionally defined gender identity based on binary oppositions (male versus female; heterosexual versus homosexual) is still being reinforced online. We are more likely to fill the virtual worlds with unusual objects or imaginary scenery than to populate them with gender ambiguous creatures. Oftentimes, in the most fantastic virtual spaces, our avatar's gender identity constitutes the most stable point of reference.

The research revolving around identity is, in most cases, based on the following key cultural and sociological markers: race, class, gender, and sexuality (Bell 2001). This chapter will focus on the question of embodiment and gender explicitly and will explore the implications of technology and cyberspace on the way gender identity is or may be constructed in virtual worlds, such as *Second Life (SL)* or *Entropia Universe (EU)*.[2]

The chapter is divided into two sections. The first constitutes a theoretical introduction and places the problem of gender identity and body in a wider cultural context, encompassing postmodern and post-postmodern concepts on identity. We are referring mainly to chosen feminist theories, as they cover the most vivid disputes over the place of gender and body in Western culture. In our understanding, feminism (or feminisms) is the crossover area of various perspectives present in the contemporary humanities. Demarcating rigid boundaries between gender studies, women's studies, queer theory, etc., is not indispensable in this chapter (disregarding the fact that oftentimes it is impossible).

In the second part, we will analyze how chosen theoretical perspectives are realized empirically in *Second Life* and *Entropia Universe*. Virtual worlds constitute communication technologies, enabling their users to create arbitrary identities; hence we selected them as our focus points. We decided upon such reference points as new communication technologies (NCTs) make perfect tools for the creation of arbitrary identities. Because in cyberspace we are not constrained by real bodies (see Denise Doyle's chapter, this volume) and we create our virtual bodies from scratch (although the metaphorical 'meat' has not been left behind), we could start the process of identity construction anew, entering the age of post-humans and cyborgs, existing beyond gender constraints in a post-gender world (Haraway 1991).

Our aim is to examine whether users devoid of certain constraints in constructing themselves create new identity models or whether they duplicate the ones present in reality. If so, what models will they be? A similar point was raised by Lisa Nakamura and Daniel Punday, who speculated whether 'the Internet [can] propagate genuinely new and nonracist (and nonsexist and non-classist) ways of being, or [whether] it merely reflect[s] our culture at large' (quoted in Nakamura 2002: xii). Nakamura further notices that the Internet may be viewed twofold: either as a progressive tool used to implement social change or as a 'purveyor of crude and simplistic stereotypical cultural narratives' (xiii). In order to conduct a thorough and well informed analysis, and to place the research on the continuum between those bipolar attitudes, it is crucial to narrow the focus to a specific rhetorical space related to the Internet. Taking into account the diversity of online applications and considering Nakamura's valid point, we contained our study within the boundaries of virtual worlds only, disregarding other spaces, such as chat rooms, websites, or fora. Observing the avatars in *Second Life* and *Entropia Universe*, we will explore the question of identity construction online, and try to determine whether users creating their characters in cyberspace are 'electing to perform versions of themselves as raced and gendered beings' (Nakamura 2002: xiv) or whether they develop their cybertypes irrespective of various stereotypes, which are already at work in the offline world.

Fluid Identity

In accordance with classic theories put forward by the sociologists of culture, such as Zygmunt Bauman (2000a, 2000b, 2007) and Anthony Giddens (1991), identity is perceived as fluid and changeable, and its creation as a never-ending task. As Bauman notices, nowadays '[. . .] everyone has the right to choose who they want to be or become' (Bauman 2007a: 27); '[...] everything may happen and all can be done [...] there are few footings in this world, which could be recognized as solid and trustworthy' (2000: 49). For Giddens, identity '[...] is not something that is just given, as a result of the continuities of the individual's action-system, but something that has to be routinely created [...]' (Giddens 1991: 52).

Such a state is, on the one hand, the consequence of the *Entzauberung der Welt* (Weber)—referring to rationalization and discovering the illusory nature of fundamental concepts—and on the other—the result of real civilization changes, which loosened up traditional national, religious, or social ties. Globalization and the phenomenon of eradication influence 'the stability and durability of identity, which under its influence become as "'mobile"' as the world itself; changeable and unstable; evasive and elusive; uncertain and fluid' (Bauman 2001: 11). A community model, in which a group assigned a particular identity to the individual on the basis of constant cultural standards, ceased to exist. It has been replaced by 'hybrid identities' (Mamzer 2007: 8) comprising various elements, no longer inherited but constructed in accordance with individually chosen criteria.

It seems that the human body could be a stable support for the fixed identity. Inborn and irremovable, the body allows others to recognize our sex and race, which constitute the basis of self-determination for our selves. However, recently various practices have disturbed the cultural status of the body (particularly with reference to sex/gender), depriving it of its durability and certainty.

The Body

Since the turn of the 19th and 20th century onwards, in the Western humanities the importance of embodiment has been increasing up to the point where it has become impossible to associate a human being with pure consciousness and, following Descartes, to separate it from its corporeal foundation.

Beforehand, the body connecting the human with temporality, unforeseeable natural forces, and the biological, perishable dimension of our existence, constituted an obstacle on the way to perfection, which—depending on the current philosophical or religious ideologies—was associated with the world of philosophical ideas, God, or reason. According to Elizabeth Grosz, the Cartesian division of a human being into distinct substances (body as *res extensa* and mind as *res cogitans*) originates from Plato's somatophobia (Grosz 1994: 5), and its final intensification was gained in the Age of Enlightenment.

For the next 300 years following Descartes, philosophy sought to 'tame' the body, which more recently has begun to be perceived as something more than the vehicle for the mind. The following statement by Maurice Merleau-Ponty marks a symbolic end as well as the beginning of a new chapter in corporeality: 'I am not in front of my body [. . .] I am in it, or rather I am it' (Merleau-Ponty 2002: 173).

Interestingly, the first attempts to embody the subject were almost automatically associated with its sexualation. The Cartesian privilege of the mind was questioned by the assumptions of Freud's psychoanalysis. Not only did he refute an idealized image of human consciousness, spotlighting its subconscious areas, but he also emphasized human corporeality (sexuality). In *The Mystery of Second Sex*, Paweł Dybel claims that it is due to psychoanalysis that 'referring to the universal, sexually neutral subject has become problematic' (Dybel 2006: 7).[3]

The question of the sexed body has been mostly scrutinized by feminism, from both its sociopolitical as well as academic standpoint. Dealing with the aforementioned issue seemed inevitable, as it was determined by the culturally well established interpretation of the relation between the feminine and the corporeal, which are perceived to be of equal value (we will discuss this point in further paragraphs). Feminism could not have stayed indifferent with reference to this fact. Its relation to the body has been always ambivalent in that a successful liberating strategy could have consisted in the body's radical transgression or, quite on the contrary, in its full cultural reconstruction. Due to such an extremely diverse attitude towards the body (as well as various other fundamental differences), we should not refer to feminism as a homogenous concept, but we should rather talk about feminisms.[4]

Nowadays, it seems almost impossible to fully embrace all the diversity of feminism. The body, perceived as the basis for female identity, constitutes a criterion which allows for partial systematization of all the branches. It should be stressed that the dualism of the body and mind—an order attributed to nature and culture respectively—is automatically followed by yet another dichotomy, that of femininity/masculinity. 'Sometimes a woman is defined with the word "sex"; she constitutes the body, delight, and danger' (Beauvoir 2003: 174). In the 1940s, Simone de Beauvoir pointed to the preceding, exemplifying the cultural leveling of a man with the sexually neutral category of a human being, as opposed to a woman, who is always referred to as the Other. The causes and results of the aforementioned assumptions were analyzed in the 1970's classic academic article of a significant title 'Is Female to Male as Nature Is to Culture?':

> Because of woman's greater bodily involvement with the natural functions surrounding reproduction, she is seen as more a part of nature than man is. [. . . .] Since men lack a 'natural' basis (nursing, generalized to child care) for a familial orientation, their sphere of activity is defined at the level of interfamilial relations. (Ortner 1974: 76–79)

Because it is men, not women, who are associated with culture (in opposition to nature) and as Ortner notices by creating it, men compensate for their reproductive incapacity, the culture embodies predominantly male subjectivity. Man becomes the universal symbol of humankind, an everyman combining all the plethora of human experiences in his self. 'Identifying the cultural *neutrum* with a man is such a common practice that it has become imperceptible. Taking into consideration language [. . .] male-oriented politics, history, literature, art and culture in general [. . .] the universal and the common to all mankind is that which is masculine' (Walczewska 2006: 125, authors' translation). Femininity, being associated first and foremost with corporeality,[5] constitutes only one of the possible scenarios of humanity. Similarly to nature, which has to succumb to culture, a woman needs to accept male dominance. An alternative for this is for women to enter into the cultural sphere and fully participate in its creation. Allegedly, the preceding scenario may be realized twofold. 1. 'As a woman' the subject is defined with reference to sex, but it is done anew and not in opposition to what is masculine. 2. The second strategy assumes entering into the culture 'as a man', which is possible only once the binary oppositions have been invalidated and traditional concepts on femininity and masculinity deconstructed.

Thus, a legitimate entanglement between the concepts of femininity and corporeality would form a stem from which various feminism branches sprout. Elaborating on the figure of feminism as a tree, its boughs seem to bifurcate into two interpretative tendencies: the affirmative and the deconstructive one.[6] Historically, the first tendency originates in naturalistic and biological essentialism (1960s and 1970s) whereas the second one in Cultural Theory representing the body as an entity formed by culture.

Early essentialism, focusing on the universal nature (essence) of femininity, in its subsequent phases has been surpassed and turned into a multidirectional 'sexual difference theory'. Sexual difference feminism is still looking for the specific character of femininity on the basis of female corporeality, albeit in a less biological and more symbolic sense, for instance by examining the 'language' or common experiences of women. Corporeal feminism, represented predominantly by Elizabeth Grosz or Susan Bordo, would constitute the most recent branch, in which the mind/body hierarchy has been turned upside down. It is the body, not the mind, that constitutes the basis for the subject formation, and the dualism itself has been rejected in favor of a fluid body/mind consolidation. Corporeal feminism is an alternative to some concepts of postmodernism, which disregard the corporeal dimension and thus constitute the opposing branch of the bifurcation in feminism we have mentioned previously.

Its symbolic beginnings date back to Cultural Theory or constructionism (a movement in anthropology), which perceives every human action as influenced by culture. The rudiments were established in the 1930s by Marcel Mauss or Margaret Mead, who demonstrated how body and gender are constructed in different societies. On the basis of similar assumptions, the differentiation between sex and gender could have been made and the faith in full biological determinism could have been questioned.

Inspired by the poststructuralist concepts, over time constructionism developed into 'gender theories', questioning all material foundations of femininity (and masculinity), and pointing to their relative and performative nature. Gender is treated as a category created by means of either sociocultural practices (see Michel Foucault and 'power-knowledge', Foucault 1991) or discourse (see the concept of 'différance' introduced by Jacques Derrida). The traditional concept of subjectivity has been also broken down, and as a result queer theory (with Judith Butler as its precursor) and gender transgressions have come into being.

None of the aforementioned tendencies constitutes a coherent whole. However, it may be observed that their bifurcation duplicates the academic opposition of sex vs. gender; as the first trend defines femininity by means of widely used biological categories, the second one by their sociocultural counterparts. Such a distinction gives rise to the problems of theoretical and political nature. Theoreticians supporting sexual difference feminism are accused of secondary sex polarization, and deriving gender identity from the body seems to be somewhat controversial. For instance, Grosz claims that gender cannot exist in the body of the opposite sex, and the surgical change performed by transsexuals constitutes a mere 'crude transformation' (Grosz 1994: 207–08; see also Hyży 2003: 249). On the other hand, the deconstruction of sex and the affirmation of fluid identities contribute to the very dispersion of the category of a woman, which comprises the basis for feminist activity. If we assume that gender is not determined by the body, but depends entirely on our choices, practicing the politics of equality becomes even more difficult. Yet another accusation may refer to the abstract nature of theories, which do not adhere to real life. The *status quo* just discussed has been very accurately summarized by Inga Iwasiów (a well-known Polish feminist), who commented on Braidotti's vision of 'nomadic subjects' in the following words: 'While nomadology is a romantic and postindustrial adventure, concrete persons fight for their identity, in the world of which having a passport is a privilege/burden' (Iwasiów 2004: 194).

However, does constructionism belong entirely to the academic utopia? We should refer here to two different standpoints. Not only have they approached identity from different perspectives, but also turned out to be practically applicable, which makes them an inspiring starting point for further reflections.

The first and most obvious association is connected with Judith Butler, one of the most distinct representatives of postmodernity. According to Butler not only gender but also sex is artificial and constructed, and so the opposition between the two is eliminated. Butler does not undermine the existence of biological differences and does not negate real bodies, but rather questions their 'reality'. For her, the bodies are the carriers of cultural significance. Although they are not fictitious in themselves, it is the fiction that constructs and signifies them. Using the word 'fiction' we refer to cultural norms connected with gender—the norms which do not originate from the bodies, but are imposed upon them. Defining the body as either male of female places it in the heteronormative social order. In the light of Butler's concept, the question of 'being' a woman or a man is not considered in terms of fate, but emphasizes its performative dimension. Gender may be treated as a corporeal style. It is also a space for all the subversive acts—dressing-up, parody, stylization—treating sex instrumentally (drag queens, drag kings, cross-dressing). Butler not only changes the established interpretation of sex/gender, but also describes people, for whom gender instability (transgender, ambigender, non-gendered, gender-neutral, gender liminal, agendered, etc.)[7] forms the basis of their identity. These people refer to gender irrespective of their sex. The following quotations clearly illustrate the point made by Butler (although being from two entirely different sources, they describe the same bodily reality). The first one constitutes the philosophical description of the bodily condition in postmodernity as understood by Monika Bakke:

> Disregarding anatomy, humans have the possibility to embody various cultural genders, without the necessity to support one of the sites. By doing so they gain a multiple social identity. The assumption that one body corresponds to one cultural gender is no longer in force, which leads to gender relativism. (Bakke 2000: 148)

In the latter one, members of a domain-specific portal for cross-dressers have turned the complex academic cultural theories into a few straightforward sentences describing their lived experience as individuals freed from gender constraints:

> There are no boundaries. There are no divisions into men and women. There is no grammatical gender connected with sex. We play with names; with verbs; with language. There is no feminine or masculine. Everything just is. (All about crossdressing, comment posted on 15 May 2006)

An equally revolutionary concept was introduced by Donna Haraway (1991), although its character is somewhat different. Instead of the academic interpretation of the category of gender, Haraway creates a vision of its final transgression by creating a post-gender or post-human body. The strategy of surpassing corporeality may be achieved by a cyborg, being a combination of a man (woman) and a machine, and creating a hybrid organism, which guarantees the elimination of natural differences existing between the sexes. If the skin is no longer the borderline for the body, the cyborg has the power to subvert the natural order. This blurs the boundary between the body and technology, between nature and culture, and thus between femininity and masculinity. As Agnieszka Gajewska notices, this shift is achieved by means of a 'patriarchal and military' product, which 'has been used against their fathers' (Gajewska 2008: 82). The myth of a cyborg is developed by Sadie Plant, who created theoretical foundations of cyberfeminism—a multilayered women's activity in the Internet.[8] Acting in alliance with technology, women can become fully emancipated, as their common ground lies in being subordinate to men (Plant 1996, 1997). The activity of cyberfeminists, oftentimes controversial and subversive (as in the case of 'cybergrrls'), corresponds to the previous statement. Women unite in groups—such as the most popular Old Boys Network and VNS Matrix—and their activity surpasses the boundaries of cyberspace and encompasses, for instance organizing international conferences in real life.

Preliminary Conclusions

The postmodern discussion on sex/gender oftentimes includes the convergence of theory and practice. We cannot disregard people for whom the evident transgressing of gender boundaries, or manifesting it in opposition to the well-established social norms, constitutes the basis for self-definition. In the light of the preceding observations, we are posing the following question: Are gender and corporeal transgressions only appealing to minorities or do they reflect the universal longing of the postmodern human for fluid identity? Bearing the aforementioned issues in mind, we will analyze these relations focusing on two of the most popular virtual platforms (*Second Life* and, to a lesser degree, *Entropia Universe*). We will perceive these virtual worlds as the areas in which the virtual equivalent of real[9] life is created.

The question of 'net utopianism' has been raised by quite a few researchers (e.g., Wilding 2001; Hayles 1999; Haraway 1991) and so our aim is neither to reformulate it nor to use it as our own original idea.[10] In this chapter we will, however, focus on concrete examples. In so doing, we seek to examine the role of body in cyberspace, concentrating on the experience of avatars, taking into account avatars' interaction with the interface elements.

CASE STUDY: VIRTUAL WORLDS

The question of gender in two of the most popular virtual platforms (e.g., *Second Life* and *Entropia Universe*) seems to be inextricably connected with graphical representations of our virtual personas, i.e., avatars. Social interactions in those worlds are no longer achieved by means of text-based descriptions only (as it was in case of multi user dungeons—MUDs, which we will briefly discuss in the following paragraph), but include visual stimuli and virtual body language as well. Because our perceptions and categorizations with respect to gender, race, and class are based on appearance, the importance of a corporeal dimension in virtual worlds cannot and should not be down-played. Prior to a closer analysis of embodiment and re-embodiment and its interdependence with the process of avatar creation, we would like to delineate the distinction between virtual worlds (VWs), virtual realities (VRs), and virtual environments (VEs), as well as discuss briefly the notions of the real, the virtual, and the actual (Boellstorff 2008: 20–21).

VIRTUAL WORLDS, VIRTUAL REALITIES, OR VIRTUAL ENVIRONMENTS?

In order to be terminologically consistent, we would like to emphasize the differentiation between the following terms: virtual world (VW), virtual reality (VR), and virtual environment (VE). In the 1990s Sherry Turkle (e.g., in *Life on the Screen: Identity in the Age of the Internet*) referred to text-based virtual communities (MUDs) as virtual realities. Although she did mention the importance of hardware (helmets, goggles, data gloves), she decided to refer to MUDs as to 'text-based, social virtual reality' (Turkle 1995: 181). Richard Bartle narrows down the definition and notices that '[. . .] virtual reality is primarily concerned with the mechanisms by which human beings can interact with computer simulations; it is not espe-cially bothered by the nature of the simulations themselves' (Bartle 2004 quoted in Boellstorff 2008: 20). In other words, the sense of immersion in VR is triggered by interface technologies, e.g., data gloves or goggles, which constitute the basis for the VR reception. Virtual worlds, on the other hand, rely mainly on the users' experience generated by means of graphical interface or in the earlier days—a text-based one (see: MUDs and Object Oriented MUDs, i.e., MOOs). Thus, taking into consideration Bartle's remark, *Second Life* or *Entropia Universe* should be referred to as virtual worlds, not virtual realities (although some researchers might use the category of VR here). Another term we would like to call into ques-tion is a virtual environment (VE), or to be more specific, a collaborative virtual environment (CVE), which exemplifies an immersive virtual reality. As Jeremy Bailenson points out, 'CVEs are systems that track verbal and nonverbal signals of multiple interactants and render those signals onto avatars, three-dimensional, digital representations of people in a shared digital space' (Bailenson 2006: 255). CVE might be perceived as the next step in videoconferencing techniques in that it maps the movement in the physical world to the one taking place in the virtual environment. Just as in the case of VR, it is the mechanisms and interface technologies that play a crucial role here.

The distinction just discussed between the three different terms referring to the virtual sphere may seem somewhat simplistic, but our intention is to merely outline the idiosyncrasies and clarify the choice of terminology, so as to make it more consistent. Therefore, in this chapter, we are using the terms virtual worlds, virtual platforms, or, alternatively, virtual universes (the latter one used specifically in reference to *Entropia Universe*).

The Virtual, the Real, and the Actual

Conducting research in the virtual, it seems almost inevitable not to juxtapose it with the concept of the real. However apparent the virtual-real opposition may seem at first, the phenomenon is far more complex. The issue has been raised by Boellstorff in one of the most recent publications on *Second Life*. Drawing on extensive analyses concerning the virtual made by other researchers (e.g., Taylor 2006; Deleuze 2004; Markham 1998), Boellstorff concludes that the virtual is in fact real and should be rather opposed to the actual instead. He agrees with the presumption that our experiences online (in virtual worlds) are perceived and felt as real, and may turn out to be as meaningful as the ones encountered offline. 'In other words, "real" often acts simply as a synonym for "offline", and does not imply a privileged ontological status [. . .]' (Boellstorff 2008: 20). The virtual thus becomes part of the real, and both states are opposed by the actual world. Nevertheless, in our understanding the categories of the virtual and the real belong to two mutually exclusive orders—the former focusing on what is created, the latter on what is experienced. Boellstorff does emphasize the same question, evoking the etymology of the adjective 'actual', which originates from the verb 'act' (from L.L. actualis 'active', adj. form of L. actus; cf. 'act').[11] He does so, however, to stress the fact that both these terms (the virtual and the actual) belong to the same order and hence they qualify to be juxtaposed. We, on the other hand, argue that because the virtual and the real are governed by different rules and express divergent levels of our existence (that which is made/created and that which is experienced), the distinction between them does not disrupt the understanding of the virtual-real relation. Also, because we are referring to the question of corporeality (corpus from L., lit. 'body'; reality from L.L. realis; meaning 'real existence'),[12] bringing up the real instead of the actual makes our argumentation more consistent. Thus, directing the reader's attention to the allegedly problematic distinction between the virtual and the real, we have decided not to introduce further terminological confusion and simply use the virtual when referring to the virtual worlds, and the real when referring to the 'actual' world.

VIRTUAL BODIES, OR 'DO AVATARS DREAM OF ELECTRIC STEAK?'[13]

Having introduced some theoretical background and hopefully clarified major terminological issues, we are now moving on to the second part of our chapter, in which we shall look for reference points of chosen theoretical standpoints in the empirical process of creating one's gender identity in *SL* and *EU*.

In the first few paragraphs we will focus on the corporeal dimension of avatar creation and their very existence within virtual worlds, i.e., *Second Life* and *Entropia Universe*. Referring to Kristeva's notion of abject, we will touch upon the question of the virtual body and its gender constraints exemplified in the aforementioned platforms. The avatar will constitute our starting point in the discussion on fluid identity, disembodiment, and re-embodiment, and the utopian dream of a post-gender world as evoked by [e.g., Donna Haraway in 'A Cyborg Manifesto' (1991). To put some order into this multilayered discussion, we have arranged it in terms of three main thematic areas. First, we will focus on the process of avatar creation (body creation) in *Second Life* and *Entropia Universe*. Our second area will revolve around the question of experiencing the avatar's body through the interface. And finally, we will concentrate on the social dimension of bodily interaction and examine the phenomenon of gender-restricted regions in *SL*. All of the phenomena discussed earlier by us belong to the visual channel of communication. We will not focus on text-based or auditory channels.[14]

Creating the Avatar's Body

The notions of embodiment or disembodiment or re-embodiment became particularly important and relevant as soon as virtual worlds moved from the era of text-based 'chat rooms' (MUDs) to complex graphical spaces inhabited by avatars equipped with perceptible cyberbodies. Because the focus shifted from the textual to the graphical, the process of creating one's virtual persona has considerably changed. The purely verbal dimension (performing a socializing function) prevalent in MUDs has been moved to the background. In graphical virtual worlds 'embodiment [has] become central to online selfhood [. . .]' (Boellstorff 2008: 134). Among four prime needs of *SL* avatars for instance, the communicative and interpersonal one constitutes 24%. The predominant need (41%) tends to be the aesthetic one, based on the avatars' appearance (Ensslin, this volume). Such a shift, both from the textual to the graphical and what follows from the interpersonal (text-based) to the performative, marks great changes in the construction of gender as well. It seems as if our imagination was constrained by visual means of description and as a result avatars became more standardized, restricted in their bodily form and gender. In the early text-based virtual worlds (MUDs), users were given the possibility to choose from up to 10 different gendered and agendered identities, represented by a pronominal system:[15]

> Neuter: it, it, its, its, itself
> Male: he, him, his, his, himself
> Female: she, her, her, hers, herself
> Either: s/he, him/her, his/her, his/hers, him/herself

Spivak: e, em, eir, eirs, eirself
Splat: *e, h*, h*s, h*self
Plural: they, them, their, theirs, themselves
Egotistical: I, me, my, mine, myself
Royal: we, us, our, ours, ourselves
2nd: you, you, your, yours, yourself (Rosenberg 1992)

As Boellstorff rightly notices, 'these "genders" refer to linguistic gender and assume lack of visual embodiment' (2008: 140). Even though the majority of MUD residents would categorize themselves as either male or female (Rosenberg 1992), there were other more flexible possibilities for the ones wishing to transgress the obvious gender boundaries. Having more advanced tools at our disposal, we have apparently moved from flexibly gendered MUDs to virtual platforms, such as *SL* or *Entropia Universe*, where the user's choice is oftentimes limited to two genders only. Although in *SL* it is possible to change one's embodiment (e.g., into an animal or an inanimate object) just the way one would change their t-shirt or haircut, there are only two gender options available in the 'Appearance' tab (either male or female), which restricts a fully malleable agendered process of creation of our virtual personae.

> While the Second Life platform required avatars to be either male or female, it was easy to take on an embodiment that did not clearly mark gender (a box, for instance, or a blue ball of light, or an androgynous figure). (Boellstorff 2008: 143)

In this sense, it seems as if our online bodies in *SL* were prima facie subject to flexibility and fluidity. Also, in *Second Life* one can switch between the available genders and modify the appearance of one's avatar repeatedly during the avatar's virtual life. The name of the avatar, once chosen, cannot be altered, so in order to disguise oneself efficaciously, it is advisable to pick a neutral name.

The fact that the appearance of one's avatar in *SL* may be altered at any time implies the possibility to create one's identity beyond the constraints of corporeality. It is, however, the virtual community that imposes the restrictive rules on its users. Because the avatar's name cannot be altered, every possible permutation of its body is still assigned to a particular virtual persona, entangled in fixed social relations. Because frequent appearance modifications are not highly approved by the *SL* community, most of the avatars keep their visual representations stable throughout their *SL* lives.

Entropia Universe is even more restrictive. Not only can the user choose between two genders only (either female or male), but once created, the appearance of the avatar cannot be changed. The announcement on the welcome screen states the following: 'You will not be able to make changes once you "accept" your appearance'. As declared by the *EU*'s developer, enhancing the avatar's appearance may be performed only by a hair dresser or by a face or body sculptor. When it comes to 'sculpting' the avatar's body, in both *SL* and *EU*, it is possible to adjust particular body parts, and so our female avatar may exhibit masculine body features (and vice versa). It is worth noticing, however, that the very framework is still very limited; our avatar will not be extremely fat (a certain degree of obesity is possible), bony, or wrinkled. The 'Randomize' option in *SL*, on the other hand, allows us to follow a standardized masculine or feminine embodiment, which succumbs to the stereotypical representation of females and males— slim waist and wide hips versus muscular shoulders in the latter case.

The representations of femininity and masculinity in the aforementioned virtual worlds seem to comply strongly with socially acceptable norms and further reinforce gender classifications. This stereotyped visual bipolarity, as Schmieder (2009: 8–9)[16] rightly notices, depends on the decisions made by the designers and/or programmers of a particular platform. Gamers/ users, however, do play a crucial role in the process of creation. It is their attitude that is taken into consideration by the producers during 'alpha' and 'beta' tests.

Having briefly looked at the process of avatar creation in *Second Life* and *Entropia Universe*, we will now move on to some theoretical reflections questioning the supposedly flexible nature of virtual worlds and cyberspace. In the light of some postmodern as well as post-postmodern theories we will refer to in this section, new technologies seemingly empower us to create our identities (and cyberbodies) from scratch. Our enacted bodies (real-life bodies placed in front of the computer screen, cf. Hayles 1999) impose a certain social identity on us. We are recognized and judged by others on the basis of our sex, race, ethnicity, social status, among many others, regardless of whether these categories comply with our own perception of ourselves.

In cyberspace, on the other hand, it is us who decide what data (e.g., bodily categories) we want to disclose to others as our virtual bodies are fully formable or at least this is the way we would like it to be. We impose a particular image of ourselves (in case of *SL* or *EU*, that image is reflected in our avatar) on the online society. It seems as if virtual worlds enabled us to be highly creative in constructing our identities. Because in cyberspace we are devoid of enacted bodies, we could re-embody and re-create ourselves blurring the boundaries at will. However, we do not seem to be making use of this opportunity, and instead we create a mere virtual equivalent of the well known reality. Even though the Internet allows us to impersonate different identities and genders, most of the time we do not dispute the well established identity based on binary oppositions—feminine vs. masculine, hetero- vs. homosexual, etc. The Internet, the virtual, although being a technology of great potentiality, is still based on the heteronormative cultural, social, and political order. The tool that could be well used to implement revolutionary ideas existing in theory becomes the tool promoting the essentialist point of view. So, how may the process of avatar creation in *SL* or *Entropia Universe* be analyzed in the context of fluidity or a utopian post-human and post-gender cyberspace?

As mentioned in the previous paragraphs, graphical virtual worlds have shifted our attention to the corporeal dimension of virtual existence (however contradictory the juxtaposition may seem). In the light of the Cartesian body-mind split prevalent in, e.g., cyberpunk fiction (cf. *Neuromancer* by William Gibson 1984), disembodiment is considered to be the ideal form of virtual existence. The so-called 'jacking in' (leaving the 'meat' behind) presupposes abandoning the body and uploading the consciousness into the virtual, ipso facto enabling a pure connection with the technological medium.

A similar attitude towards the body as a limitation was also present in the academic discourse revolving around the post-human view, in which a human being was perceived '[. . .] as a set of informational processes' (Hayles 1999: 4). As Katherine Hayles further explains, 'Embodiment has been systematically downplayed or erased in the cybernetic construction of the post-human [. . .]' (Hayles 1999: 4). The information pattern, the code, the mind were regarded as the superior components of post-human existence. Evoking Gibson's metaphor again, the post-human body may be described as 'data made flesh'. The body, if considered at all, acts as a prosthesis controlled by our consciousness. Yet again, in the dialogue between nature and culture, the latter one turns out to be taking the helm. In 'A Cyborg Manifesto' Haraway refers to '[. . .] the utopian tradition of imagining a world without gender; [. . .] the cyborg [being] a creature in a post-gender world [. . .]' (Haraway 1991: 154). And although the body is present in her dream, it is not constrained by the organic wholeness and has no origins in Western thought. It is a merger between humans and machines, which questions the binary oppositionist nature of our existence. 'The dichotomies between mind and body, animal and human, organism and machine, public and private, nature and culture, men and women, primitive and civilized are all in question ideologically' (Haraway 1991: 151). The concept of a cyborg is supposed to liberate women from the patriarchal order, which is responsible for the present gender, race, or class consciousness. Haraway notices that communication technologies give women the possibility to recraft their bodies and create new social relations, new meanings, not necessarily encapsulating female embodiment within the role of the mother. In the case of women, therefore, the notions of becoming disembodied or cyborg-like signify freedom from the constraints of the patriarchal social system.

Eventually, all those abstract theories and literary dreams had the chance to realize themselves online (in text-based MUDs), where the textual body could have been re-crafted, redefined, or abandoned altogether. A similar situation took place in the late 1970s and prevailed in the 1980s (with the outburst of MUDs), when, as Sherry Turkle observes, the abstract philosophical ideas of the decentered and multiple self were concretized by experiencing online communities. 'The disjuncture between theory (the unitary self is an illusion) and live experience (the unitary self is the most basic reality)' was brought down to earth (Turkle 1999: 646). There is, however, one crucial difference between the two scenarios—whereas in the latter case purely theoretical assumptions found their practical counterpart online, the dream of a disembodied cyborg devoid of gender never came true.

As it turned out, the physical body situated in front of the screen cannot be disregarded, and ignoring its importance will not help women in building a more independent social image. It seems as if the reflection on the body in cyberspace has proceeded from leaving the 'meat' behind to its rehabilitation and reformulation of its importance. The body has been moved from the periphery to the center of analysis (especially in corporeal feminism, cf. Grosz 1994). After all, the body made of flesh and bones sits in front of the screen and interacts physically with the computer in order to launch the mind into the virtual and re-embody itself. This phenomenon may be referred to as the double-situatedness of the body, which 'implies, on the one hand, that user-readers are "embodied" as direct receivers, whose bodies interact with the hardware and software of a computer. On the other, user-readers are considered to be "re-embodied" through feedback that they experience in represented form, e.g., through visible or invisible avatars [. . .]' (Ensslin 2009: 158). The concept of the human-machine cybernetic feedback loop has become settled in the academic discourse in recent years and seems to be giving justice to both, mind and body. Not only has the Cartesian dualism long gone, but the importance of the body itself has been revived. Human-machine interaction is as dependent on the cognitive processes as it is on physical reciprocity.

The theories discussed previously constitute just a fraction of various attitudes that have sprung up in recent years. For the purpose of this chapter we decided to focus on a few, which seem to track the changes cybernetics and body studies have undergone. Some of the ideas presented in this paragraph had the chance to move from theory into practice and be concretized in cyberspace (e.g., the fractured and multiple self), and some remained in the sphere of pure theory. As said previously, although new communication technologies give us the possibility to become even more flexible and escape binary oppositions, we use them to reinforce the already existing ones. We re-embody female or male avatars; we create gender-restricted regions (in *SL*); we form societies and rules corresponding to the ones valid in real life. And even though our *SL* avatar may become a ball of light or an androgynous figure, from the level of the interface we are still either male or female. Our eccentric outfit (texture) becomes one of the clothing items we may put on. In MUDs (as mentioned in the previous paragraphs) some attempts were made to give more gender freedom to its users. However, because we have moved from text-based virtual platforms to graphical worlds, such as

SL or *EU*, gender arbitrariness seems to have become restricted. It may be due to the fact that these platforms are no longer created by online communities, but by commercial companies, which are not focused on fulfilling the needs of niche users.

Experiencing the Virtual Body

We will now move on to the second thematic area revolving around the subject of experiencing the virtual body, and focus briefly on the interface elements in *SL*, discussing their significance in creating the stereotypical heteronormative model of avatar behavior. Because experiencing the real body by going beyond its rigid and stable boundaries (various body fluids, which cross the body's surface, i.e., skin) constitutes an extremely important dimension of our corporeal existence, we will draw on Kristeva's notion of the abject with reference to avatars' bodies as well.

Stereotyped heteronormative bipolarity in *SL* is not only reinforced by means of graphical representation, but is also reflected in our avatar's motor skills, such as walking, sitting, dancing, or making gestures. As it turns out, experiencing the virtual world and interacting with its objects and other avatars by means of *SL* interface is to a large extent determined by our avatar's sex. As part of our methodology of research involved spending several hours in *SL* and interacting with its content, we encountered numerous instances supporting the point made previously.

The most discernible manifestation of heteronormativity refers to our avatar's walking style. In *SL*, those motor skills are clearly dependant on the avatar's sex. Our female avatar swayed her hips gently, whereas its male counterpart plodded along in a stereotypically masculine manner, invading the cyberspace self-confidently with his straight-up chest and wide arms. Interestingly, the way avatars sit also exhibits their physicality dependent on sex. It is not possible for a female avatar to walk or sit like a man. To communicate with one another, avatars may also use a plethora of gesture patterns. Apart from the standardized gestures, we have a number of female or male shrugs, cries, or chuckles to choose from. Some gestures are also accompanied by auditory effects accordingly. 'Dance balls' constitute one of the most entertaining phenomena relating to gender and sex movement manifestations. The two round objects placed above the dance floor may be activated by clicking. The pink dance ball is meant for female avatars and blue for males. We made our avatar dance in the Fabglitter Woman's Club (a place for women only) by clicking on the 'Intan Feminine Dance Ball' and browsing through many different dance styles for female avatars, e.g., easy kneesy, boogie, or lime jelly. There are also dance balls intended for couples (abiding by heterosexual norms only). Even in *SL* gay clubs, the couple dance balls are divided corresponding to either male or female dance styles. One can, however, activate a male dance ball for a female avatar, which may be perceived as the manifestation of fluidity, at least to a certain extent.

Having browsed through various gesture patterns, we came across 'female cry'. We double-clicked the gesture to play animation and sound. To our astonishment, the avatar, although crying out loud in a very realistic manner, did not shed literal tears (the same applies to avatars in *EU*). This experience pointed us in the direction of examining the avatar's body, taking into consideration its fluids and what follows, Kristeva's notion of the abject. As Grosz notices, '[T]he abject is what of the body falls away from it while remaining irreducible to the subject/object and inside/outside oppositions' (Grosz 1994: 192). The idea of the abject is closely related to body fluids (i.e., tears, sweat, menstrual blood, saliva, vomit, etc.), which 'attest to the permeability of the body, its necessary dependence on an outside, its liability to collapse into this outside [. . .] to the perilous divisions between the body's inside and its outside'(Grosz 1994: 193). The avatars' virtual bodies in *SL* and *EU* are empty and therefore stable and fixed in that they do not secrete bodily fluids. Because they are deprived of their fluid and unstable dimension, they may be defined by and reduced to binary oppositions, such as inside/outside or subject/object. Lack of bodily fluids with reference to avatars may be also an interesting point, when it comes to the way body is (or bodies are) idealized in our culture—body as a stable object regulating the influence of fluids (in our case completely withstanding their influence) is perceived as pure and clean. Therefore, the virtual bodies in *SL* or *EU* may be regarded as superior to their real counterparts. The concept of the pure and idealized body links to the remark on the avatars' bodies made in the previous paragraphs—*SL* and *EU* avatars cannot be obese or bony, and they never get old. In case of virtual bodies in the aforementioned platforms, certain parts and functions have been privileged, whereas others have been minimized or left underrepresented (Grosz 1994: 192). As Grosz explains, '[I]t is the [. . .] culture [that effectively intervenes] into the constitution of the value of the body' (192). In other words, the avatar's body may be referred to as the proper social body; the reflection of the process of cultural codification and construction.

Sexual relations between the avatars of both sexes, analyzed with reference to the abject theory, constitute another interesting point. As Grosz notices, '[I]n certain cultures each of the sexes can pose a threat to the other, a threat that is located in the polluting powers of the other's body fluids' (Grosz 1994: 193). In *Second Life* the avatars may have sexual intercourses and the genitals are easily visible, however, no transfer of sex fluids occurs. In the light of Grosz's remark, we may assume that the role of the female body and the notion of sexual difference in virtual worlds has been shifted. Because the avatars do not secrete any fluids (and may be thus perceived as empty or two-dimensional only), the uncontrollable element of the female body—connected with leaking and lack of self-containment (Grosz 1994: 203)—is no longer in force. Female avatars' bodies may no longer be treated as containers or vessels. The distinction between women as corresponding to nature and men to culture has been also undermined with reference to virtual worlds. Pushing these conclusions even further, we may say that the female body has been thus reconstructed and re-embodied in the virtual, thus regaining control and an equal cultural status with the male body.

However, because there is no exchange between the inside and the outside, and the avatars' bodies are two-dimensional only, a crucial question arises—can they be treated and interpreted as legitimate bodies at all? Maybe it is more reasonable to refer to the avatars' skins, which points to the surface and thus the outer (and only) layer of these virtual bodies.

Moving from virtual worlds to the realm of video games, it is worth noticing that in some of them the superficiality of the virtual bodies is transgressed to a certain degree and graphical representations of selected bodily fluids do occur. As Ensslin accurately points out, '[f]ood and energy provision, intake and expenditure have a crucial function in the macro-structure of a large number of videogames' (Ensslin forthcoming: n.p.). This does not mean, however, that the avatar's body in every game is subject to physiological processes. One of the most interesting examples, from the point of view of the abject theory, is *The Sims 2* (EA Games, 2004), where Sims succumb to the following needs: hunger and bladder. The latter case is particularly interesting as '[. . .] visits to the toilet are not tabooed or semiotically erased' (Ensslin forthcoming: n.p.). This adds a highly realistic dimension to the life of the Sims and metaphorically fills their bodies and enables the interaction between the inside of their bodies and the outside world. Apparently, Sims can also get sick, in which case vomiting takes place. The instances of abject, however, are very rarely depicted in video games. Food consumption—be it organic, synthetic, or abstract—is a very popular interface element in many games, but hardly ever is it interlinked with the processes of excretion.

Gender-Restricted *SL* Regions

As we have presented in the preceding paragraphs, gender fluidity in *SL* or *EU* may be and is restricted by means of the very interface. In such case, the users do not have a direct influence on that process and in order to interact within the virtual world, they have to follow the rules established by the producers. On the other hand, *SL* allows its users to create their own land, clubs, shops, and other venues, for which the guidelines or terms of use are established by the users themselves. Theoretically, with the help of given interface elements, one might create an unconventional region devoid of traditional social constraints or gender restrictions. Yet again, users do not eradicate identity based on binary oppositions. The model of Internet identities merely mirrors the model of the ones present in the real world. Hence, *SL* is filled with gender-restricted regions, which further contributes to the limitation of flexibility. The phenomenon related to generating such places reflects very accurately one of the viewpoints presented by cyberfeminists. As the cyberspace seems to be a zone predominantly governed by male users, it is understandable that women demand a fair share in its creation. Women try to conquer and seize this new space, stereotypically being in the possession of men. In the light of such arguments, the creation of gender-restricted regions in SL seems justified to a certain degree. To examine how this phenomenon is realized in virtual worlds, we have explored a few SL regions for women only. Having visited the Isle of Lesbos, for instance, we found out that land rental in the district of 'Whispering Big Pines' is intended exclusively for women. One of the points in the agreement states the following: 'In order to rent on the Whispering Big Pines region you must be female' (Linden Lab). Clearly, this regulation is in force with reference to the avatar's appearance. It operates, thus, on the virtual level only, and one should not confuse it with the actual person sitting in front of the computer screen.

FabGlitter Women's Club operates in accordance with even more limiting and restrictive rules. Again, FabGlitter is a male-free zone. There are certain exceptions to the rule, but in such a case male avatars need to wear special tags not to be banned from the region. It is surprising how exclusive such places may be when it comes to the avatar's appearance. Avatars are most welcome to FabGlitter 'as long as they are in a female shape (butch or androgynous is welcome just not male specific shapes)' (Linden Lab). After hours of research, we have stumbled upon Venus Beach, whose rules have struck us yet again as being extremely gender restrictive. The beach allows heterosexual, bi-sexual, lesbian, as well as transsexual/transgender women. Also, its owners do specify what exactly they mean by a male avatar—'Our basic definition of a man is an AV with a penis, and/or having an obvious masculine physical form' (Linden Lab 2003: n.p.).

Male avatars, once entering the beach, are ejected and/or banned. The virtual body as the indicator of one's sex and presumably gender turns out to be a determinant factor in restricting one's access to certain regions or sites.

CONCLUSIONS

The question of embodiment, gender, and fluid identity may be scrutinized from numerous perspectives. Taking into account the size constraints of this chapter, we have focused on gender and body with relation to virtual worlds. Having examined the preceding notions, concentrating on a purely visual channel of virtual worlds (as opposed to the textual and the auditory ones further elaborated on by Schmieder 2009), we have touched upon the following thematic scopes: the avatar's body, experiencing it through the interface, and finally its placement in *SL* gender-restricted regions. Extrapolating from various theories relating to identity (Dybel 2006; Merleau-

Ponty 2002; Bauman 2000a, 2000b; Giddens 1991), gender (Hyży 2003; Butler 1999; Hayles 1999; Haraway 1991), or net utopianism (Wilding 2001), among many others, we conclude that cyberspace is not liberating users from heteronormative and phallocentric constraints. However, this current situation is not rooted in the nature of the medium, which does allow for flexibility, but in the users themselves who re-create their social, cultural, and political experiences of the real world in their cybernetic communities. Theoretically, we have the facilities to enter an age of gender-free cyborgs liberated from bodily constraints, but the question is whether the post-human reality is a dream projected by a handful of researchers that does not seem to reflect general tendencies present in the postmodern society.

The topic we have examined from one of many possible perspectives has a lot of potential and constitutes rich material for future research. Possible thematic ramifications may concentrate on various other online phenomena. Body rehabilitation and its reconstruction as understood by corporeal and cyberfeminism can be linked with the fact that women are taking the helm of originally masculinist cyberspace. Regaining cyberspace by women takes place on many different levels. They establish varied support groups or cultural projects, such as Old Boys Network, Wise-Women, the Bitch magazine, or ArtWomen.[17] Excluding virtual worlds, massively multiplayer online role-playing games (MMORPGs) and video games in general also constitute fertile ground for gender analysis. As far as gaming and women support groups are concerned, Grrl Gamer comprises one of the most interesting cases relating to the fact that women begin to find their legitimate place in the gaming field, originally a male dominated zone.[18]

There are many more examples of the aforementioned kind, which only adds strength to the fact that gender related issues do make up an extremely broad field. We hope our perspective on the role of gender and body in virtual worlds contributed to a greater understanding of the phenomena discussed herein and the way they function online. Although we have discredited the fluid nature of cyberspace, we do hope that one day it will turn into a zone unrestricted by essentialist social order and its undisclosed potential will come into force. As for now, however, the virtual worlds remain mere reflections of the already familiar reality, and cyberspace cannot be 'regarded as an arena inherently free of the same old gender relations and struggles' (Wilding 2001: n.p.).

NOTES

1. After Grosz (1994).
2. *Second Life* is a virtual world developed by the American company Linden Lab and launched in June 2003. *Entropia Universe* is a virtual world created by the Swedish software company MindArk and released in January 2003.
3. Paweł Dybel is a Polish philosopher and a member of the Polish Academy of Sciences.

4. That terminological issue has been emphasized by Robyn Warhol and Diane Prince Herndl (the editors of *Feminisms: An Anthology of Literary Theory and Criticism*), who stated the following: "[. . .] [W]e've used the plural form "feminisms", rather than "feminism", to acknowledge the diversity of motivations, methods, and experience among feminist academics" (Warhol and Herndl 1997, x). The plural form is also used in the volume edited by Sandra Kemp and Judith Squires (see Kemp and Squires 1998).

5. Referring to essentialism, naturalism, and biologism, misogynous thought confines women's role to biological needs connected with reproduction; assuming that women are somehow more biological, corporeal, and natural than men (Grosz 1994).

6. For the purpose of this chapter we have simplified the distinction, disregarding various fluctuations present within those movements. We also refer to subject in a general way, excluding the variation of contexts, in which this term may be analyzed in contemporary philosophy.

7. It is impossible to discuss the problem of transgenderism and its various subcategories within the confines of this single concept. Academic definitions may be found, for instance, in the writings of Stryker (e.g., 1994). However, because arbitrariness forms the basis for this phenomenon, the terminology is also diverse and unstable. Usually, the differentiations between certain concepts are based on subjective and fluid criteria. Establishing one's gender irrespective of sex is the linking point.

8. No unified definition of cyberfeminism exists; even its founders describe it through negation. The manifesto of the movement is included in "100 anti-theses" formulated at the First Cyberfeminism International in Kassel in 1997 (http://www.obn.org/cfundef/100antitheses.html [accessed 15 July 2009]).

9. Or 'actual' after Deleuze. We will explain the distinction between reality and actuality in a later section of this chapter.

10. Net utopianism is characterized by anti-corporeal discourse, which '[. . .] declares cyberspace to be a free space where gender does not matter—you can be anything you want to be regardless of your "real" age, sex, race, or economic position—and refuses a fixed subject position. In other words, cyberspace is regarded as an arena inherently free of the same old gender relations and struggles' (Wilding).

11. Actual. (n.d.). *Online Etymology Dictionary*. Retrieved 17 May 2009 from Dictionary.com. http://dictionary.reference.com/browse/actual.

12. Corpus. (n.d.). *Online Etymology Dictionary*. Retrieved 17 May 2009 from Dictionary.com. http://dictionary1.classic.reference.com/browse/corpus. reality. (n.d.). *Online Etymology Dictionary*. Retrieved 17 May 2009, from Dictionary.com. http://dictionary1.classic.reference.com/browse/reality.

13. Cf. Astrid Ensslin (forthcoming), '"Do avatars dream of electric steak?"—Games, energy supplies and the cybernetic body'.

14. For the analysis of the three channels (visual, textual, auditory), see Schmieder (2009).

15. Spivak pronouns are gender-neutral pronouns in English, which were introduced by Michael Spivak and became popular as one of the numerous genders available in MUDs and MOOs. Splat pronouns are formed by using an asterisk to replace the letters used in standard English pronouns; for instance, instead of him or her, we may type in h*.

16. In his article Schmieder (2009) focuses on *World of Warcraft* (an MMORPG—massively multiplayer online role-playing game). However, the process of decision making and designing may be applied to other platforms of similar kind as well; *SL* and *EU* in our case.

17. 'OBN is regarded as the first international Cyberfeminist alliance and was founded in 1997 in Berlin. OBN is a real and a virtual coalition of Cyberfeminists. Under the umbrella of the term "Cyberfeminism", OBN contributes to the critical discourse on new media, especially focussing on its gender-specific aspects'. http://www.obn.org (accessed 10 April 2009).
   Wise-Women is a world-wide, online community of web designers, developers and programmers'. http://www.wise-women.org) (accessed 10 April 2009).
   Bitch: Feminist Response to Pop Culture, a print magazine devoted to feminist analysis and media criticism. Bitch features critiques of TV, movies, magazines, advertising, and other elements of pop culture. We also interview feminist pop culture makers, review new books and music, and lots more' http://bitchmagazine.org (accessed 5 April 2009).
   A website cumulating 'visual art and feminist cultural production across and between disciplines and geographical boundaries'. http://www.artwomen. org (accessed 10 April 2009).
18. From http://www.grrlgamer.com (accessed 25 March 2009).

REFERENCES

All about crossdressing. Online. Available HTTP: http://www.crossdressing.pl/main.php?lv3_id=551&lv1_id=25&lv2_id=52&lang=pl (accessed 15 July 2009).
Bailenson, NJ (2006) Transformed social interaction in collaborative virtual environments. In *Digital media: Transformations in human communication*, ed. P Messaris and L Humphreys, 255–56. New York: Peter Lang.
Bakke, M (2000) *Ciało otwarte. Filozoficzne interpretacje kulturowych wizji cielesności* [*The open body. Philosophical interpretations of cultural corporeal visions*]. Poznań: Wydawnictwo Naukowe Instytutu Filozofii Uniwersytetu im. Adama Mickiewicza.
Bauman, Z (2000a) *Liquid modernity*. Cambridge: Polity Press.
———. (2000b) *Ponowoczesność jako źródło cierpień* [*Postmodernity as the source of suffering*]. Warszawa: Wydawnictwo Sic!
———. (2001) Tożsamość—jaka była, jest i po co? In *Wokół problemów tożsamości* [*Around the problems of identity*], ed. Aldona Jawłowska, 8–26. Warszawa: Wydawnictwo LTW.
———. (2007) Tożsamość ze sklepu, tożsamość ze spiżarni [Identity from the shop, identity from larder]. In *W poszukiwaniu tożsamości. Humanistyczne rozważania interdyscyplinarne* [*In search of identity. Humanistic interdisciplinary reflections*], ed. H Mamzer, 27–32. Poznań: Wydawnictwo Naukowe Uniwersytetu im. Adama Mickiewicza.
Beauvoir, S (2003) *Druga płeć* [Le Deuxième Sexe], trans. G Mycielska and M Leśniewska. Warszawa: Jacek Santorski and Co.
Bell, D (2001) *An introduction to cybercultures*. New York: Routledge.
Boellstorff, T (2008). *Coming of age in Second Life: An anthropologist explores the virtually human*. Princeton: Princeton University Press.
Butler J (1999) *Gender trouble: Feminism and the subversion of identity*. New York and London: Routledge.
Deleuze, G (2004) *Difference and repetition*. London: Continuum.
Derrida, J (1978) *Writing and difference*. London: Routledge.
Dybel, P (2006) *Zagadka 'drugiej płci'. Spory wokół różnicy seksualnej w psychoanalizie i feminizmie* [*The mystery of 'second sex'. Disputes over sexual difference in psychoanalysis and feminism*]. Kaków: TAiWPN UNIVERSITAS.

Ensslin, A (2009) Respiratory narrative: Multimodality and cybernetic corporeality in 'physio-cybertext'. In *New perspectives on narrative and multimodality*, ed. R Page. London: Routledge.

Ensslin, A (forthcoming) 'Do avatars dream of electric steak?'—games, energy supplies and the cybernetic body. *Journal of Gaming and Virtual Worlds* 3, no. 1.

Foucault, M (1991) The Foucault reader: An introduction to Foucault's thought. London: Penguin.

Gajewska, A (2008) *Hasło: feminizm* [*Entry: Feminism*]. Poznań: Wydawnictwo Poznańskie.

Gibson, W (1984) *Neuromancer*. New York: Ace Books.

Giddens, A (1991) *Modernity and self-identity: Self and society in the late modern age*. Stanford, CA: Stanford University Press.

Grosz, E. (1994) *Volatile bodies: Toward a corporeal feminism*. Bloomington and Indianapolis: Indiana University Press.

Haraway, D (1991). A cyborg manifesto. Online. Available HTTP: http://sfs.scnu. edu.cn/blogs/linghh/uploadfiles/2006928221222229.pdf (accessed 25 April 2009).

Hayles, NK (1999) *How we became posthuman: Virtual bodies in cybernetics, literature, and informatics*. Chicago: University of Chicago Press.

Hyży, E (2003) *Kobieta, ciało, tożsamość. Teorie podmiotu w filozofii feministycznej końca XX wieku* [*Woman, body, identity. Theories of subject in the feminist philosophy of late 20th century*]. Kraków: TAiWPN UNIVERSITAS.

Iwasiów, I (2004) *Parafrazy i reinterpretacje. Wykłady z teorii i praktyki pisania (eseje naukowe)* [*Paraphrases and reinterpretations. Lectures on the theory and practice of writing; academic essays*]. Szczecin: Wydawnictwo Naukowe Uniwersytetu Szczecińskiego.

Kemp, S and J Squires, eds. 1998. *Feminisms*. Oxford: Oxford University Press.

Mamzer, H (2007). Introduction: How to conceptualize the notion of identity? In *W poszukiwaniu tożsamości. Humanistyczne rozważania interdyscyplinarne* [*In search for identity. Humanistic interdisciplinary reflections*], ed. H Mamzer, 7–19. Poznań: Wydawnictwo Naukowe Uniwersytetu im. Adama Mickiewicza.

Markham, NA (1998) *Life online: Researching real experience in virtual space*. Walnut Creek, CA: Altamira Press.

Merleau-Ponty, M (2002) *Phenomenology of perception*, trans. C Smith. London: Routledge.

Nakamura, L (2002). *Cybertypes: Race, ethnicity, and identity on the Internet*. New York: Routledge.

Ortner, SB (1974) Is female to male as nature is to culture? In *Woman, culture, and society*, ed. MZ Rosaldo and L Lamphere, 68–87. Stanford, CA: Stanford University Press.

Plant, S (1996) Feminisations: Reflections on women and virtual reality. In *Clicking In. Hot links to a digital culture*, ed. L Hershman-Leeson, 37–42. Seattle: Bay Press.

———. (1997) *Zeros + ones: Digital women + the new technocultures*. New York: Doubleday.

Rosenberg, MS (1992) Virtual reality: Reflections of life, dreams, and technology: An ethnography of a computer society. Online. Available HTTP: http://www.eff.org/Net_culture/MOO_MUD_IRC/rosenberg_vr_reflections.paper (accessed 20 March 2009).

Schmieder, C (2009). World of warcraft vs. world of queercraft? Communication, sex and gender in the online role-playing game 'World of Warcraft'. *Journal of Gaming and Virtual Worlds* 1, no. 1: 5–21.

Stryker, S (1994). My words to Victor Frankenstein above the village of chamounix: Performing trransgender rage. *GLQ: A Journal of Gay and Lesbian Studies* 1: 237–54.

Taylor, TL (2006). *Play between worlds: Exploring online game culture.* Cambridge, MA: MIT Press.

Turkle, S (1999). Looking toward cyberspace: Beyond grounded sociology: Cyberspace and identity. *Contemporary Sociology* 28, no. 6: 646.

Walczewska, S (2006) *Damy, rycerze i feministki. Kobiecy dyskurs emancypacyjny w Polsce Polsce [Ladies, knights and feminists. Feminine emancipatory discourse in Poland].* Kraków: Wydawnictwo eFKa.

Warhol, RR and DP Herndl, eds. (1997). *Feminisms: An anthology of literary theory and criticism.* New Brunswick, NJ: Rutgers University Press

Wilding, F (2001) Where is feminism in cyberfeminism? Online. Available HTTP: http://faithwilding.refugia.net/wherefem.html (accessed 20 April 2009).

LUDOGRAPHY

EA Games (2004). *The Sims 2.* Online. Available HTTP: http://www.thesims2.ea.com (accessed 2 April 2009).

Linden Lab (2003). *Second Life.* Online. Available HTTP: http://www.secondlife.com (accessed 12 March 2009).

MindArk (2003). *Entropia Universe* Online. Available HTTP: http://www.entropiauniverse.com (accessed 12 March 2009).

5 The Body of the Avatar
Constructing Human Presence in Virtual Worlds

Denise Doyle

INTRODUCTION

> VR bodies are thin and never attain the thickness of flesh.
>
> —Ihde (2002: 15)

A debate surrounding the recent growth in virtual worlds, and a concern this chapter explores, is how human presence is constructed through our avatar representation in virtual space. Many of us now regularly participate and interact in the virtual space of our computer screens through our avatar forms, whether it is organizing a raid in *World of Warcraft*, chatting with our friends in *Habbo*, or exploring an island in *Second Life*™ (*SL*). This chapter focuses, in particular, on the *SL* platform created by Linden Lab. Launched in 2003 with barely 1,000 users (Rymaszewski et al. 2007: 5), the number of *SL* users with an account has grown to over 16 million.[1] Following the logic of the 'real' world, it follows most of the rules of our space, providing earth, sky, water, gravity, day and night, moon and sun within a three-dimensional networked grid. Experienced through an avatar, many users choose to represent themselves in human form, although other forms are readily available. The question of how we are now creating and living Second Lives as our new avatar selves, and indeed, how we are creating new virtual communities on these shared virtual platforms is the wider debate that surrounds the representation of the self in virtual-world space.

To explore these issues and concepts of presence, both Eastern and Western philosophy are drawn upon, from Benedict de Spinoza and the writings of Gaston Bachelard, and from recent discussions of the Dalai Lama on the mind-body relationship, against the backdrop of the virtual world of *SL*. I explore the relationship between visualization practices in certain meditational traditions and the imaginary itself. I question how, and if, our experience of virtual spaces allows us to rethink the experience of the mind and body relationship. Central to both the trained experiences of visualization in meditation and our experience of presence in virtual worlds is the imagination. Both experience virtual and imagined spaces as real, whereas they are not actual. Finally, I explore the relationship to the represented self in virtual space.

THE BODY OF THE AVATAR

The virtual embodiment of people as avatars is a term used in many online worlds, according to Tom Boellstorff (2008: 128). Avatar is the Sanskrit word originally referred to the incarnation of a Hindu god and particularly the god Vishnu (Boellstorff 2008: 128). However,

> While 'avatar' [. . .] historically referred to incarnation—a movement from virtual to actual—with respect to online worlds it connotes the opposite movement from actual to virtual, a decarnation or invirtual-ization. (Boellstorff 2008: 128)

He further suggests that as 'avatars make virtual worlds real, not actual: they are a position from where the self encounters the virtual' (Boellstorff 2008: 129). Using the terms the virtual, the real, and the actual, Boellstorff links his ideas to Bergson's examination of the real and the virtual in the early part of the 20th century. Bergson makes this distinction between the real and the actual, which reframes his concept of the virtual. Whatever the change in use of the term avatar towards the invirtual, how do we begin to examine this represented self in virtual space, and how do we approach the term the 'body of the avatar'? Speaking of virtual reality bodies in 2002, Ihde compares the virtual body with the real body. Virtual bodies are less than the real, as they can never attain even the thickness of flesh (Ihde 2002: 15). Further discussion of Ihde's investigations of virtual bodies can be found later in the chapter.

My own virtual counterpart, or avatar, Wanderingfictions Story, has developed significantly since her 'birth' in 2006. In Figure 5.1 she sits contemplating, already with glasses, which later becomes a central feature of her identity in virtual space. She has developed from the original newbie state.[2] Later she finds her fully-fledged identity following a project where she discovers that she is comfortable in a skin unlike her own. More recently, experiments in realizing her as a digital object have created interesting results.[3]

The two avatar sisters presented in Figure 5.2 are examples of highly developed avatars in *SL*. In fact Chingaling Bling and her sister China have become part of a narrative, which sees them operate together in *SL* as sisters.[5] This was one of Jacquelyn Morie's first social experiments: Using two computers she logged on as both sisters to see if participators would believe they were two different people. They did. Morie, herself a veteran of the *SL* space, describes herself to have 'a closet full of avatars to match her multifaceted personality' (Doyle 2008: 12).

Figure 5.1   Wanderingfictions Story in *SL* (2007).

Figure 5.2   Two avatar sisters in *SL* (2008).[4]

THE BODY AND THE IMAGINATION

It can be hard to find words to explain the meaning of the imagination. One thing is for certain: We have all imagined; we have all day dreamed at some point in our lives. What role does the imagination play in our acceptance of our represented presence in virtual space, through the body of our avatar? Moira Gatens and Genevieve Lloyd suggest that the imagination, for the 17th-century philosopher Spinoza, has 'a powerful ontological dimension—a direct and strong contact with bodily reality' (Gatens and Lloyd 1999: 12). His version of the imagination has an equally strong emphasis on the reality of the mental and:

> [. . .] the figments of the imagination are just as real—just as appropriate objects of systematic investigation—as the modifications of matter. Imagination involves the coming together of mind and body in the most immediate way: *mind is the idea of body* [my emphasis]. (Gatens and Lloyd 1999: 12)

So the imagination, according to Spinoza, is rooted in the body, or to put it slightly differently: The body has a mind of its own. It is interesting to note that there is an emphasis here on the relationship between the body and the mind, and that the mind does not exist without the body.

In *Air and Dreams*, Bachelard (1988: 4), writing in the 20th century, proposes that 'the imaginary is imminent in the real, [and] how [there is] a *continuous* [original emphasis] path [that] leads from the real to the imaginary'. In *Water and Dreams* he writes that by following the daydreams of a man:

> [. . .] who abandons himself to the imagination of matters, [. . .] a substance will never seem sufficiently worked over for him because he never stops dreaming of it. Form reaches completion. Matter, never. Matter is a rough sketch of unrestricted dreams. (Bachelard 1983: 113)

The meaning of the 'material imagination' for Bachelard, according to Steve Connor, is described through two intersecting ideas: firstly, that the material world is imagined by everyone all of the time and this is termed the 'imagination of matter' (Connor 2004: 40); and secondly, that imagination is itself:

> [. . .] always implicated in the world that it attempts to imagine, made up, like the gingerbreadman enquiring into his dough, of what it makes out. This is not least because the merely visual or image-making faulty suggested by the word 'imagination' is always toned and textured by the other senses. (Connor 2004: 40)

According to Bachelard (1969: 203), what we imagine works on our being, in our substratum. Connor suggests that the phrase material imagination 'must signify the *materiality of the imagining* [my emphasis] as well as the imagination of material' itself (Connor 2004: 41). Of the skin, Connor writes that, '[it] provides a good opportunity for enquiring into the material imagination because it is bilateral, both matter and image, stuff and sign' (Connor 2004: 41).

Brian Massumi suggests that imagination is the mode of thought that is most suited to the virtual. And further that the:

> Imagination can also be called intuition: a thinking feeling. Not feeling something. Feeling thought [. . .] Imagination is felt thought [. . .] the mutual envelopment of thought and sensation, as they arrive together. (Massumi 2002: 134)

To draw these ideas together, it appears that Spinoza and Massumi agree that there is a strong relationship between the body and the imagination. Bachelard talks of the material imagination, although his poetic theory of the imaginary is often about an elsewhere, that is not here, not a place that begins with the body. However, if we dream over the material, we must also dream over the body. Idhe sees only a thinness to the surface of a virtual reality body, with no possibility of skin, of substance. But what of avatar representations that are closely connected to a person's identity? Some avatars that physically very closely represent a person are actually recognizable to another person. What if the representation of the avatar is physically completely different, but to the person is closer to the way they see, or experience themselves?

VISUALIZATION AND EMBODIED EXPERIENCE

With an emphasis on embodied experience in virtual worlds, parallels can be drawn with yogic practices, and in particular, the practice of Tantra. The imaginary landscapes generated by visualization practices and meditational techniques such as those in the Vajrayana tradition of Tibetan Buddhism or from the Hindu Tantric tradition are deliberate in their virtuality. With their focus on the particularity of the image these landscapes are not intended to be materialized; their pristine and deliberate virtuality is used as a tool for developing and transforming the body and mind.

In Tattwa Shuddhi, a tantric practice of inner purification, there are a number of stages to the meditational practice, which requires the participant to visualize each stage in a particular way. It is explained that in Tattwa Shuddhi rapid progress depends on the tantric aspirant's ability to apply a detailed process of visualization.

This imaginative and creative inner visualization which tantra emphasizes, is not chosen at random, but is deeply related to, and based on, the world of the psyche, which is a world of symbolism. (Saraswati 1984: 78)

The five elements earth, water, fire, air and ether are represented through one of five corresponding tattwas.[6] The practitioner must work with their breath and through visualization place the tattwas on the corresponding part of the body. In the final stage of Tattwa Shuddhi, you are guided to visualize 'a vast red ocean with a large red lotus on it. Seated on that lotus is the form of Prana Shakti. Her body is the color of the rising sun, and is decorated with beautiful ornaments' (Saraswati 1984: 100).

THE DALAI LAMA

Of the relationship between the body and mind, the Dalai Lama writes that even in:

> [...] extremely subtle states of consciousness, the mental state must have a physical base, however subtle it may be. Sometimes there is a tendency among Buddhists to think of these very subtle states of consciousness as if there were no embodiment or material basis for them [...] the brain is the basis for all cognitive events. Without the brain there is no cognitive function of the mind. (Quoted in Harrington and Zajonc 2006: 96)

It is interesting to consider the relationship between Spinoza's and the Dalai Lama's emphasis on the relationship between the body and the mind, that one cannot exist without the other. The contemplative texts of the Sutra system acknowledge the cultivation of heightened awareness in relation to two senses, visual and auditory perception. However, as the Dalai Lama notes, the other senses are not considered. Drawing parallels with modern technologies he comments that:

> [...] You can project images on a television screen, or you can project sounds through radio waves, but you still cannot transport smell and tactile sensations. But in the Vajrajana tradition [...] there is an understanding that it is possible for advanced yogis to gain mastery over these physiological elements. Those bodily energies that are normally confined to the function of specific sensory faculties can actually be co-opted or transferred. (Quoted in Harrington and Zajonc 2006: 97)

Does the interface with virtual-world technologies give us a glimpse of the effects of the co-opting or transferring of our sensory facilities as suggested by the Vajrajana tradition? Does this translation of the senses occur when we interact with virtual worlds? Can we sense this experience through our avatar?

IMMERSION, TELEPRESENCE, AND THE VIRTUAL BODY

In the introduction to *Changing Space* (1997) Char Davies suggests that the medium of immersive virtual space offers the potential for 'exploring consciousness as it is experienced subjectively, as it is *felt* [original emphasis]' (Davies 1997: 1). She likens much of her work to the experience of meditational practice and focuses on the nature and experience of virtual space. In *Osmose* (1995), the participant, or 'immersant', must concentrate on their breath as a device to navigate vertically through the spaces represented. Many immersants can relate their experience to Mark Hansen's when he explains that:

> You are floating inside an abstract lattice [. . .] you have no visible body at all in front of you, but hear a soundscape of human voices swirling around you as you navigate forward and backward by leaning your body accordingly [. . .] Exhaling deeply causes you to sink down through the soil as you follow a stream of tiny lights illuminating the roots of the oak tree. (Hansen 2006: 107–08)

Davies says that within her work, 'within this spatiality, there is no split between the observer and the observed' (Davies 2003: 1). She argues that this is not tied to the Cartesian paradigm, rather allowing 'another way of sensing to come forward, one in which the body feels the space very much like that of a body immersed in the sea' (Davies 2003: 1). As Hansen explains, there is no visible, visualized body in front of the immersant, representing their presence in the space. In virtual worlds there is not the kind of immersive experience that is possible in virtual reality, and in particular in the works of Char Davies. Rather, the virtual world is a mixed experience of the sense of presence and absence, a mix of objective 'looking' and a subjective sense of 'being', which suggests a more complex set of relationships.

Whereas Char Davies has no represented observer as the basis for her immersive installation work, Don Ihde, in *Bodies in Technology*, investigates the duality of the notion and experience of, what he terms, the here-body and the image-body. In asking questions of our phenomenological experience of virtual space he observes that:

> A(n) analysis shows a variation between what would be called full or multidimensional experience and a visual objectification of presumed

body experience. Where does one feel the wind? Or the vertigo in the stomach? Can it be felt 'out there' in the disembodied perspective? The answers quickly show partial primacy to the embodied experience. (Ihde 2002: 4)

The here-body is where we can have a full, multidimensional experience and 'gestalts in the here-body of the embodied perspective, whereas the visual objectification out there is spectacle like' (Ihde 2002: 4). The image-body is where the body of the avatar lies. As Ihde explores the ambiguities experienced in virtual space, particularly when our presence is identified through a third person avatar perspective he suggests that this is 'the opening to a sliding perspective from the multidimensional experience of my here-body toward the image-body perspectives lie within these ambiguities (Ihde 2002: 6).

Toni Dove, an artist who uses responsive interface technologies, describes the charged space of telepresence as, 'the space through which the body extends itself in to the movie or virtual space. It is the invisible experience of the body's agency beyond its apparent physical edge' (2002: 210). Ihde draws the comparison to actual skin which he says is 'at best polymorphically ambiguous, and, even without material extension, the sense of the here-body exceeds its physical bounds' (Ihde, 2002: 6). If the here-body exceeds its physical bounds, does the image-body have a sense of materiality that enables us to dream over it, and in turn, have a sense of the body of the avatar?

THE SL BODY EXPERIENCE OF
WANDERINGFICTIONS STORY

Wanderingfictions Story, if translated back into physical space, would be over seven foot, brown skinned, with a wardrobe full of saris. The author is often asked why she represents herself in *SL* in this way. This was the result of a piece of performative writing undertaken in collaboration with the artist, Taey Kim, in 2007.

In *Embodied Narrative: The Virtual Nomad and the Meta Dreamer* (2007), in conversation with Dongdong whose presence is in Web 2.0 space, Wanderingfictions Story attempts to describe her experience of 'being' in *SL* space. Seen through new eyes, comparisons were made between the early travelers exploring and discovering new lands. However, of her identity she writes:

At the beginning I looked like lots of other people here. That was shocking at times; when I was someplace and another 'me' was there too. Over time my shape seemed to change, though I only really found my identity when my skin changed. It's a brown shade now. Oh, and I wear glasses. (Doyle and Kim 2007: 214)

Figure 5.3   Wanderingfictions Story in a sari in *SL* (2008).

Inspired by a description of cyberspace, Wanderingfictions goes to search for 'place' in *SL*. In *A Sideways Look at Time*, Jay Griffiths claims that in cyberspace there is no Africa:

> [...] no mud, no beads or wells or such humanity in the very air. There's no India in cyberspace, no jasmine, no gupshop, no sari, no desert. There's no swampy, mucky, messy stuff, no tadpoles, no owls. There's no nature in the synthetic element. (Griffiths 2004: 269)

So Wanderingfictions tries to find India on the *SL* platform. She discovers that the Taj Mahal has been built somewhere, at some time. But India itself, with its jasmine and gupshop, is not so easily found.

In Figures 5.3 and 5.4, Wanderingfictions is now dressed in a sari. She explains:

> Yesterday I searched again for India and in a way found it. There was no Taj Mahal, no sign to tell me. I changed my clothes so I could imagine India a little more. It seemed to work. (Doyle and Kim 2007: 218)

Exploring what is particular to her experience in *SL*, she explains her experience of flying:

Figure 5.4 Looking for India in *Second Life* (2007).

Of course I can fly here. But it's like having invisible wings that you cannot really spread widely or fully or freely enough. Sometimes I fly upwards as fast as I can, so I can feel that sensation of freedom, and I can dream of flying a great distance along the horizon. Eventually I get to a point where gravity pulls me back down, but I do seem to be able to have the fantasy of escaping gravity, at least for a moment. (Doyle and Kim 2007: 214)

She has discovered the joy of flight, although it does not give her that full sense of freedom, as she cannot fly far along the horizon.

There is no doubt that the experience of Wanderingfictions Story as my virtual counterpart, who has developed this particular identity, has been a rewarding experience. Not able to present this identity in a physical way in the real world, this particular identity has 'stuck' following the performative writing experiment. This process, of exploring an(other) identity distinct from my own, has given me an opportunity not only to understand my own character, but to understand another through 'virtually' sitting in their skin.

ONTOLOGIES OF VIRTUAL BODIES AND SPACES

In 'Performing in (Virtual) Spaces' (2007), Jacqueline Morie begins with the ontological assumption that the body has been recontextualized in the age of digital technology. Morie claims that there is a specialized and intrinsic set of qualities of 'Being' in immersive virtual environments, and suggests that there has been a paradigm shift in what humans are now able to experience. She points to the research of visual and performance artists and their contribution to the exploration of virtual environments as key to our future understandings of ourselves in the physical and digital domains (Morie 2007: 123).

Morie, in agreeing with Hayles, identifies the body as an integral part of the concept of the post-human, and also sees the body as container. Hayles suggests that the virtual body needs 'bits of information as well as bits of flesh and bone' (Hayles in Morie 2007: 124). Morie claims that 'there would be no mind as we know it without the body that engenders, contains and nurtures it' (Morie 2007: 124). She suggests that the act of emplacing a body into an immersive environment signifies 'a shift to a dualistic existence in two simultaneous bodies' (Morie 2007: 127) and claims that, now, the lived body has 'bifurcated and become two' (Morie 2007: 128).

In her article she explores the representation of the body, or presence, in virtual environments in five ways: as no representation/no avatar, as the mirrored self, as a partial or whole graphical personification, as a third person/observed avatar, and as experience in shared environments. According to Morie, using the observed or third person avatar, in this form of embodied image the participant takes on:

> [...] an experiential locus that is outside their perceptual self. An avatar appears, at some distance out in front of the experient's physical and imaginal locus. (Morie 2007: 132)

For Morie a representation or metaphor of her body icon may compete with her own inner representation of herself in inhabiting an environment, and suggests that virtual environments such as those created by Char Davies become a

> [...] sacred, encompassing space, where mind transcends body even as it references the body, the felt organism even in visual absence. This body, as felt phenomenon, is how we know the world, true as much within the virtual as in the real. (Morie 2007: 133)

She returns to Merleau-Ponty's phenomenological standpoint as he views the body as 'the common texture of which objects are woven' (Merleau-Ponty in Morie 2007: 13), but suggests that he did not have to grapple with 'new forms of immaterial bodies beyond the phenomenal' (Morie: 2007: 133) as we do now in light of new technologies.

CONCLUSIONS

If these new immaterial bodies can be experienced through new technologies, we can also experience ourselves in virtual worlds through embodied presence. However, the virtual-world experience is an interplay of a number of elements: of ourselves experiencing telepresence, our imagined presence in virtual space, and of ourselves switching to the disembodied perspective of Idhe's 'image-body'. This double experience relies on a complex set of relationships between the body and the mind. At the centre of this is the imagination.

Morie's claim is that the centre of our understanding is our body, and through this felt phenomenon, we know the world. Yet, according to Morie, the avatar perspective still has an experiential locus, even though is 'out there'. For Char Davies, it is essential for the body to experience virtual space in a more direct, and most strongly imagined way, within the physical body, rather than 'through' the body representation in space. Yet we see, for Wanderingfictions Story's real-world counterpart, her sense of presence in the *SL* space is rooted in the identity of the represented avatar, in the image-body presented.

The imagination, as Massumi describes it, is thought and sensation arriving together (2002: 134). This concept has echoes in the Dalai Lama's view of the relationship between the body and the mind and opens up ideas surrounding the advanced yogi's techniques of co-opting the senses. The senses are, or can be, interconnected with an imaginary of their own. Virtual worlds are contributing to new dimensions of experience, and at its centre lies the experience of the body of the avatar as a complex construction of human presence in virtual worlds.

NOTES

1. Statistics from http://secondlife.com/whatis/economy_stats.php. Accessed 30 December 2008.
2. A term referring to a novice in *SL*.
3. Wanderingfictions Story has been presented as a digital object, from data extracted from *Second Life*, and exhibited at the Golden Thread Gallery, Belfast.
4. Used with kind permission of Dr Jacquelyn Ford Morie/Chingaling Bling and her sister China.
5. Dr Morie is a Research Scientist from the University of Southern California.
6. Tattwa means energy in Sanskrit.

REFERENCES

Bachelard, G (1969) *The poetics of reverie: Childhood, language and the cosmos.* Boston: Beacon Press.
———. (1983) *Water and dreams: An essay on the imagination of matter.* Dallas: The Pegasus Foundation.
———. (1988) *Air and dreams: An essay on the imagination of movement.* Dallas: The Dallas Institute Publications.
Boellstorff, T (2008) *Coming of age in Second Life: An anthropologist explores the virtually human.* Princeton: Princeton University Press.
Connor, S (2004) *The book of skin.* London: Reaktion Books.
Davies, C (1997) Changed space: Virtual reality as an arena of embodied being. In *Multimedia: From Wagner to virtual reality*, ed. RJK Packer. New York: W. W. Norton.
———. (2003) Landscape, earth, body, being, space, and time in the immersive virtual environments *Osmose* and *Ephemere*. In *Women, art and technology*, ed J Malloy. Cambridge, MA, and London: MIT Press.
Dove, T (2002) The Space Between: Telepresence, Re-animation and the Re-casting of the Invisible. In *New Screen Media: Cinema/Art/Narrative*, eds. Reiser, M and Zapp, A. London: BFI.
———. (2006) Swimming in time: Performing programmes, mutable movies—notes on a process in progress. In *Performance and place*, ed. LPH Hill. Basingstoke: Palgrave Macmillan.
Doyle, D (2008) *Kritical works in SL exhibition catalogue.* Morrisville, NC: Lulu.
Doyle, D and T Kim (2007) Embodied narrative: The virtual nomad and the meta dreamer. *International Journal of Performance Art and Digital Media* 3, no. 2–3: 209–22.
Gatens, M and G Lloyd, eds. (1999) *Collective imaginings: Spinoza, past and present.* London: Routledge.

Griffiths, J (2004) *A sideways look at time.* New York: Penguin.

Harrington, A and A Zajonc (eds) (2006) *The Dalai Lama at MIT.* Cambridge, MA: Harvard University Press.

Hansen, M (2006) *Bodies in code: Interfaces with digital media.* New York: Routledge.

Ihde, D (2002) *Bodies in technology.* Minneapolis: University of Minnesota Press.

Massumi, B (2002) *Parables for the virtual: Movement, affect, sensation.* Durham and London: Duke University Press.

Morie, J (2007) Performing in (virtual) spaces: Embodiment and being in virtual environments. *International Journal of Performance Arts and Digital Media* 3, no. 2–3: 123–38.

Rymaszewski, M, WJ Au, M Wallace, C Winters, C Ondrejka, B Batstone-Cunningham, and Second Life residents from around the world (2007) *Second Life®: The official guide.* Indianapolis, IN: Wiley.

Saraswati, SS (1984) *Tattwa Shuddhi: The tantric practice of inner purification.* Bihar: Bihar School of Yoga.

6 The Grips of Fantasy
The Construction of Female Characters in and beyond Virtual Game Worlds

Isamar Carrillo Masso

INTRODUCTION

> We may be toying with the body when we play, but we remain flesh as we become machines. (Lahti 2003: 169)

Virtual worlds and computer games (CG) in general seem to provide users myriad choices to create ('write') their own 'Second Lives'. It is arguable, however, that the choices and tools we receive as users of New Media are more limited than they appear at first, and that the gendered messages that are semiotically and linguistically encoded in virtual worlds and CG, by virtue of their being naturalized in the mainstream discourse about CG, not only affect our experience of gameplay, but also define the construction of gamers' identities and create a gate-keeping mechanism that ultimately determines the extent to which virtual communities become (or not) gender-inclusive.

Female characters in some computer games seem to finally have moved away from being the damsel in distress, but in many others their roles have not progressed much. If anything, they seemed to have fallen into different clutches, in somebody else's grips: the grips of fantasy.

I intend to determine in a methodical and in-depth fashion how female characters are represented in the context of *Diablo* and *World of Warcraft* (*WoW*), two immensely popular games, by their developers in Blizzard Entertainment and by the games' players, and how this representation differs from the representation of male characters.

As I have discussed elsewhere (Carrillo Masso 2009), in order to understand the representation of female characters in computer games, one has to begin by understanding the nature of computer games, the way they are perceived, how they can be studied, and the way the identity of gamers is both signified and constructed. In order to do this I will start by giving an overview of the previous research done in this area in the following section. It will be easier to classify it and organize this information by grouping related topics around a focus given by the most relevant terms in this study. Second, I will explain in detail the methodology used in this study, from the initial stages of data collection to the creation of a corpus. Third, I will present the results shown by the data. Finally, I will analyze the results and draw some conclusions.

DIABLO AND WOW: TWO TYPES OF ROLE-PLAYING GAME (RPG)

RPGs as we know them today started as pen-and-paper games based on the art of participatory storytelling (Kelly 2004). Although both *Diablo* and *WoW* are generally seen as forms of RPGs, there are some basic differences that make them very different games, and which affect the 'gameplay'—the total experience of playing the game (Dovey and Kennedy 2006). The main difference is the number of players that can participate. In a game of *Diablo*, up to eight players can play at the same time (each player from their own computer, with one computer acting as a server). This makes *Diablo* a minimally multi-player online RPG, or MORPG. *WoW*, on the other hand is a massively multiplayer online RPG, or MMORPG (pronounced like *morgue*, [Kelly 2004]). This means you participate in the game along with millions of other players at the same time, although you might only share one server with about half a million (Kelly 2004).

The second most important difference has to do with the storyline. In *Diablo* players move their avatars through a series of levels, completing a number of quests to obtain more weapons, and eventually defeat what(ever) awaits them in the last battle level. The storyline is fairly linear, as players are consistently constricted in their choices to make them move ahead in the game. The player wins by finishing the last level. In the most difficult mode, avatars have only one life, meaning there are no second chances if the player makes a mistake.

In *WoW*, on the other hand, there is basically no storyline as such. After designing an avatar, the game will generate a full-motion video introducing the player to the 'cultural' context of their avatar's race and alignment, and obtain instructions on how to play. As players move through the *WoW* world, they gain experience points (XPs) and improve. Players can complete quests to move ahead, but this is not essential or mandatory after a certain level. If they get 'killed', there are several ways to be resurrected. There is no ultimate goal and no way to win.

Computer-mediated communication (CMC) has been defined by different scholars in different ways but it can be defined as 'the interaction between two or more people who interact using individual computers via a network connection' (Gardina 2006). CMC studies both 'synchronous' and 'asynchronous' interactions. A synchronous interaction occurs when the participants react to each other in real time; that is, the communication is almost instant. When participants have a time gap between interactions (as in when interacting on an online forum), then the interaction is said to be asynchronous.

RPGs (in both their MORPG and MMORPG incarnations) have started to become the objects of study for both synchronous and asynchronous communication scholars in the field of CMC. In this particular study, the bulk of the user-edited or user-generated data will come from asynchronous CMC; particularly game-centered forums.

The use of corpora to study CMC tends to lean towards project-specific raw-data corpora compilation (Beißwenger and Storrer 2008), and I will keep to this tendency, which means I will use a corpus built specifically for this one project and that uses only unannotated texts, meaning that grammatical features in these texts in the corpus will not be tagged.

USING CORPORA AS A TOOL FOR THE CRITICAL DISCOURSE ANALYSIS (CDA) OF CMC

A corpus is a collection of texts (Thompson 2007). An electronic corpus can serve many purposes, but its main purpose is to allow researchers to observe what is central and typical within the data, by means of a concordancer (Thompson 2007). It can provide us with quantitative information about language use, and frequency of occurrence of lexical (vocabulary) items. It also provides the opportunity to examine patterns of regularity in large quantities of text, which are too difficult or time-consuming to obtain by other means.

Critical discourse analysis (CDA) is the social analysis of discourse through a variety of approaches and methods, each depending on the nature of the research being carried out (Pêcheux 1982; Wodak and Meyer 2001; Orpin 2005). CDA combines interdisciplinary, as well as transdisciplinary techniques to analyze texts and to look at the way dominant discourses not only represent the world, but also *construct* the world through texts.

CDA can be used in different ways to deconstruct institutionalized gender representations in given discourses, and the way these discourses are inculcated and operationalized. I chose CDA for this reason, and for its flexibility, meaning that it can be combined with other methods and techniques in a hybrid approach.

The methods commonly classified as part of CDA offer a way to interpret a problem, to narrow down a topic, and to see the motivations behind the discourse in and through different 'readings' of a text. CDA in itself is then not a single quantitative or qualitative research method, but rather a critical approach to research methods that seeks to eliminate inequality expressed and legitimized through language use (Wodak and Meyer 2001: 2) by exposing it, and to make social changes through social understanding (Van Dijk 1993: 252).

CDA, according to Fairclough (1992, 1993, 2003) and Chouliaraki and Fairclough (1999), can be performed by examining a text as the basic unit of discourse and looking at its context and surrounding elements. This context refers not only to a text's accompanying images, which should never be disregarded in an analysis (Kress and Van Leeuwen 1996), but to the discourses that exist around (and inside) the text and the accompanying images, and the sociocultural practices that envelope them both.

CDA has traditionally focused on the ideologies present in discourses, both as 'representations of how things are and have been, as well as imaginaries—representations of how things might or could or should be' (Fairclough 2003: 207). The main focus in this analysis of the representation of female characters in CG will be the way the node discourse 'woman' creates other discourses that shape mainstream representations of females, and how this is translated inside the text.

New Media Studies scholars and narratologists have devised and adapted different methods of study that attempt to deal with CG's unique features, as well as with the features they see as common to other media. This 'hybrid approach' combines methods and tools from a wide variety of fields in the social sciences (Dovey and Kennedy 2006; Carr et al. 2004), and has proven successful for studying a number of games at least at the level of representation (Jenkins 2001; Dovey and Kennedy 2006; Frasca 2003), which is our main concern here.

To those who argue that games and traditional narrative texts have nothing in common, because, they argue, the player's choices determine the outcome of the narrative, I must say that they forget that the possible outcomes are not endless. They are constricted to the number and type of outcome that was designed and made possible by the CG's designers, as well as by the number of choices available to the player. In this view, the behavior of a player is 'programmed' or 'modeled' (in the semiotic sense, as in Cobley and Jansz 1997: 86) by a 'series of limitations of choices of operations' which produce the 'text' as gameplay. I believe that a number of games (like *Diablo*, and the questing sections of *WoW*) follow this simple narrative style that can be linked to multiple-ending story books (like the *Choose Your Own Adventure Series*, popular in the 1980s), and therefore many of the analysis tools that apply to narrative can be recycled and adapted to this genre.

Ludologists, however, seem entirely focused on rules and resolutely ignore any features of the game that can be said to 'represent' something or someone outside the game rules, holding a position that is almost always determinedly 'a-historical' (Dovey and Kennedy 2006). Those who champion this position, although convincingly defending the need for new tools that aid researchers in the study of the phenomena of immersion (a deep engagement in gameplay) and simulation (the representation of real-life systems through a computer interface) (Frasca 2003) have still not been able to remove representation from the equation. Dovey and Kennedy (2006) summarize the state of this 'schism' (Newman 2004: 91) in the field of Games Studies thus:

> By and large, the game interface is still representational; for many games, perhaps most, representation has not disappeared and cannot easily be argued away. Even though the representation content may only be an interface to the simulation of the game engine, even though action might be more significant than connotation, even though the textual meaning of the representation is secondary to the compulsive engagement with improved game performance—despite acknowledging all this, researchers working within these frameworks insist that most games still use representation; despite 'the Tetris Defense', it hasn't gone away. Whilst games use representation, they remain contextually aligned with operations of power; however, this alignment is certainly of a different order to the relations of meaning production encountered in novels, cinema or television. (Dovey and Kennedy 2006: 101)

Studying the representation of female characters in CG using a 'hybrid' theoretical framework to study CG as media texts is then not only possible, but a necessary feature of this type of study, at least for the present.

Scholars who have developed and refined the Social Constructionist Theory (SCT) departed from traditional perspectives of a fixed sex and a fixed gender (and a fixed gender assigned to a fixed sex), and tried to deconstruct how these widely held notions of sex and gender originate, and their political implications (Butler 1990; Bucholtz and Hall 1995; Lorber 1994; Foucault 1980, 1988; Bucholtz et al. 1999; Epps and Katz 2007).

Two essential elements of SCT are the fact that gender is 'done' by enacting strategic gender discourses, and that these discourses are often invisible, or 'assumed' (Fairclough 2003: 47), as they conform with what has been 'naturalized', and made 'factual or objectively real' (Tolman and Diamond 2001). These discourses are enacted both through individual choice (that is, when confronted with choice in a situation, individuals tend to choose to 'do' their assigned gender consistently), and through the social implementation of 'difference', that is, the consistent and institutionalized interpretation of men's and women's actions as inherently different (Lorber 1994).

The fact that CG are the virtual offspring of contexts that have traditionally been coded as 'highly masculine' (Dovey and Kennedy 2006) is very significant in the way power structures have been used to keep the status quo within this field, and to use this coding as a gatekeeper that prevents females to access the technology more freely. Jenkins (2001) and Graner Ray (2004) suggest that when a team of designers is predominantly or all-male, their decisions (those that will affect the way characters will look as well as gameplay) are going to be 'intuitively different' from those made by a well-balanced team (in terms of gender).

Even those women who manage to enter the almost-exclusively-male realm of CG design are rendered invisible. Often female CG developers find their work 'overlooked or ignored' (Kirkup and Smith-Keller 1992; Stewert Millar 1998; Jenkins 2001; Dovey and Kennedy 2006).

Women are also largely ignored as consumers of CG, despite statistics proving beyond all possible doubt that women make a sizeable portion of all gamers (Atkins, 2003; Stewert Millar 1998; Jenkins 2001; Graner Ray 2004; Taylor 2006; Dovey and Kennedy 2006). According to Dovey and Kennedy (2006), the reasons for this invisibility are twofold: an attempt by those belonging to the 'dominant technicity' (those who own, create, use, and control technology in a way accepted by mainstream society) to ignore other technicities, followed by a sort of forced mass delusion to ignore these alternative technicities and make them conform to the established norms. In their words:

> The power of hegemonic dominance is such that, first, technicities that do not fit the dominant model are made invisible by those that do and, second, that those of us who do not belong to the dominant group also internalize their power and make ourselves invisible. (Dovey and Kennedy 2006: 81)

THE 'IDEAL' CG PLAYER/CONSUMER: THE CONSTRUCTION OF THE SUBJECT POSITION OF AN 'IDEAL GAMER' IN MAINSTREAM MEDIA

There is arguably a stereotypical idea of what a 'typical gamer' looks like. He (for it is always a 'he') is white, is in his late teens, has no social life, is a computer 'geek', and does nothing but play games all day. This is the image most typically seen in the media to portray a gamer, and we have all more or less come to accept it as 'true'. Statistics, however, show that this image is not entirely true. It has been demonstrated that empirical research 'reveals a rich and diverse range of technicities in play at any point in cultural history' (Dovey and Kennedy 2006: 80).

But according to the IDSA, women make up at least 43% of all PC gamers and 35% of console gamers, and our numbers are rising (Women Gamers 2008; Kelly 2004). Women also make up 70% of casual gamers, and in countries like Korea, 69.5% of all women play games (Women Gamers 2008). And women gamers are more likely to play online games (53%) than male gamers (46%) (Women Gamers 2008). Women are, however, largely ignored as an audience, and even as a buying force, by game developers. These developers insist on designing and advertising games to teenage boys, and justify their programming choices by saying that 'women don't play games, anyway' (Kirkup and Keller 1992; Stewert Millar 1998; Jenkins 2001; Dovey and Kennedy 2006).

This myth of the 'typical gamer' exerts a big influence in the market, both determining and constricting who will be an active participant in the technology (as a game producer and as a gamer/consumer) and who will have minor roles in mainstream CG. The word 'myth' here is used in the semiotic sense of something that conveys a distorted political message about the world, by eliminating or 'forgetting' other possible alternative messages, 'so that the myth appears to be simply true' (Bignell 2002: 21).

The 'ideal gamer' myth not only concerns CG as products, as the term 'gamer' itself can be said to form part of a larger context in which 'lifestyles' (Fairclough 2003) or 'neo-tribes' (Bauman 1993) place the gamer/consumer in a niche with other products to consume that contribute to the 'pre-packaged identity' of gamers (Fairclough 2003) by surrounding them with a cohesive array of paraphernalia to consume.

CG producers and advertisers certainly continue to perpetuate this myth by attempting to target a small segment of consumers, and to position them as 'subjects' using what Fairclough (1989) calls 'synthetic personalization'. This strategy serves to select between 'targets' (the segment of the population targeted by advertisers), by having consumers identify themselves with the Ideal (Gamer) and accept the position of subject, or understand that this position has been built for someone else and disregard it. Thus, in this 'simulated intimacy' (Baudrillard 1998) between advertisers and consumers, gamers and advertisers of game products and products for gamers have reached a sort of 'artificial consensus', an assumption, of who a 'real gamer' is. As stated previously, those who do not conform to this mythical representation will be made invisible, and will make themselves invisible (Dovey and Kennedy 2006; Graner Ray 2004).

Female characters in CG have been traditionally construed as one or the other in the form of a Damsel in Distress as opposed to a Foxy Heroine or Foxy Villainess. These two femininities are embodied by remarkably similar avatar types, all of them characterized by similar features, to the extent that they can be actually said to be one single figure with different props surrounding it. Macdonald (1995) explains this apparent sameness of representation that uses one single body by stating that 'the diversity of real women, potentially challenging to male authority, is transformed into manageable myths of "femininity" or "the feminine"' (Macdonald 1995: 2).

In CG and virtual worlds in general (e.g., *Second Life*™), humanoid female avatars share the same characteristics. Particularly, in both humanoid and non-humanoid female characters, breasts are a very prominent feature. Brownmiller (1984) expounds the 'semi-public, intensely private status' of breasts in cultural representations of women, and argues that the representation of women in the media make women understand that breasts

> belong to everybody, but especially to men. It is they who invent and refine their myths, who discuss breasts publicly, who criticize their failings and extol their wonders, and who claim to have more need and more intimate knowledge [of them] than a woman herself. (Brownmiller 1984: 41)

Other shared characteristics include having large eyes, being very young and slim, being usually significantly shorter and thinner than their male counterparts, and having long hair. Where evolutionary psychologists might argue that some of these characteristics in the representation of women are the embodiment of 'biological preferences', they have never been able to argue their case convincingly (Grogan 1999: 164; Itzen 1986: 126). According to SCT these 'attractive feminine characteristics' are more of an 'acquired taste' by means of socialization.

The 'biological' sexual dimorphism that characterizes the Races (species) that populate *WoW* was examined by Rubenstein (2007). Rubenstein looked at pictures contrasting the males and females of the playable Races in *WoW* (in both their alpha versions—i.e., prior to release—and their beta or current versions). This study determined, using CDA techniques, that the male figures resemble the bodies of real-life human male athletes. As the avatars are subjected to similar 'physical' conditions and pressure, regardless of gender, Rubenstein had expected the female avatars to also resemble human female athletes in proportions. She found this to be true only in the least played Races (Dwarves and Gnomes). The other female avatars more closely resembled supermodels; indeed, 'the body types of the female avatars seem to be closer to those of *Zoo Weekly* models than actual body builders' (Rubenstein 2007). Originally in several of the Races (in the alpha version) there was no such dimorphism, and males and females wore equivalent armor (meaning that the avatar's body was covered in more equal proportions in both cases than it is now).

What seems to signal most effectively a character's femininity, and as importantly, the place of a particular CG character in the Saint/Whore dichotomy (as explored in Holland 2006) seems to be the way she is dressed. This tension between two extremes of a feminine continuum is echoed in the main tension of real life fashion: the tension between modesty and display, which shows 'ambivalent orientations toward the erotic and the chaste' (Davis 1992: 98). The imbalance between these two orientations results in what was termed 'the theory of the shifting erogenous zone' (Flugel 1930). According to this widely accepted fashion theory, social changes exert influence on the way eroticism is translated in fashion, and this will subtly (and not so subtly) shift the focus on different body parts by displaying them and keeping others hidden from view. I will devote more attention to the way avatars are dressed in *Diablo* and *WoW* later.

Regardless of the type of femininity embodied in a female CG character, CG always seem to construct this character as the Other, and to underline assumptions and myths of Difference (Kennedy 2002; Dovey and Kennedy 2006). Kennedy (2002) explores the idea that this very Otherization or sexual objectification of female avatars is founded on the (male) player's 'attempt to deny any identification with [a female avatar]'. It has been argued that this exaggerated construction of the feminine Other is merely one more sign of misogyny and backlash, and it is a response to a crisis of 'masculinities', as their value has been brought into question (Turner 1984; Giddens 1992; Cameron 1990; Kirkup and Keller 1992).

There is, however, a complementary explanation that helps adapt this view to the nature of the representation of women in CG as hypersexualized (and usually just 'token') characters. Sedgwick (1993) wrote on the problems men have reconciling the homosocial within a context that despises the homosexual. Following Levi-Strauss, Sedgwick (1993) argues that the use of female characters in computer games has traditionally been one that serves only to create a 'strategic erotic triangle', in which one man (the male gamer) and another man (the male character) are in a simulated competition over a woman (the female character) to justify the fact that their 'real interest is in each other' (Sedgwick 1993 in Wolf and Perron 2003:178). There is no data at present on how this theory applies to homosexual and female gamers and their male or female avatars.

The hyper-sexual but ambiguous female character drives potential female players away from a game (Graner Ray 2004; Kirkup and Keller 1992; Stewert Millar 1998; Jenkins 2001; Dovey and Kennedy 2006). According to Kelly (2004) female characters are simply more visually appealing to some male players. To some other players (those keen on engaging in 'identity tourism' [Nakamura 2002]), playing a female character has the advantage of receiving more friendly treatment from other players, as well as free items and more information and help. Most gamers are surprised when they realize that playing with a female avatar means receiving sexual invitations constantly. Many players eventually abandon their female characters, as the continuous 'condescension and stalking becomes too much to bear' (Kelly 2004: 54).

Playing a female avatar with these characteristics, then, definitely affects the gameplay and the audience that will choose (or will be allowed) to play a particular CG. The 'text' produced by such gameplay is very likely to be different from one in which the player can choose an avatar that is not highly sexualized, or one in which there are at least other possible 'readings'.

METHODOLOGY

This section will be devoted to giving a brief overview of the research methodology followed in this study. Before moving on I must state here the research questions that I will attempt to answer in the final section:

- How do the game makers of *Diablo* and *WoW* and their gamers use language and images to represent the female characters in the games?
- How do these representations differ from the representation of male characters in these games?

An eclectic method, also known as 'multi-method' (Wodak 1996), combining features of qualitative text and image analysis from CDA and quantitative text analysis using corpora tools, and the use of questionnaires to complement the corpus created, was especially devised to suit this particular study.

The data for this study was collected from a variety of sources, and in this sense the process of data collection was as eclectic as the methods of data analysis employed. The data was taken from three main sources: questionnaires about *Diablo* and *WoW* answered by volunteers, websites about the games, and the content of the games themselves.

The questionnaire was designed for, and applied to, 65 adult respondents who were familiar with both games, and had played them both for at least six months within the two years previous to this study. Due to time constraints, and the added language barrier of the setting, I deemed it more practical to apply for students' and workers' participations during school and working hours. This maximized the returned questionnaires, and made the application time more efficient.

I approached several schools and companies in Prague via email, sending them a cover letter in both English and Czech, as well as the questionnaire the students and employees would be answering if permission to proceed was granted. A date and time were scheduled to apply questionnaires to different groups, also via email. The questionnaire design, cover letter, and my introductory speech made it clear to the participants that the focus of the study was to explore the way CG characters were portrayed by developers and gamers. To avoid any intentional or unintentional bias, however, participants were not told that the focus would be on female characters, or that the paper would explore the issue of sexualization. The constraints and problems faced during the design and application of this instrument will be discussed in detail later.

The participants were given instructions on how to access the questionnaire posted on a server. They were told to open it, and save it in their own desktops by changing the file name. Then they were told to open the questionnaire to make sure the file was working. The file consisted of 60 questions, divided into four sections. The first section dealt with the participants' personal information. The second section had to do with the characters in *Diablo I, Diablo II,* and *Diablo II: Lord of Destruction.* The third section had to do with the characters in *WoW* and *WoW: The Burning Crusade.* The final section had to do with characters in CG in general.

The instructions were to fill out the questionnaire by providing the first three terms that came to mind in each case in association with each character. If they could not remember the word in English, they could ask for help or use an online dictionary. If they felt unable to answer one question, they could skip it, and move forward to the next one.

After identifying the websites that were relevant for this study, an email was sent to their webmasters to request permission to use text and images contained in them. Most webmasters replied in due course granting their permission, as long as their sites were credited as sources, and that the data was not used for commercial purposes. It was impossible to contact the webmasters who run Blizzard's official sites, but nothing in their terms and conditions prevents using their data for academic purposes.

Once permission to use the relevant websites was obtained, I proceeded to bookmark the home page. When this had been done for all sites, and with the corpus record grid open, I proceeded to create a text file with each page, by copying and pasting the relevant text, or by re-typing the information when copying was not possible. Once the text was in a ASCII format, I proceeded to paste it onto an empty Microsoft Word document to use the word count tool, because ASCII files lack this feature. With all the information, each ASCII file was given a code name that was entered in the grid. Each ASCII file's name also contained its number of words (e.g., '001_DB_BZ_G_176'). Online texts were extracted from websites related to both games. Five different types of website were used for this study: Blizzard-produced or Blizzard-approved websites (also called 'official' websites), gamer-produced or gamer-edited websites, informational and advertorial websites, and online forums.

The websites chosen for the study were selected using the following controlled variables:

- Language: The sites had to be in English.
- Popularity: The sites chosen must be the most popular ones regarding number of hits or subscribers.
- Availability: The sites' content had to be available for academic use, as per their terms and conditions or by obtaining permission from the webmaster/mistress.
- Target Audience: The chosen sites' stated target audience was 'gamers in general'. Websites that address very specific gamer populations (such as GayGamers.com) were not to be taken into account.
- Updates: The sites chosen were 'active' as opposed to 'defunct'.

The online data sources were chosen over a two-year period of time. Different grids were designed to record information for the corpora while still choosing and classifying the websites into separate categories. Five text sub-corpora and two image corpora were created from these online sources. The text corpora included a questionnaire response corpus, two corpora based on information from *Diablo* and *WoW* official websites and on each game, and two corpora based on user-edited sites. An image corpus was assembled for each game, including screenshots from in-game events.

All corpora were balanced against the others and resized accordingly, to ensure that comparable data was produced. I then proceeded to download and test AntCon 3.2.0 (a free concordancer available online) and tested it to make sure all the text files were readable for the concordancer, and that all the records had been kept accurately for my own reference.

I obtained *quantitative* results by using key node words related to gender (he, she, him, her) as well as character names. These results, especially in terms of the number of hits obtained per pronoun and character name, provided some insights into the number of male and female characters and their relative importance in the texts. These searches were performed using both the full corpus, as well as separate parts of it (only Blizzard-produced texts, or only questionnaire answers, for example).

More node words were entered into the concordancer. A random sample of concordance lines was selected for analysis, depending on the amount of data obtained in each search, and from these concordance lines information was obtained on what is 'central and typical' in the texts contained in the corpora. I found, for example, what words usually accompany the third person pronoun 'she' as opposed to its masculine counterpart. I then proceeded to examine the concordance lines provided by each corpus to find regularities and patterns.

Once these images were collected, a random sample was chosen using an automatic number generator to select two images representing each playable character in both games. To handle the images in the image corpora I created a grid to be able to record details with as much objectivity as possible, based loosely on the idea of a summary table as described by Miles and Huberman (1994). The grid, I found, was of the utmost importance. Without it, the visual aspect of the representation of women and the element of difference would have been very difficult to deconstruct and analyze.

Additional information was obtained by doing the following:

- Playing both games, and keeping note of other texts and images contained in them (these were added to the corpus as a separate section). I played each game for 65 hours, until I felt I had familiarized myself with the games well enough to be able to discuss them and understand them. NOTE: I had not played either of these games prior to this stage. I had, however, played other games that use the same type of interface, so as to 'train myself' in the use of the controls and not be distracted by these technicalities during gameplay.

• Keeping notes of gamer-gamer and gamer-NPC (non-player characters) in-game interactions (by means of taking screenshots whenever possible).

• Playing both games using both male and female characters, and taking notes of other players' reactions to my avatars' appearance (by means of taking screenshots whenever possible).

• Keeping record of my own reactions and experience when trying out these games. I feel this can provide very detailed insights into the participant's perspective that some pieces of research might otherwise lack. This information can also be very useful for 'comparing notes' if this piece of research is replicated.

I have now explained the steps I followed for the method I designed for this study, and justified my choices in this respect. Next, I will give a very brief description of the most relevant results yielded by the data, and then will move on to their analysis.

RESULTS: FREQUENCY AND COLLOCATION

On *Diablo*'s official websites female and male characters were mentioned in the frequency shown in Table 6.1.

The frequency of the term 'warrior' would at first sight make it seem like the Warrior is the most popular playable character in *Diablo I*. This figure is misleading, as 'warrior' is used both as a noun and an adjective

Table 6.1   Frequency of Male and Female Characters' Names in Official *Diablo* Websites

DIABLO OFFICIAL WEBSITES			
MALE	*HITS*	*FEMALE*	*HITS*
WARRIOR	173	ROGUE	74
SORCERER	23	SORCERESS	119
BARBARIAN	160	AMAZON	136
NECROMANCER	136	ASSASSIN	101
DRUID	98		
PALADIN	134		
BAAL (DEMON)	98		

Table 6.2 Frequency of Male and Female Characters' Names in Unofficial *Diablo* Websites

DIABLO GAMERS' WEBSITES			
MALE	*HITS*	*FEMALE*	*HITS*
WARRIOR	46	ROGUE	22
SORCERER	15	SORCERESS	25
BARBARIAN	37	AMAZON	48
NECROMANCER	44	ASSASSIN	25
DRUID	45	ANDARIEL (DEMON)	6
PALADIN	38		
BAAL (DEMON)	120		

to refer to other characters in the game. I had expected the Sorcerer and Rogue to be mentioned many more times, as they also appear in *Diablo II* as NPC and monsters. The least popular character of all time in *Diablo* seems to be the Sorcerer from *Diablo I*, as he was only mentioned 23 times. (Notice that I worked with the names of only two monsters, one male and one female).

Table 6.2 demonstrates the frequency of characters' names in unofficial *Diablo* websites. It is obvious that Baal is mentioned several times more than any other character. I can explain this only by saying that Baal is the only character on the list who appears in the background story. In my perusal of websites during data collection I did notice that the game's background story was a popular topic of discussion, and this seems to prove it.

My third session of searching for concordance lines was devoted to the pronouns 'he' and 'she', as it was apparent after examining the data that these words would be highly significant for my analysis, because I am not looking at the way only individual female characters are represented, but rather at how they are represented in general. Table 6.3 shows the results of that search.

I will first show here, in Table 6.4, the results for my search of the male and female pronouns in the *WoW*-related corpora.

During the search for concordance lines I had to proceed in a somewhat different way from what I did with *Diablo*, as *WoW* character Races and Classes can be both male and female.

In the case of the questionnaires, for practical reasons, I decided to combine a manual search with a search using the concordancer, and to classify all terms used into two categories: terms for male characters and terms for female characters (see Tables 6.8 and 6.9 in the Appendix).

Table 6.3 Frequency of Male and Female Pronouns in *Diablo* Corpus (All)

COMBINED SUMMARY (DIABLO)	
MAIN COLLOCATES (INCLUDING MAIN VERBS, AUXILIARY VERBS AND MODALITY)	
SHE (193)	HE (559)
IS (28), CAN (22), HAS (19), WILL (18), MUST (6), SHOULD (3), UNDERSTANDS (4), LOOKS (3), DIES (3), COMPENSATES (3), NEEDS (2)	IS (50), CAN(43), HAS (36), WAS (29), WILL (25), WOULD (13), HAD (11), COULD (9), MAY (8), SHOULD (7), BELIEVES (8), SAID (5), USES (6), NEEDS (5), MUST (5), BECAME (5), COMMANDS (4), WITNESSED (3), WANTS (3), LIVES (4), ATTACKS (3), UNLEASH (2), WALKED (2), TOOK (2), REQUIRES (2), POSSESSES (2), REACHES (2), IDENTIFIES (2), DROPS (2), DIES (2), CONTINUES (2), CLAIMED (2), APPEARS (2)
OTHER LEXICAL COLLOCATES AND UNIQUE (UN-NUMBERED) COLLOCATES	
SHE (193)	HE (559)
SKILL (4), REALITY (4), COMBAT (4), SERVICE (3), JAVELIN (3), HEART (3), DAMAGE (3), SPELLCASTER (2), HEALER (2), GRIEVES (2), WEAPON, WALKS, TRAVELS, SUMMONED, SUBSTANTIAL, STUDIES, PHYSI-CALLY, PROGRESSES, MUSCLES, MANA, MASTERMINDED, INTER-VENED, INFLICTS, IMPLORED, HOUSE, HUT, HATRED GROUND GORE, AGREED, CASTS, ARMY, BECOMES, ATTACKS, CARRIES, DEADLY, FIRES, EXPENSES.	GAME (4), COMBAT (4), SKILLS (3), SHIELD (3), REASON (3), ELDER (3), OPPONENTS (2), MONSTERS (2), KNIGHTS (2), FRIEND (2), DAMAGE (2), ABILITIES (2), ZEALOT, UNPARALLELLED, TRAVELS, TRANSFORMING, TRANCES, TORMENTED, TOXIFIES, TOOLS, THROWS, THRASHING, THINKS, TELEPORT, TECHNIQUE, STRUGGLE, STRONGEST, STRONGER, SELFLESSLY, SECRETS, RIDDLES, RETAINS, RESIDES, RESCUED, RAPES, PETS, PALADIN, OPEN, NOOB(S), MISERY, MINIONS, MEANING, MATTER, MASTER, LOVED, LOOKED, LACKS, KILLS, IMPROVES, FACES, CONFESSES, DEALS, BATTLE

Table 6.4   Frequency of Male and Female Pronouns in *WoW* Corpus (All)

COMBINED SUMMARY (WoW)	
MAIN COLLOCATES (INCLUDING MAIN VERBS, AUXILIARY VERBS AND MODALITY)	
SHE (193)	HE (559)
IS (19), STARTS (8), HAS (5), HAD (5), WILL (4), WOULD (3), WAS (4), FELT (4), TRAINS (2), SAID (2), RESEOLVED (2), LED (2),	WAS (21), HAD (20), STARTS (11), WOULD (9), COULD (8), HAS (5), WILL (4), LEARNED (4), FELT (4), WARNED (3), BELIEVED (3), SOUGHT (2), SAYS (2), RUNS (2), RELAYED (2), REALIZED (2), PROMISED (2), LOVES (2), HASTENED (2), GOT (2), FOUND (2), ENTERED (2), ENCOUNTERED (2), DEPARTED (2), DECIDED (2), CREATED (2), CONTACTED (2), CAN (2), AGREED (2), ACCEPTS (2),
OTHER LEXICAL COLLOCATES AND UNIQUE (UN-NUMBERED) COLLOCATES	
SHE (101)	HE (245)
STORMWIND (6), ORGRIMAR (6), EVENT (2), WISHES, WISH, VOWED, UNCHECKED, SWORE, SURE, STUNNING, SLEPT, REMAINED, REGULATES, REGARD, CAPTURE, REASON, PROTECTION, PASSED, ORC, LEARNED, INVITED, MERELY, HUNT, HAND, GRASP, GOVERNMENT, FREEDOM, FREED, FORCED, EARTHMOTHER, DRAGONS, ELVES, ELEMENTALS, DIED, DRUIDS, DECIDED, DESIRES, CREATURE, COULD, COST, CLAIMS, BELIEVED, BECOMES, APPROVED, ABANDONED	UNDEAD (5), ORGRIMAR (5), STORMWIND (4), ELVES (4), SURVIVORS (2), POWER (2), LOYALTY (2), CHARACTER (2), ARMY (2), YEARS, WATERS, VINDICATED, VISTOR, VICIOUS, VENTURED, VENGEANCE, TWISTED, TRAVELS, THOUGHTS, TAUREN, TECHNIQUES, SUNSTRIDER, STUDIED, STRONHOOF, STRENGTHENS, SILENT, SHARED, SENTENCED, SCHMUCK, SAVAGE, RULED, RELIEF, REFUSED, RECLUSIVE, RANKS, RACE, QUESTS, PROUDMOORE, PROBLEM, POOR, PLAN, PARDONED, OPPORTUNITY, OFFERED, NAMED, MISSION, MILLENIA, MAGIC, LOVED, LOST, LIKE, LAUGH, LATE, KNOWLEDGE, INVADED, IMPRISONED, HELP, HEARD, GREW, GRASP, GLADLY, GAVE, GATHERED, FOLLOWED, FESTIVAL, EXPERIMENTATION, ETERNITY, ESCAPED, DISASTER, DEFILED, DEMONS, DESTINY, CREATION, COURTED, CONVINCED, CONTINUED, CONSUMED, CONFESSED, CAUGHT, CARRIED, BITTER, APPRENTICES, ALIVE, ALLIANCE, ALONE, AFFAIRS

VISUAL REPRESENTATION OF CHARACTERS

Diablo characters are less frequently seen on the Internet than the ones in *WoW*, for reasons I will discuss in my analysis as follows. The images available tend to be repetitions of the same few pictures produced by Blizzard when the game first appeared, and these tend to be replicated in every website. This certainly made the work of deciding on what visual material to use for my in-depth analysis very easy. I examined two images for each playable character following criteria on a grid I had previously designed for this purpose (see Table 6.8.1 in the Appendix). There were several important differences between the ways both genders were represented, which I will discuss later.

On the other hand, characters in *WoW* can be customized by selecting two professions during the game, and it is advisable to choose a primary and secondary profession that complement each other or are compatible. Most of these professions have an equivalent in real life. I examined the online manual for the game to see how the Classes and Professions were represented, and the results are expressed in Table 6.5.

Table 6.5 Representation of Professions Using Male and Female Characters

IMAGES IN ONLINE MANUAL (OFFICIAL WEBSITE)			
CLASS	*REPRESENTED BY*	*PROFESSION*	*REPRESENTED BY*
DRUID	MALE N. ELF	ALCHEMY	MALE UNDEAD
HUNTER	MALE TROLL	BLACKSMITHING	MALE HUMAN
MAGE	FEMALE B. ELF	COOKING	FEMALE ORC
PALADIN	MALE DRAENAI	ENCHANTING	MALE N. ELF
PRIEST	FEMALE HUMAN	FIRST AID	FEMALE HUMAN
ROGUE	MALE UNDEAD	ENGINEERING	MALE GNOME
SHAMAN	MALE ORC	FISHING	MALE TROLL
WARLOCK	MALE GNOME	HERBALISM	FEMALE N. ELF
WARRIOR	MALE DWARF	JEWELCRAFTING	FEMALE B. ELF
		LEATHERWORKING	MALE ORC
		MINING	MALE DWARF
		TAILORING	FEMALE DWARF
		SKINNING	MALE TAUREN

Table 6.6 Image Analysis Grid for *Diablo* Avatars

CHARACTER	IMAGE ANALYSIS GRID (*Diablo* GROUP IMAGE/ CHARACTER SELECTION SCREEN)														
	HAIR		FACE				BUILD			ARMOR					
	S	N	SCARS Y	SCARS N	LINES Y	LINES N	M	L	N	SHOULDERS	CHEST	UPPER ARMS	TORSO/MIDRIFF	BUTTOCKS	THIGHS
WARRIOR	X		X		X		X			X	X	X	X	X	X
SORCERER		X	X		X			X		X	X	X	X	X	X
ROGUE	X			X		X		X	X	X	X	O	X	O	O
AMAZON	X			X		X		X	X	O	X	O	X	O	O
PALADIN	X		X		X		X			X	X	X	X	X	X
NECROMANCER	X		X		X		X			X	X	X	X	X	X
BARBARIAN	X		X	X	X		X			X	O	O	O	X	O
ASSESSIN	X		X		X			X	X	X	O	X	X	O	O
SORCERESS	X		X		X			X	X	X	O	X	O	X	O
DRUID	X		X		X			X		X	X	X	X	X	X

HAIR: S= STYLED/STYLIZED N=NON-STYLED/NON-STYLIZED   BUILD: M=MUSCULAR L=LIGHT (NO VISIBLE MUSCULATURE)

ARMOR: X=COVERS OR PROTECTS THIS AREA O=ALMOST NO PROTECTION

Table 6.7 Image Analysis Grid for *WoW* Avatars (Sample) Internal Analysis

IMAGE ANALYSIS GRID BY CLASS (LEVEL 1 CHARACTERS)

CLASS / WARRIOR	HAIR S	HAIR N	POSTURE S	POSTURE E	POSTURE S	WRINKLES Y	WRINKLES N	MAKE-UP	JEWELRY Y	JEWELRY N	BUILD M	BUILD L	CLOTHING SHOULDERS	CHEST	UPPER ARMS	MID-RIFF	HIPS	THIGHS
MALE																		
HUMAN	X			X						X	X					X	X	X
DWARF		X		X		X				X	X					X	X	X
GNOME		X		X		X				X	O					X	X	X
DRAENEI		X		X		X				X	X			X		X	X	X
NIGHT ELF		X		X		X		?		X	X			X		X	X	X
ORC	X				X	X				X	X				X			
TROLL		X			X	X				X	X							X
TAUREN		X			X	X				X	X				X			X
UNDEAD		X			X	X				X	X				X			X
BLOOD ELF											N.A.							
FEMALE																		
HUMAN	X			X			X	X	X			X				X	X	X
DWARF	X			X			X	X	X		O					X	X	X
GNOME	X			X			X	X	X		O					X	X	X
DRAENEI	X			X			X	X		X		X		X			X	X
NIGHT ELF		X		X			X	X	X			X			X	X	X	X
ORC	X			X			X	X	X		O				X			X
TROLL	X			X			X	X		X		X			X			X
TAUREN	X			X			X	X		X	O				X		X	X
UNDEAD	X			O			X	X	X			X			X			X
BLOOD ELF											N.A.							

HAIR: S= STYLED/STYLIZED N=NON-STYLED/NON-STYLIZED   BUILD: M=MUSCULAR/HEAVY   L= LIGHT (NO VISIBLE MUSCULATURE) O=HEAVIER THAN OTHER FEMALES, BUT MUCH LIGHTER THAN MALE OF SAME RACE/ VERY DIFFERENT FROM MALE, MORE SIMILAR TO OTHER FEMALES   JEWELRY: Y/N   CLOTHING: Y/N   CLOTHING: X=COVERS OR PROTECTS THIS AREA   BLANK: ABSENT/N.A.

I designed two similar grids to systematically examine the appearance of the different playable characters in both games. Because of the large numbers of data produced (each Race in *WoW* has at least four Classes, and they can be customized by changing five physical characteristics), I decided to select a random sample within the image corpus. I selected one random image from each Race, Gender, and Class—as screenshots were taken using every customizable change of color, hair and angle possible—and the images were examined using the grids in Tables 6.6 and 6.7.

In the case of *Diablo*, the fact that the masculine pronoun is used three times as often as the feminine one might have been immediately justified because of the unequal numbers of male and female characters and their distribution and roles within the story. There are no important female roles in the background story to the game as portrayed in the game cinematics. Indeed, there are no female characters in the main storyline.

I was very surprised, however, to obtain almost exactly the same correlation between the two pronouns from the *WoW* sub-corpus as I got from *Diablo*. Unlike *Diablo*, *WoW* has the option of playing as a male or female with every Race and Class, so I had originally thought that this alone would make a significant difference to the data. The unequal frequency (in the case of the official websites) can be attributed to the background story. The most significant characters are all male, or exist only in the background story, and do not appear during gameplay. This leads me to conclude that there is a form of exclusion of female characters (Fairclough 2003: 145) in which they are both suppressed from the story, or 'backgrounded', which means their presence has to be inferred by the player.

The unequal frequency of terms for male and female characters in the data yielded by questionnaires is puzzling (see Table 6.9, in the Appendix), given that there is exactly the same number of questions for both. One possible explanation was hinted at by one of the respondents, who answered 'same as men' to the questions about female characters, which could mean she had interpreted the questions about the male representatives of one Race as questions about the whole Race, and did not feel a distinction was necessary. Even if this rather simplistic explanation went unchallenged, the lexical items in the data themselves tell a different story. Take these two phrases from the data:

A) '[THEY] STRONGLY PROTECT THEIR WOMEN'.
B) 'THEY LEAVE ALL THE WORK TO MEN AND TAKE CARE OF THEIR HOMES AND FAMILY'.

In each case the same pronoun—'they'—was used, but was contrasted with a different lexical item (women or men). Even without the context provided by my questions, one can safely assume that 'they' in A means 'men' and in B 'women'.

I would not have been surprised to find these answers to questions about a traditional patriarchal community, with clear divisions of labor. To find these answers to describe an imaginary society in *WoW*, an MMORPG that gives you that choice to be a warrior of either gender, is highly significant. I turned my attention to the character Classes and Professions in *WoW* to examine what images were chosen to illustrate them (see Table 6.7).

There are nine Classes available in *WoW*. Seven of them are represented by male characters in the official website, and only two are represented by females. I believe that it is also highly significant that the Classes these female characters illustrate are ones in which combat is done primarily in a non-physical way; that is, the character attacks from afar. Indeed, from all the data I examined when gathering the corpus, I gained the insight that more often than not female characters in these two games are shown as having some sort of skill or power that would eliminate or reduce their need to 'jump in the fray'. If we take this back to *Diablo II*, a point in case would be the fact that the three female characters have no need to get close to the enemy: The Amazon throws spears or shoots arrows, the Sorceress casts spells, and the Assassin sets traps.

Out of 14 Professions, 5 are represented by females doing activities traditionally thought of as feminine: cooking, nursing, sewing, herb gathering, and wearing jewellery to illustrate respectively the *WoW* Professions of Cooking, First Aid, Tailoring, Herbalism, and Jewel Crafting. Again, this being an imaginary world where attributed or rationalized biological constraints of relative physical strength do not apply, one would expect to see a different order of things.

When playing *Diablo I* with the Rogue, or *Diablo II* with the Amazon, there was also a large difference between the genders. If you have ever watched a horror movie and felt annoyed at the character who hears a macabre laughter next door and runs over to her doom in the dark, unarmed and in her pajamas, you will understand what I mean: If I am about to enter an underworld populated by all the forces of Hell, armed only with a cheap sword or bow because I am only level one, why in the world would I wear a thong to do it?

In *WoW* the clothing available to level-one avatars is almost identical to males and females. There are differences in customization, as in the different available hairstyles, and the options of facial hair or jewellery (no facial hair options for females, and no jewellery options for males). The biggest difference between male and female characters' appearance in *WoW* seems to be size, and this observation agrees with the ones made by Rubenstein (2007). I believe Rubenstein focused more on height than total mass in her observations because (by her own admission) she had not played the game, but during both customization and gameplay I noticed a marked difference between male and female characters. When playing with a male character (especially in the case of the male Tauren), it was usually impossible to see the enemy clearly unless I moved the point of view to a sharper angle above the avatar, as the width of his back would completely block most enemies from view.

POSITIONING THE TEXTS IN RELATION TO GENRES

A genre combines both a more or less explicit purpose to a discoursal activity and an internal 'generic structure' (Fairclough 2003). To find the genres being operationalized through a text Fairclough (2003) proposes asking the question 'what are people doing discoursally here?'

As games are very complex texts, they can be treated as heads of 'genre chains' ('chains or networks of texts') (Fairclough 2003). A chain of texts for a game can be represented as shown in Figure 6.1.

These texts can be classified into different genres according to their purpose, e.g., Promotional Genre, Narrative, Argument, Conversation, etc. There will inevitably be overlaps, as in an interaction with an NPC which is both a simulated conversation and part of the Narrative, or a fan video which simultaneously enacts Narrative and promotes the game itself or the gamer's allegiance to an in-game faction.

Most of the texts included in the earlier representation are part of CMC. This mediation is both the product and the mechanism for 'recontextualization' of these genres (the movement of meaning-making from one area to another). Many elements of the real world are recontextualized and enacted *through* and *in* these games: war, play (in its many forms), power, religion, gender, conflict, learning, fun, work, friendship, death, to name a few. I

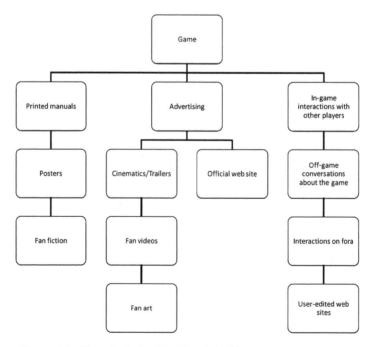

Figure 6.1   Text chain for *WoW* and *Diablo*.

am of course concerned here with how gender is 'done' discoursally within these games, and with the operationalization of gender difference.

CONCLUSION

It is apparent from the data that there is a discourse of marked gender difference operating in these two games, and that it is realized through the exclusion or suppression of female characters (see earlier discussion), and through other features of discourse, such as the fact that the masculine pronoun collocates with many more different verbs than the feminine one (even taking into account the different frequencies), which provides the idea of males being either more diverse in their activities, or simply more active than females. This idea seems confirmed when one looks at the accompanying image corpus, and the way discourses of difference are further recontextualized by gamers in other media, such as the forums and the gamer-edited websites.

Fairclough (2003: 41) identifies a particular orientation to Difference (among five), that of a '[c]onsensus/normalization/ acceptance of difference of power (which suppresses differences of meaning and norms)'. The data seems to point out that the orientation to gender difference in these games is based on legitimized assumptions about what gender is, and how it is 'done' based on cultural expectations outside the game.

My analysis indicates that female characters in *Diablo* and *WoW* are both excluded from many aspects of the narrative and suppressed from others (textually and visually). Furthermore, there is a strong discourse of gender difference when they are present in the text, which constructs women as the 'other', different from the male norm, that needs to be protected, or whose sexuality is emphasized at all times, be it contextually appropriate or consistent or not.

This discourse is operationalized through different aspects of the texts, including images that seem to operate under assumptions of naturalized and legitimized inequalities of power distribution between the genders. The discourse is further enacted and recontextualized by Blizzard and gamers outside of gameplay as part of promotional texts, accompanying narratives, and CMC between gamers, which reinforces its legitimization.

This discourse of difference is not inevitable. There is nothing pre-determined in a computer game as a genre that programmers, game designers, and consumers cannot change. There is no evidence to date that a discourse of gender equality would detract in any way from an enjoyable experience of gameplay. Further research into the discourses operating in CG as new media is both desirable and necessary; particularly because everything seems to indicate that we will be spending more and more of our time interacting through them. It becomes a more pressing matter, then, to be able to identify possible issues that are beginning to arise within and through CG in the construction of social identities.

APPENDIX

Table 6.8   Questionnaires' Respondents

QUESTIONNAIRES			
GENERAL INFORMATION ON THE SAMPLE (50)			
PARTICIPANTS	MALE	FEMALE	NO ANSWER
TOTAL NUMBER	28	16	6
PLAY GAMES REGULARLY	23	9	2
DON'T PLAY REGULARLY	7	6	2
PLAY REGULARLY, BUT NOT THESE GAMES	8	9	2
DAMAGED FILES/INCOMPATIBLE	-	-	1

Table 6.9   Lexical Items Associated by Participants with Male and Female Characters

QUESTIONNAIRES	
WORDS USED BY GAMERS TO DESCRIBE	
MALE CHARACTERS	*FEMALE CHARACTERS*
CHALLENGING)	AGGRESSIVE
ALLURING	ANNOYING
ALMOST DEAD MAGICAL EVIL	ATTRACTIVE
ANDROGYNOUS	AVERAGE
ARMORED	BEAUTIFUL
ARROGANT	BEEFY, MUCH MORE THAN NORMAL WOMEN
AVERAGE	BETTER VARIATION
BEST HERO	BORING
BEST MAGIC	BORING
BIG	CALM
BIG RESPECT FOR NATURE	CARING
BLUE	CLASSIC ADDITION
BORING	CLEVER
BRAVE	COLD
BRUTAL	CRITICAL
BULKY	CRUEL
CAN HAVE COOL HAIRSTYLES	CUTE
CAN SEE THEIR BONES	DANGEROUS
CAN TRANSFORM	DECISIVE
CARE ABOUT THEIR HONOUR	DIFFICULT
CHARISMATIC	DIRTY
CLASSIC	DOMINATING
COURAGEOUS	ECCENTRIC
CRAFTY	ELEMENTALIS
CREATIVE	

(continued)

Table 6.9   (continued)

QUESTIONNAIRES	
WORDS USED BY GAMERS TO DESCRIBE	
MALE CHARACTERS	FEMALE CHARACTERS
CRUEL	FEMALE CHARACTERS GET AWAY WITH MORE
DANGEROUS	
DARK	FORSAKEN
DEMONIC	FRUSTRATING
DULL	FUN TO BATTLE
DUMB AS A BRICK	FUNNY
DURABLE	GLAMOUROUS
ECCENTRIC	GOOD
ELITIST	GOOD ATTACK
ENTERTAINING	GOOD FOR FIRST FEW LEVELS
ENTHUSIASTIC	HORRIBLE LOOKING, TOO MASCULINE
EVIL	I LOVE THEM
FAST	I WOULDN'T PLAY ONE MYSELF
FAT	IDIOTS
FLAWED	IMPOSTRUOUS
FOUL	INSANE
FOUL	LIKE MEN
FRIENDLY (TO THEMSELVES)	LINEAR
FUNNY PLAYING WITH THEM	MAD
GAY	MASCULINE
GOOD AT SUMMONING	MYSTERIOUS
GOOD AURA	NASTY
GOOD CLASS	NICE
GOOD FIGHTER	NICE (PRETTY)
GOOD IN MULTI-PLAYER	NOBLE
GOOD LOOKING	OVERRATED
GOOD MAGIC	PASSIONATE
GOOD TO PLAY THEM AS A WARRIOR	POWERFUL
GRATING VOICES	PRETTY COOL
GREEN	PROUD
GREEN-EYED	QUICK
HAIRY	QUICK DANGEROUS
HALF-NAKED	QUIET
HARD PASSION FOR MAGIC	QUIRKY
HAS SOME GOOD SPELLS	ROUGH
HAVE A NICE CAPITAL CITY	RUTHLESS
HAVE GOOD ABILITIES	SAVAGE
HEADSTRONG	SELFISH
HOLY POWER	SELFISH BUT FRIENDLY

(continued)

Table 6.9   (continued)

QUESTIONNAIRES	
WORDS USED BY GAMERS TO DESCRIBE	
MALE CHARACTERS	FEMALE CHARACTERS
HOMOSEXUAL	SEXY
IMMUNE	SHOWED THEIR ASSES WHEN THEY DIED
IMPOSING	SMART
INCOMMUNICATIVE	SPIRITUAL
INTERESTING	SPITEFUL
LANKY	STEALTH
LIKE NATURE	STRONG
LIKE TO LIVE ALONE	STRONG
LINEAR	SUBSERVIENT
LITTLE HP (HIT POINTS)	THE SAME AS MEN
LITTLE MP (MAGIC POWER)	THEY LEAVE ALL THE WORK TO MEN AND TAKE CARE OF THEIR HOMES AND FAMILY
LOOK VERY NICE	
LOVE MECHANICAL THINGS AND INVENTING NEW MACHINES	THEY LOOK LIKE NIGHT ELVES BUT THEY'RE WONDERFUL
LOVE NATURE, MAINLY FLOWERS	THEY LOOK NICE AND PRETTY
LOW ARMOR	THEY LOOK NICE BUT I DON'T LIKE THEM
LUSTFUL	
MALE MONSTERS ARE MORE DANGEROUS	THEY LOVE ARCHITECTURE AND AMAZING HAIRSTYLES
MANY HEALTHS	THEY LOVE COOKING AND HOUSE-KEEPING
MEN ARE STRONGER AND I LIKE HEAVY CHARACTERS	
MILD	THEY TAKE CARE OF THE MEN AND PREPARE THEM FOR BATTLE
MY FAVOURITE	THIN
MYSTERIOUS	THOUGHTFUL
NOBLE	TIME-CONSUMING
NORMAL	TRADITIONAL
OLD	UGLY
OVERUSED	UGLY
PLEASANT	UNDERRATED
POWERFUL	UNIVERSAL
POWERFUL	UNORIGINAL
PROUD	UNORTHODOX
PYROMANIAC	UNPOPULAR
QUIETLY (QUIET)	USING JUST SPELLS TO FIGHT
REALLY LIKE THE WAY THEY'RE ANIMATED	VERY FRIENDLY
RELIGIOUS	VIOLENT
RESORCEFUL	VULNERABLE
RUDE	VULNERABLE
RUTHLESS	WEAK
SAVAGE	WEAK COMBOS

(continued)

Table 6.9 (continued)

QUESTIONNAIRES	
WORDS USED BY GAMERS TO DESCRIBE	
MALE CHARACTERS	FEMALE CHARACTERS
SILLY	WHEN I STAND AGAINST A WOMAN, I THINK SHE'S WEAKER
SKILLFUL	
SLIM	WILLOWY
SMALL	WISPY
SMART	WORST RACE
SMELLY	WOULDN'T PLAY
SNEAK	YOU CAN SEE THEIR BONES
STOCKY	
SNEAK	
STOCKY	
STRANGE	
STRONG	
STRONGLY PROTECT THEIR WOMEN	
STUN ENEMIES	
STUPID	
SUMMONER/SUMMON MONSTER OR CORPSE	
TALL	
TALL	
THE BEST RACE	
THEY LIKE BEER AND THEY'RE SELF-ISH	
THEY LOOK WEAK BUT THEY'RE STRONG	
THEY WANT KILLING AND DEAD(DEATH) FOR EVERYBODY	
THIN	
THOUGHTFUL	
TINY	
TOUGH GUY	
UGLY	
UNCREATIVE	
UNIVERSAL	
UNORIGINAL	
VERY STRONG	
VICIOUS	
VITALITY	
VOICE LIKE A RUSSIAN	
VULNERABLE	
WEAK	
WEAK ATTACK	

(continued)

Table 6.9   (continued)

QUESTIONNAIRES	
WORDS USED BY GAMERS TO DESCRIBE	
MALE CHARACTERS	FEMALE CHARACTERS
WEEDY	
WILD	
WIS	

REFERENCES

Atkins, B (2003) *More than a game: The computer game as a fictional form*. Manchester: Manchester University Press.
Baudrillard, J (1998) *The consumer society: Myths and structures*. London: Sage.
Bauman, Z (1993) *Postmodern ethics*. Malden, MA: Wiley-Blackwell.
Beißwenger, M and A Storrer (2008) Corpora of computer-mediated communication. In *Corpus linguistics: An international handbook*, ed. A Luedeling and M Kyto. Online. Available HTTP: <http://www.michael-beisswenger.de/pub/hsk-corpora.pdf> (accessed 4 November 2007).
Bignell, J (2002) *Media semiotics: An introduction*, 2nd ed. Manchester: Manchester University Press.
Blizzard Entertainment Official Website. 2010. Online. Available HTTP <http://www.blizzard.com> (accessed 28 January 2008).
Bucholtz, M and K Hall (eds) (1995) *Gender articulated*. New York: Routledge.
Bucholtz, M, AC Liang and L Sutton (1999) *Reinventing identities: The gendered self in discourse*. Oxford: Oxford University Press.
Butler, J (1990) *Gender trouble: Feminism and the subversion of identity* (Thinking Gender Series). London: Routledge.
Brownmiller, S (1984) *Femininity*. New York: Linden Books.
Cameron, D (ed.) (1990) *The feminist critique of language: A reader*. London: Routledge.
Carr, D, G Schott, A Burn, and D Buckingham (2004) Doing game studies: A multi-method approach to the study of textuality, interactivity and narrative space. *Media International Australia* 110: 19–30.
Carrillo Masso, I (2009) Developing a methodology for corpus-based computer game studies. *Journal of Gaming and Virtual Worlds* 1, no. 2: 143–69.
Chouliaraki, L and N Fairclough (1999) *Discourse in late modernity: Rethinking critical discourse analysis*. Edinburgh: Edinburgh University Press.
Cobley, P and L Jansz (1997) *Introducing semiotics*. Cambridge: Icon Books.
Davis, F (1992) *Fashion, culture and identity*. Chicago: University of Chicago Press.
Dovey, J and HW Kennedy (2006) *Game cultures: Computer games as new media*. Maidenhead: Open University Press.
Epps, B and Katz, JD (2007) *Monique Wittig at the crossroads of criticism*. London: Duke University Press.
Fairclough, N (1989) *Language and power*. New York: Longman.
———. (1992) *Discourse and social change*. Cambridge: Polity Press.
———. (1993) Critical discourse analysis and the marketization of public space: The universities. *Discourse and Society* 4, no. 2: 133–68.

———. (2003) *Analysing discourse: Textual analysis for social research.* New York: Routledge.

Flugel, JC (1930) *The psychology of clothes.* London: Hogarth Press.

Foucault, M (1980) *The history of sexuality*, Vol. 1. New York: Vintage.

———. (1988) *The history of sexuality*, Vol. 3. New York: Vintage.

Frasca, G (2003) Ludologists love stories, too: Notes from a debate that never took place.In *Level up: Digital game research conference proceedings*, ed. M Copier and J Raessens, 92–100. Utrecht: University of Utrecht Press.

Gardina, A (2006) *Use of computer mediated communication in massively multi-player online role-playing games.* Ithaca, NY: Ithaca College. Online. Available HTTP: <http://www.ithaca.edu/rhp/portfolio/p26/mmorpg.pdf> (accessed 20 December 2007).

Giddens, A (1992) *The transformation of intimacy: Sexuality, love and eroticism in modern society.* Cambridge: Polity Press.

Graner Ray, S (2004) *Gender inclusive game design: Expanding the market.* Hingham, MA: Charles River Media.

Grogan, S (1999) *Body image.* London: Routledge.

Holland, J (2006) *Misogyny: The world's oldest prejudice.* London: Constable and Robinson.

Itzen, C (1986) Media images of women: The social construction of ageism and sexism. In *Feminist social psychology*, ed. S Wilkinson, 119–34. Milton Keynes: Open University Press.

Jenkins, H (2001) *From Barbie to Mortal Kombat—further reflections.* Online. Available HTTP: <http://culturalpolicy.uchicago.edu/conf2001/papers/jenkins.html> (accessed 17 July 2009).

Kelly, RV (2004) *Massively multiplayer online role-playing games.* Jefferson, NC: McFarland.

Kennedy, HW (2002) Lara Croft: Feminist icon or cyberbimbo? On the limits of textual analysis. *Game Studies* 2, no 2. Online. Available HTTP: <http:www.gamestudies.org/0202> (accessed 17 December 2006).

Kirkup, G and L Smith-Keller (eds) (1992) *Inventing women: Science, technology and gender.* Oxford: Blackwell.

Kress, G and T van Leeuwen (1996) *Reading images: The grammar of visual design.* London: Routledge.

Lahti, M (2003) Corporealized pleasures in video games. In *The video game theory reader*, ed. MJP Wolf and B Perron, 169. London: Routledge.

Lorber, J (1994) *Paradoxes of gender.* New Haven, CT: Yale University Press.

Macdonald, M (1995) *Representing women: Myths of femininity in the popular media.* London: Edward Arnold.

Miles, MB and AM Huberman (1994) *Qualitative data analysis: An expanded sourcebook*, 2nd ed. London and Thousand Oaks: Sage.

Nakamura, L (2002) *Cybertypes: Race, ethnicity and identity on the Internet.* New York: Routledge.

Newman, J (2004) *Videogames.* London: Routledge.

Orpin, D (2005) Corpus linguistics and critical discourse analysis: Examining the ideology of sleaze. *International Journal of Corpus Linguistics* 10, no. 1: 7–61.

Pêcheux, M (1982) *Les Vérités de la Palice* [Language, semantics and ideology: Stating the obvious]. London: Macmillan.

Rubenstein, A (2007) Idealizing fantasy bodies. In *The Iris gaming network.* Online. Available HTTP: <http://www.theirisnetwork.org/archives/12> (accessed 10 January 2008).

Sedgwick, EK (1993) Gender asymmetry and erotic triangles. In *Feminisms: An anatomy of literary theory and criticism*, ed. R Warhol and D Price Herndl, 507–532. New Brunswick, NJ: Rutgers University Press.

Stewert Millar, M (1998) *Cracking the gender code: Who rules the wired world?* Toronto: Second Story Press.

Taylor, TL (2002) Living digitally: Embodiment in virtual worlds. In *The social life of avatars: Presence and interaction in shared virtual environments*, ed. R Schroeder, 40–62. London: Springer-Verlag.

Thompson, P (2007) *MAAL corpora in applied linguistics materials* (Module Materials), 1–7. Reading: University of Reading.

Tolman, DL and LM Diamond (2001) Desegregating sexuality and research: Cultural and biological perspectives on gender and desire. *Annual Review of Sex Research*. Online. Available HTTP: <http://findarticles.com/p/articles/MI_QA3778/IS_200101/AI_N8944785> (accessed 3 January 2008).

Turner, BS (1984) *The body and society*. Oxford: Blackwell.

van Dijk, TA (1993) *Élite discourse and racism*. New York: Sage.

Wodak, R (1996) *Disorders of discourse*. London: Longman.

Wodak, R and M Meyer (eds) (2001) *Methods of critical discourse analysis*. London: Sage.

Wolf, MJP and B Perron (2003) *The video game theory reader*. New York: Routledge.

Women Gamers Official Website (2008). Online. Available HTTP: <http://womengamers.com> (accessed 7 January 2008).

World of Warcraft Official Website (2008). Online. Available HTTP: <http://www.worldofwarcraft.com/index.xml> (accessed 1 February 2008).

Part III
Creating Second Spaces

.

7 Second Chances
Depictions of the Natural World in *Second Life*™

Joseph S. Clark

INTRODUCTION

As we create and inhabit spaces within three-dimensional virtual worlds, we simultaneously create unique places that foster the development of communities, as users return to and inhabit the same electronic locales over time. These sites then become aspects of identity for both avatars and the human beings behind them, in much the same way that one identifies with a neighborhood, workplace, or hometown in the non-virtual world. Furthermore, most of these virtual sites contain both 'built' and 'natural' elements, and the near-ubiquitous presence of these reminders of real-life nature attests to their importance to those who are constructing and inhabiting Second Lives. And as with other media—from advertisements and architecture to chat rooms and wikis—these virtual places become important means of cultural transmission, political activity, and creative work. The 'virtually natural' thus offers a three-dimensional rhetoric of nature that can be read and interpreted.

Many of these virtual environments are pre-built spaces, especially in game spaces such as *World of Warcraft*. More recently, however, a number have taken a less directed path, serving as more or less blank slates. Users can then express themselves by designing and creating sharable, immersively realistic spaces in which to interact with others. This democratization of virtual-world construction extends rhetorical agency to a larger community of users than has been the case with past virtual environments. Even though the resulting spaces often represent entirely fantastic or fictional worlds, cities, and landscapes, at their most fanciful they still tend to contain at least a modicum of the world as we know it. Buildings, highways, parks, seacoasts, and forests in these virtual worlds may be utopian or not physically possible in real life, but they are still, like any other creative endeavor, reflective of the hopes and dreams—and the bias and ignorance—of their designers. They perform ideologies just as sculptures, movies, monuments, and buildings do in real life, and are thus rhetorical constructions.

Given the power to create artificial worlds, what choices do we make? Do we become completely post-human, or do we retain a connection with the embodied life, including its necessary interconnections with biological and physical systems of our natural environment? In a real world in which threats to these systems are widely acknowledged, what do our virtual-world constructions say about our view of nature?

The role of virtual environments in our constructions of 'The Environment' will likely become at least as powerful as that of movies, magazines, television, and other forms of popular culture. In 2008, the Gartner Group predicted 70% of organizations will have their own private virtual worlds by 2012 (Gartner Group 2008), and a number are under active development. As virtual-reality technology grows powerful enough to create phenomeno-logically real spaces, the impact on our perceptions of reality (including the natural world) can be profound. In this chapter I will describe depictions of nature in *Second Life*, one of the most popular and groundbreaking of these online worlds.

Second Life

Whereas its long-term viability remains a continual matter of disagreement, *Second Life* was the target of often breathless hype in 2005–07, when it experienced significant growth—for example, 35% per month in user accounts and 15% per month in economic activity in 2006 (Jana and McConnon 2006). One source described the *Second Life* growth curve in late 2005 as 'closer to that of the adoption of a communication technology rather than that of a game' (Jones 2006: 27). Data on actual usage trends is highly controversial, but *Second Life* is undeniably the most popular non-game, user-built virtual environment as of this writing, and as such offers a preview of what such platforms might offer in the near future.

Second Life is a visually rich 3-D virtual space containing imitations of real-life artifacts and activities, as well as utopian (and dystopian) fantasies and alternative realities. It has a relatively impressive pedigree. According to Jones (2006), it grew out of a 'Metaverse' concept described in Neal Stephenson's novel *Snow Crash*: 'Stephenson was the first to describe an online environment [The Metaverse] that was a real place to its users, one where they interacted using the real world as a metaphor' (Jones 2006: 2):

> *Second Life* not only grew out of a particular cultural discourse but also out of an ancestry of publicly available virtual worlds, marrying the user creativity and sociability of text-based Multi-User Dungeons/ Domains (MUDs) with the graphic richness of Massively Multi-Player Role Playing Games (MMORPGs). MUDs and MMORPGs contributed greatly to what Second Life is today, and sets Second Life apart from other currently available virtual worlds. (Jones 2006: 16)

Although its depictions are at times cartoonish and fanciful, participants often describe it as being immersive enough to feel 'real' to its participants, and it can replicate real-world spaces (such as Paris in 1900, or a forest of conifers) with enough fidelity to allow users to suspend disbelief.

It may also represent a new manner of web-based interaction: According to *Fortune*, 'what it really may represent is an alternative vision for how to interact with information and communicate over the Internet' (Kirkpatrick 2006). In fact, *Second Life* founder Philip Rosedale 'sees *Second Life* as a platform, in the same sense as MySpace. In the future, Rosedale sees *Second Life* as a possible 3D Web browser' (Jana and McConnon 2006). As such it becomes both a place for and a medium of interaction; not simply an alternate, created world but a means of communication for humans in the real one—with corresponding potential to frame and influence perceptions.

Second Life consists of a number of internetworked, three-dimensional 'islands' or 'sims', each of which is actually a web server (and thus the spaces are comparable to 2-D websites). Basic user accounts are free; access requires downloading the free browser tool, connecting to the Internet, and logging on with a sufficiently powerful computer. Users who visit this space are represented by (and see others as) more or less cartoon-like 'avatars' that move, walk, fly, gesture, and communicate via text chat, or more recently, via stereo audio channel that renders voices spatially, indicating both direction and distance. The appearance of avatars is fully customizable, from realistically humanoid to creatures from the wildest flights of fantasy, and they have demigod-like powers that allow them to fly over terrain and 'teleport' instantaneously across large distances. Avatars never need food or drink, and cannot be injured or 'killed' as in many role-playing games such as *World of Warcraft*.

A space such as *Second Life* generates new forms of social behavior, or twists on old ones: 'griefing' (pranks and harassment), cultural collisions between humanoid avatars and 'furries' (animal-like avatars), and gender-bending are just some of the more well known. According to *Second Life: The Official Guide*, as many as 15% of the male users of *Second Life* are represented by female avatars (Rymaszewski et al. 2006: 76)—perhaps because they find social advantages in doing so.

One particular form of social behavior that has received plentiful attention is economics: Not only can users buy and sell items within *Second Life* using 'Linden dollars' (Linden Labs is the software company behind the virtual world), but this currency exchanges for real-world money and thus creates substantial real-world incomes for a select few. For example, *Second Life* real-estate mogul Anshe Chung is estimated by Linden Lab to have pulled in $150,000 *per year* from sales and rentals of virtual space (Rymaszewski et al. 2006: 253). Furthermore, real-world companies like Reuters, Mercedes-Benz, and Starwood Hotels have used the virtual world to test and market products (Brady and McConnon 2006).

Settings for exploration, interaction, and other activities include night-clubs, flying castles, classrooms, libraries, shopping malls, residences, rail-roads, yacht clubs, airports, and used-car lots—all created by users:

It took a radical approach to design from the beginning. It offered itself as a mere platform for the creations of its occupants. Essentially everything seen inside the software today was created by its users. All that the company that operates Second Life, Linden Lab, sells is server time and network capacity. (Kirkpatrick 2006)

According to Jones (2006),

It is by giving its users tools for creativity that Second Life gives the users' experience particular meaning and makes the world more interactive and realistic. Second Life creates a new type of producer-consumer (prosumer), similar to the thousands of people who are mixing their own music, making their own movies or publishing their own art or texts on the Internet. (Jones 2006: 19)

Before examining how these virtual texts depict the natural environment, though, it's worthwhile to examine previous work on representations of nature.

Embodiment and Virtuality

The literature on virtual reality and on the way nature is represented, constructed, and experienced in real-life museums, theme parks, and tourism reveals a complex interconnection between the real and the virtual, with possibilities for both clarifying and distorting.

No matter how phenomenologically real virtual worlds may be, most authors agree that the virtual is not ontologically equal to reality. Book (2003: 20) states that virtual worlds are 'liminal spaces, existing somewhere between work and play, conscious and subconscious, real and unreal'. No matter how realistic they may seem, their 'otherworldly qualities' are continuous visual cues that remind the user that he or she is in a virtual space.

Yet, as Stewart and Nicholls (2002: 85) assert, this unreality need not be cause for dismissing them as false and misleading (a 'shabby facsimile of reality'). Echoing the work of Sherry Turkle (1995) on Internet identities, they argue that a virtual experience can 'facilitate an improvement in the way one actually experiences the world' (85) and potentially 'transform the "reality" in which we presently live for the better' (96).

The experience of virtual reality may not even be clearly distinct for the user. Whereas there is a tendency toward disassociation and disembodiment that arises from a camera-like, third person view, Stewart and Nicholls argue that the virtual body and an engaging virtual narrative can result in 'one phenomenal body' that melds the virtual and the real identities. This further implies a virtualizing of the physical body when it starts to perform real actions 'within the actuality of its transformed social space'

(87). In short, virtual experiences are ontologically real, and the real can extend into virtual spaces.

Asserting that, at least in principle, virtual experiences can 'facilitate an enhanced and more authentic relationship with actuality' (84), Stewart and Nicholls point to the phenomenon of 'virtual vacations' and compare this with real travel and tourism, which has also 'traditionally required normative justification' (84)—like virtual reality, it has often had to explain its real-world value. Their insightful connection of the European Grand Tour, landscape painting, English gardens, and virtual reality is discussed in detail in a later section of this chapter.

Thus virtual realities problematize our ontological notions of the real (including continents, rain forests, and endangered animals). According to Jones (2006: 4), 'virtual reality is the contemporary and future articulation of the philosophical and psychological question of how we define (and create) reality'. He distinguishes between those virtual experiences that are artificial 'essential copies' that merely fool the senses, and those that can provide a genuine physical transcendence from physical and physiological limitations. A productive virtual experience is neither a false representation nor necessarily the unalloyed good championed by enthusiastic futurists, but a balance he calls 'virtual realism' (8). In fact, he asserts that we constantly experience the virtual:

> Virtual reality is not entirely good or bad, but one of many virtualities in our lives. [. . .] Virtual worlds rest within a discursive space that has been constructed upon the struggle between the strengthening and blurring of boundaries of corporeality and transcendence, the real and the virtual, where and nowhere, and the unitive and multiplicitous self. It is this tension that makes virtual reality and virtual worlds so compelling to the contemporary imagination. (10)

Virtual worlds are thus pragmatically real, existing between 'the extremes of transcendence and nihilism' (27). Their ability to create 'real enough' environments makes the character of those environments worth attending to, because their reality may articulate with and even alter perceptions of traditional real-world spaces that have undeniable impacts on the health and well-being of humans and non-humans. Thus advances in technology will require only increased critical vigilance of the discourses interconnecting the real and the virtual. Jones concludes that 'a true understanding will ensure that instead of being distracted by godhood and monstrosity, we can ever seek the human in whatever form it takes' (28).

Light and Vision

One enduring critique of virtually-derived realities is that they overemphasize and valorize the visual medium at the expense of other sensory modalities. Jones (2006: 7) draws a connection to an historical interplay—in culture, science, and philosophy—between the observable and the transcendent. He notes that Western culture originally looked beyond the observable to the Divine, whereas modernism changed that focus to the empirical world,

> a pursuit aided by optical technologies. This experiment furthered understandings of the way vision worked and how to create visual experiences—plays of sound and light, magic lanterns and stereoscopes, and later photography and film—that mediated the actual world and/or created realistic virtual images. In the contemporary moment, Western thought is informed by a history of seeking the transcendent, finding truth in the seen and the increasingly developed technological ability to create more visually (and aurally, and, eventually, more fully sensually) rich constructions of artifice and simulacra. It is into this context that the discourse of virtual reality and virtual worlds developed in its contemporary sense. (Jones 2006: 7)

Thus Jones asserts that virtual reality is primarily visual in part simply because it reflects modernism. The fact that virtual worlds are 'primarily experienced through screen technology' (13) means that even with aural or kinesthetic components they are 'virtual worlds of light' (11).

Patin (1999) further explores the connection of the visual with political history, noting that 'technologies of vision [. . .] serve to constitute and to reproduce the social arrangements of power' in a 'politics of nature' that includes

> the ways in which natural phenomena are also the products of the processes of categorization—of language and cultural practices. Names for natural phenomena, such as 'wilderness' and 'natural disaster' reference nature, but at the same time these terms return us to society, discursive categories, and narrative genres. (Patin 1999: 57)

This kind of 'taming of the wilderness' into linguistic and visual rhetorical constructions is, for Patin, 'a fruitful place for the beginning of an environmental politics (58).

Urry's (2002) idea of the mediating 'tourist gaze', employed by Book (2003) in her analysis of virtual tourism and photography, helps connect visuality and power; the virtual world user controls through an omniscient visual access. But like Jones, Book argues that the focus on the visual is an artifact of the medium, and exists only because virtual worlds 'do not yet fully engage the other senses' (3).

She also sees a parallel between advances in the ability of computer-based virtual worlds to replicate the real, and the increasing 'hyper-reality' (in Baudrillard's [1981] sense of *simulacra*) of real-world tourist sites. She provides an example of these two problematic realities intertwining:

a mini-golf castle in *Second Life*, designed to imitate Disney's Cinderella Castle, which is itself modeled on Ludwig of Bavaria's Neuschwanstein Castle, which is yet again another pastiche of historical and imagined antecedents (5)—all re-created with the visual presentation paramount.

Against this background—wherein reality and virtuality can coexist in a shifting, liminal state that tends towards a valorization of only that which is seen—a range of phenomena have been examined as constructed messages about what is assumed to be the natural (ontologically more real) world.

Manifestations of 'Real' and Virtual Nature

Stewart and Nicholls (2002) describe the emergence of the 19th-century English garden as 'a complex mingling of the virtual and the real—neither simulacrum nor reality' (84). Such gardens were constructed subsequent to the rising popularity of 'nonessential' travel or tourism, prior to which travel was usually considered warranted only for business, pilgrimage, or exploration (88).

During the 18th century (in a transition that might have analogies in the modern evolution of computers from tools to entertainment devices) the pedagogical and self-improvement aspects of travel, especially as experienced in the so-called Grand Tour, were often subsumed under the goal of 'maximizing subjective pleasure' (89). The instrumentality of travel became more aesthetic and spiritual.

Thoreau and others justified this form of travel as a reconnection with 'the Wild'—resulting in a complex relationship between the places traveled and ideas about those places:

> [The Wild] does not refer to any specific place—some eco-tourist destination—because a person can be in the Wild, Thoreau says, in the midst of a crowded city. The Wild, let us say, is a virtual world. And given its intimate connection with actual travel in Thoreau's context, it makes no sense to completely dissociate this world from 'reality' [. . .] [thus] any form of travel can be examined in terms of the virtual world with which it is bound, and assessed according to the reality made available by that virtual world. (Stewart and Nicholls: 90)

The very real dangers and hardships one might encounter during a Grand Tour were both depicted and relived in landscape art, which provided the model for the English garden (91). Gardeners such as Capability Brown (who designed the still-extant gardens at Blenheim Palace near Oxford) were hired by the wealthy to both recapture the literal experience of wild landscapes and evoke experiences of the Sublime (92).

The gardens were informed by a desire to re-create the real experiences (themselves mediated by preconceptions) of the Grand Tour, but were themselves unreal expressions. They modified nature under the 'ubiquitous eighteenth century term "improvement"' (93), in part because of the practice of organizing the garden experiences as a series of carefully ordered views or perspectives, which ordered the wilderness of nature into the safe, ordered garden (94). Thus:

> The English garden is appropriately conceived as the 'phenomenal body' that results from the melding of the existing physical environment and the virtual worlds experienced in foreign travel. (Stewart and Nicholls: 95)

The convergence of travel, landscape art, and gardens thus forms an early model of the virtualization of nature. This artificiality amid reality is not confined to the gardens of wealthy aristocracy, however. Ottesen (2008) similarly describes the way scenic trails are now 'deliberate, calculated, and use-less' except as homages to past working trails (pioneers and pilgrims, for example):

> Overwhelmingly, these trails appeal to our sense of aesthetics. Dramatic geographic features typify both the route and the destination: mountaintops, waterfalls, rivers, lakes, canyons—our trails invariably tend towards these sorts of locales rather than toward useful resources the trails might once have led to. (Ottesen 2008: 232)

She asserts that rather than bring humans closer to nature, trails typically separate us from it by driving away animals and by masking the impacts of trail-building from users. A complex tension that exists between giving people access to nature while minimizing the impact of this access tends to preserve distance and separation (234).

Beyond trails themselves, Patin (1999) notes that America's national parks are:

> essentially museological institutions, not because they preserve and conserve, but because they employ many of the techniques of display, exhibition, and presentation that have been used by museums to organize and regulate the vision of visitors. (41)

In addition to this continuing emphasis on the visual, Patin asserts that these structured experiences are designed to articulate natural wonders with America's cultural heritage, in much the same way that Stewart and Nicholls argue that English gardens were in part an assertion of 'Englishness'. Both illustrate the ways that representations of nature can serve ideological functions. DeLuca (1998) found a similar rhetoric in landscape photography, asserting that such images do not so much *represent* nature as *create* it within a political frame that, in the case of Yosemite National Park, comprises 'the discourses of tourism, nationalism, romanticism, expansionism, and religion' (2).

These cultural and ideological shapings persist even when efforts are being made to create depictions of a less anthropocentric natural environment than one sees in gardens and parks. For example, Hovardas and Stamou (2006) examined the perceptions of a Greek forest preserve among local inhabitants and found them to share a touristic perspective of nature. Locals regarded the preserve not for its ecological or resource value but as a 'hedonistic experience', in part because of the way the 'preserve' separates humans from their environment, which can then only be visually consumed (because it is to be 'preserved', [1765–66]). The authors note with some concern that their findings

> suggest that direct or indirect involvement in ecotourism and participation in environmental education programs and related events could not suffice to enhance environmental conservation or quality of life issues within rural communities living in protected areas. (Hovardas and Stamou: 1767)

This idealization or abstraction of even 'real nature' can influence ecological restoration projects. For example, Turnhout et al. (2004) found that idealized conceptions of nature were strongly at play in competing versions for the (re-)creation of an area of drift sands in a Dutch national park. On one side, adherents of a 'pastoral idyll' vision argued for species protection and active management for humans to experience, whereas others favored an idea of 'wilderness' that valorized an ideal pristine nature, natural processes, and nonintervention (192). Importantly, Turnhout et al. remind us that neither vision exists in the world in its pure form; neither is real (190). Both are virtual realities existing in the cultural constructions of those participating in the discourse about conserving and restoring the drift sands area.

Turning to frankly artificial and explicitly virtual experiences, several writers have addressed the pragmatic realism of experiences such as virtual tours, as well as the problematic messages conveyed about the natural world via the artifice of theme parks. Utterson (2003) examines the proliferation of webcams and web-based virtual tours, and asserts that contrary to the expectation that these experiences might be passive and distancing, they are in fact interactive, as the tourist (whom he compares to the strolling Parisian *flâneur*) navigates endless virtual environments:

> Like the space of the cinema before it, the Internet becomes the connective site for a multitude of subjective gazes. Abstracted, related to the rhetoric of moving image representation, the virtual travelogue prompts the spectator/user to take immediate possession of a series of recontextualized environments. (Utterson 2003: 200)

Book (2003) continues the notion of the engaged *flâneur* in her discussion of tourist-like behavior in 3-D virtual worlds. These spaces encourage movement, exploration, and engagement even as they promote escape from the 'humdrum reality of everyday life and workplace responsibilities' (3–4). The virtual world becomes a real space, an 'interactive canvas' in which the audience participates in creation and development. This creates a sense of attachment comparable to that associated with real places:

> Despite the fact that virtual views and landmarks are completely fabricated entities, regular visitors can become quite attached to them and even come to think of them as 'natural resources' that need protection from overzealous real estate projects and 'litter' like unsightly large signs and billboards. (Book 2003: 8)

Krug (n.d.) connects virtual and real-world tourism by noting that the virtual tour can preserve sensitive environments while allowing them to be in some sense appreciated. And he argues that the virtual tour may open an appreciation of certain places to those who cannot travel due to physical, economic, or political barriers (3). Stumpo (2008) reiterates the potential of virtual worlds as an ecologically friendly alternative, 'cleaner even than books', but says this can be so only if we develop alternative means of powering the servers these worlds run on (39).

Thus Utterson, Book, and Krug demonstrate ways in which the virtual experience can be beneficial in an environmentalist sense, despite its 'unreality'. Yet, as Krug notes, it is important to maintain a kind of eco-critical vigilance, continually interrogating the relationship between virtual nature and what it purports to represent, and asking how digital constructions may influence the consumption of actual environments (4).

This point is best elaborated by Davis (1997), who writes about Sea World and other nature-oriented theme parks, offering a strong critique of their message. She argues that these artificial environments are 'not so much a substitution for nature as an opinion about it' (241) and that they construct an inaccurate, corporate-dominated picture of the relationships between humans and marine ecosystems (10). Fantasy hides the reality of exploitation and pollution of the natural environment, takes attention away from real environmental action by providing a veneer of concern for visitors (238), and 'the possibility of alternatives collapses into the consumption of images' (239).

Furthermore, she notes that marine ecosystems are presented in purely anthropocentric ways:

> Dolphins, krill, fingerling bass, the oceans' ecosystems are not allowed to be useless or just exist beyond human fathoming: the whole natural world is there for something. (Davis 1997: 241)

For Davis, theme parks and even virtual, computerized ecosystems are simply the latest installment of nature simulations that have been an enduring component of Western culture (238), although in future they may be called upon to stand in for state and national parks as these are sold or closed. Indeed, she points out that already, entertainment companies are hired to run places like Yosemite, further blurring the line between 'real nature' and touristic, entertainment-oriented depictions and constructions thereof (236–37).

Even civic, non-corporate entities like public or nonprofit zoos, wildlife parks, and museums tend to present an ideologically bound conception of nature. Mitman (1996) observed in his analysis of parks and museum exhibits that they exemplify 'the late twentieth century's preoccupation with the re-creation of nature' in which humans are deliberately made invisible, despite their role in creating and managing the parks (143), thereby mystifying the human-nature relationship. Continuing the visual emphasis noted earlier, Mitman asserts that this 'creative invisibility' became essential to visitors' belief that the exhibits are natural because of the role of the camera in the profession of natural history after World War II; unlike landscape painting and tourist photography, the camera (and associated biotelemetry and satellite images) came to promote the human relationship to nature as panoramic and transcendent: 'an omnipresent and omniscient Being: invisible, yet ever watchful, ready at any moment to intervene and impose divine justice. They [humans] had become the divine arbiter, ensuring the police of nature' (143).

Thus on top of an already complex interaction among the real and the virtual, and an anthropocentric photo-centrism, we continue to find ideology and cultural practice embedded even in (what we are presented with as) real nature. Yet Utterson, Book, and Krug, as noted earlier, hold an at least guardedly optimistic view of virtual tourism and the virtual experience of nature. What of specific virtual-environment 'environments' available today? Whereas the depictions of natural environments in virtual worlds such as *Second Life* have not yet received much attention in the literature, two studies have examined computer games from an environmentalist orientation. Opel and Smith (2004) suggest possibilities in their analysis of the computer game *ZooTycoon*. Noting that video games are spaces where cultural norms and values, as well as notions of reality, can be constructed and affirmed by the 'culture producing industry' (10), they further observe that *ZooTycoon* in particular offers a route for examining environmental messages outside traditional news and other venues in popular culture, suggesting the emerging role of virtual worlds asserted at the outset of this chapter.

Opel and Smith's findings were not promising, suggesting a tendency towards more problematic representations. They found that animals were depicted out of context either with their ecosystems or with the processes of capture or maintenance in captivity (112), creating a 'significant barrier to environmental education' (114). Instead, they found that by reducing the player to a manager and entrepreneur, the game essentially redirects players into a commodity culture wherein notions of public and private are inverted and avarice is valorized (117). Furthermore,

> The de-emphasis on size of the animals, depersonalization, and dull portrayal seems to indicate that animals are on equal footing with the vending machines, there merely to attract paying customers. (117)

Stumpo (2008) found similar economic reductionism in the multiplayer online game *EverQuest*, wherein players must kill 'monsters' (animals, only some of which are fantasy creatures) to obtain objects needed to advance in gameplay (35). Sustainable relationships with nature, such as farming or husbandry, are not present, and even the process of obtaining 'loot' from killed monsters is sanitized. Creatures always 're-spawn' at intervals, meaning there is no such thing as extinction. The ecology of *EverQuest*, then, is 'broken' (32) and this broken ecology is reproduced in players' minds because the game 'both reflects and reinforces a view of the world that treats nature as simply one more object to be conquered, killed, or commercialized' (31):

> Here is the real intellectual danger of Norrath—it presents a nature that can be known only for its commercial or superficially aesthetic value. Being a series of signs without realities, a world that refers only superficially to this one, it educates the player that nature is utterly separate from the self, from culture, and to react to nature in a particularly limited fashion—destroy it . (36)

In contrast to the corporate dominance found in Sea World and *ZooTycoon*, one might expect that a user-created space like *Second Life* could present themes that are more diverse, even if not entirely pro-environmental. However, Jones's (2006) review of avatar behavior in more urban spaces there is pessimistic:

> Second Life is not an idyllic world, unless one envisions a capitalist paradise. From observation of Second Life, it is clear that, as in the real world, American consumerism (of a virtual sort) is everywhere. One cannot walk down the virtual street without being barraged by virtual vending machines selling virtual wares or seeing virtual advertisements for virtual casinos. As in American culture, it is this commerce that allows the system to be viable, but it also means that money can become the root of both good and evil. (20)

However, because Jones was not looking at natural-world representations *per se*, empirical questions remain, to be explored in the remainder of this chapter. On balance, do the representations of natural environments and non-human nature in *Second Life* simply reproduce a kind of hegemonic industrial/consumerist orientation? Or do they suggest alternatives and possibilities for environmental awareness and social change?

METHOD

As an exploratory approach, this study is grounded in the environmental components of simulations found in *Second Life*, which will be read and interpreted as expressions of popular culture in much the same way that previous research has examined national and theme parks and computer games. Due to the sheer size of *Second Life*, I will focus attention on aquatic environments: seashores, lakes, streams, and so on, along with their plant and animal inhabitants.

The locations were selected for analysis through what might be considered a combination of convenience and snowball sampling. After signing on to *Second Life* in late 2006, I began searching for aquatic-environment representations and 'landmarking' them in my inventory. Several methods were used to locate these: keyword searches using the internal search tool, reading the various lists and guides available 'in-world', talking with other users/avatars while visiting environmental simulations, and in some cases, scanning the in-world maps to locate water features for closer examination.

Once a location was identified, I visited it (usually via 'teleportation') and then toured the area by walking or flying, noting the landforms, water bodies, and biological components, as well as what might be considered more conventional cultural artifacts such as signs, clickable note cards, and related built structures such as tiki huts, docks, sunken vessels, and so on.

Related to this inquiry, I investigated the biophysical conditions of the virtual world itself, via direct observation, conversations with others, trial and error, and reference materials.

RESULTS

Second Nature

Second Life is indeed an unreal place, without all the constraints of a physical and biological space—a 'broken ecology' as Stumpo (2008) might describe it. As one resident put it, '[y]ou don't need a home and it never rains—in fact, you can set the sun to shine the way you like it most' (Rymaszewski et al. 2006: 197). Although not completely accurate (it can rain, but nothing gets wet), the statement conveys the overall paradisiacal nature of the virtual world.

The biophysical environment of *Second Life* is different from real life in several key ways that impact residents and their constructions. Thus whereas it has built-in physics emulation that causes objects and avatars to fall, bounce, or collide in expected ways, these actions can be modified to 'pin' objects so that they float in the air or make them 'phantom' so that avatars can move through them (Rymaszewski et al. 2006: 187). A simulated sun and moon 'rise' and 'set' at regular times, but these are not natural circadian cycles, and can be overridden so that, for example, your avatar sees a scene under full moon or sunset conditions if you so prefer it.

Atmospheric conditions include clouds, fog, and simulated precipitation (which has no effect), as well as wind, which can be heard and which 'blows' certain objects if they are so designed, contributing to a pleasant immersive feeling. On the other hand, there is apparently no similar 'current' effect in most underwater areas—even when, for example, the towering simulated tidal wave crashes over your avatar in the NOAA's simulated tsunami experience on *Meteroa* island. Astronomic and atmospheric conditions are set by the owner of a given region or 'sim'.

The owner also sets land elevations and sea levels, where *Second Life*'s 'ocean' abuts the land (*Second Life* 2007, item 054), via a process called 'terraforming' (*Second Life* 2007, items 235 and 275). To attain these titan-like powers, residents purchase land in units (the 3-D analogue to web-server storage space) from as little as $512m^2$ to entire regions—also called 'islands'—of 6.5 hectares (Rymaszewski et al. 2006: 37). Many landowners begin simply, by flattening areas to be built upon and applying a green grass texture to the undeveloped areas, although professional 'real estate developers' may create 'elaborate themed sims complete with custom-made, exotic vegetation; professionally scripted, sparkling waterfalls; and sandy beaches' (Rymaszewski et al. 2006: 240)—the touristic areas described later.

As in real life, waterfront land is often at a premium—if only because it means nothing will be built next to your property. Property owners can control access to their land by other avatars and even set 'telehubs' that restrict property entry to a specific location (Rymaszewski et al. 2006: 110) for a controlled experience, not unlike the constructed views of real-life garden viewpoints, narrative pathways through museums, or scenic overlooks.

Once the land is shaped to the owner's desires, textures such as wood, sand, and mulch (Rymaszewski et al. 2006: 116) can be added, as well as a fairly wide variety of default plants and trees, freely supplied in every avatar's inventory of clothes, boats, scripts, and other *Second Life* essentials. Plants, trees, and grasses are a special type of object; they are essentially made less 'expensive' to property owners to encourage their wide use (Rymaszewski et al. 2006: 11, 135). This suggests that the designers of *Second Life* recognized the importance of natural objects in the enhancement of immersivity; the *Official Guide to Second Life* makes this explicit: 'You'll really appreciate the contents of this folder [inventory] when you acquire your starter land and are in a hurry to make it look good' (Rymaszewski et al. 2006: 110); 'These more complex models have been added to fill out the sorts of builds that *Second Life* residents enjoy. Without them, the world would be a far blockier and less organic place' (Rymaszewski et al. 2006: 116). Custom plants can also be built, although this requires the 'highly specialized' skills employed by 'landscapers': 'A realistic looking plant involves not only delicate prim manipulation, but also scripting (so that it moves in the wind, and so on) and frequently the creation of a new custom texture or two' (Rymaszewski et al. 2006: 239).

One measure of this world's anthropocentrism is that despite all the default store of materials and developed skills related to 'landscaping', relatively little attention has been devoted to underwater aquascaping. Whereas waterfront areas abound (beaches, harbors, and so on) and, as mentioned, are in high demand, most underwater vistas are, in the words of one marine-science blogger, 'stark abyssal plains' (Robertshaw 2006) devoid of aquatic life. The default store of plants includes no aquatic varieties, and until at least mid-2007 the Second Life Knowledge Base (*Second Life* 2007) comes up empty when searched for any of the following terms: *ocean, lake, river, aquatic, marine,* or *wave.*

Yet there are many aquascapes and aquatic environments represented in *Second Life,* and several residents have created marine plants and both static and dynamic representations of vertebrate and invertebrate life forms. The movements of dynamic, scripted animals can be exceptionally lifelike within the context of the virtual space. All can be easily purchased through in-world vendors whose stores resemble virtual aquariums, nurseries, and pet stores. Specific constructed environments vary widely in *Second Life.* A large number might be termed 'natural' areas: idealized tropical islands, park-like settings, and forested lands. Most of these might be typed as either 'pastoral idyll' or 'wilderness' using Turnhout's (2004) categories. Closely related are scientific sites and museums that depict or explain natural ecosystems. Even outside these areas, there are always trees and bushes, sound loops of birds and insects, and occasional 'wildlife' all serving primarily as incidental/ background decor.

A significant number of areas can also be considered representations of the touristic 'tropical island' that Book (2003: 7) describes. She found this kind of representation to be ubiquitous in another virtual world, *There,* and argues that this is a 'perfect match' for the way the virtual setting is employed as a get-away-from-it-all tool. Book found that *Tiki* tropical islands were both popular among users and frequently used in marketing materials. In fact, she states 'there are so many virtual islands and beaches online it is nearly impossible to find a virtual world that does not have one' (7), and this is certainly true of *Second Life.* Because these are expressly human-resource uses—in which the environment is strictly there to relax visitors or create a vacation mood, I consider these neither pastoral idylls nor wildernesses. They have more in common with theme park and resort landscaping, no matter how realistic and 'natural' their appearance.

A fourth type observed might be termed critical or ironic constructions, in which the represented environment serves primarily as a direct commentary on cultural practices. I only located one locale that fits this category (to be described in detail later), but it was striking in both realism and effect.

The remainder of this section describes several of these locales in greater detail.

Tropical Tourism

Bora Bora is a tourist island where visitors can buy surfboards and tiki items, ride a virtual waveboard, lounge in a hot tub, or ride bareback on a killer whale—much like a theme park (Figure 7.1). The island's palm-tree vegetation and sandbars are realistically proportioned, although the overall effect is of a natural space completely overrun by stilt-supported tiki huts selling a variety of tropical kitsch. *Chi* is another tourist island with a scripted surfing beach a short walk from an oceanside mini-mall,

Figure 7.1   Bora Bora.

re-creating a common real-life commercialized oceanfront. Its north shore contains tranquil ponds filled with ducks and fish, and these seem less artificial in part because they are not the focus of attention. Located off the focal points of the island, they suggest the designer's need for holistic completeness to make the island feel 'real'. This kind of natural element is found surprisingly often in *Second Life*; several areas have small incidental creeks and ponds often containing fish, waterfowl, and aquatic plants.

Educational Sites and Museums

Water-themed educational sites abound in *Second Life*. These include the *Abyss Museum of the Ocean Depths*; two elaborate, simulation-filled islands called *Meteora* and *Okeanos*, run by the National Oceanic and Atmospheric Administration; and a large, detailed coral reef near the Divers' Alert Network island. *The Center for Water Studies* on *Better World Island* typifies this category and includes a wide variety of simulated ecosystems such as a coral reef, mangrove swamp, and freshwater pond, complete with scripted and animated animals (Figure 7.2). Further details grace an underwater coral reef, featuring a large number of scripted, moving animals, from jellyfish to whales. An amphitheater

Figure 7.2 A heron finds lunch.

floats overhead (although in plain sight) and is used for virtual meetings and environmental talks. Plants and animals are grouped by ecosystem, and the island includes signage, informational links, and places where avatars can be posed in realistic attitudes that harmonize with the naturalistic theme.

Calculated Ugliness

Caleta/Hobo Trainyard is a polluted harbor and dockside with a rundown appearance, complete with toxic effluent, bayside landfill, and floating oil drums (Figure 7.3). Reminiscent of an exhibit this author encountered at Monterey Bay Aquarium 10 years ago, this build represents the worst in environmental degradation, and does so with open irony and exacting detail. The site is remarkably devoid of natural life, and unlike nearly all waterfront sites in *Second Life*, there is no attempt to create a pleasant vista (unless one is a fan of industrial decay). Distant smokestacks spew dark smoke while glowing sludge empties into the harbor from an open rusty pipe at water's edge. A garbage dump full of brand-name trash and the rusting hulk of a locomotive is right by the water, and offshore the sea bottom is littered with more industrial detritus.

Figure 7.3 A polluted harbor.

DISCUSSION AND CONCLUSION

Second Life offers depictions that support both the dominant, hegemonic, resource orientation towards nature and—at least ostensibly, through museums and even incidental elements—visions of a more sustainable, 'eco-friendly' world.

The hegemonic depictions predominate in tropical tourist islands and park-like settings. Even the elaborate undersea grottoes at *Cave Rua* are hedonistic gardens for human consumption; their artfully arranged mollusks and sea fans only superficially represent anything one might encounter in an unmodified natural setting. Tropical-fantasy islands like *Bora Bora* and *Chi* share a sense of being only temporary destinations, places for fun and adventure, not ongoing habitation (although there are houses on *Chi*). They are commercial and entertainment zones, with the natural features serving to frame or enhance their entertainment value. In fact, they may do more potential damage because of their realism, which masks the constructedness of their presentation in ways that more fantastic places like *Bliss Gardens* and *Cave Rua* make obvious.

Whereas these visions may not be as duplicitous as Davis found those at Sea World to be, if only because they do not conceal their purpose behind an educational or environmentalist veneer, they nonetheless reinforce the notion that nature is something to be managed and preserved for human exploitation. The bareback whale riding on *Bora Bora* performs the same trivialization of nonhuman life that Opel and Smith found in their analysis of *ZooTycoon*.

The museum environments, on the other hand, provide a means for users to experience, vicariously, a number of aquatic and marine ecosystems that might otherwise be unavailable in such immersive ways, and allow these visits to take place in a manner that does no harm to real-world sensitive environments—both ideas mentioned by Krug. Yet even the most lifelike animals there are for the most part blocky 3-D primitives, or flat images of fish in eternal circular scripted orbits, not unlike the string-supported plastic sharks in the old *20,000 Leagues Under the Sea* ride at Walt Disney World in Florida. They are, at best, scenic elements rather than artificial life—even (or perhaps especially) when they are beautiful and impressive, such as the elaborate spouting whales that can be found at the *Center for Water Studies* and offshore from the *Commonspace for Progressive Organizations*. In fact, the very replication of this virtual right whale, the quality of which has made it 'the whale' for marine simulations, becomes part of a message that says nature is replicable, purchasable, and deployable (Figure 7.4).

The *Center for Water Studies* attempts to be realistic and scientifically accurate, as do the Abyss Museum, DAN, and NOAA sims, but they tend to be zoo-like in their concentration of a number of ecosystems in an unrealistically small place. They remain managed views, and the Abyss and NOAA

Figure 7.4   All manner of wildlife for sale.

sims tend to place technology on an equal footing with nature by focusing on the equipment used in exploration and environmental monitoring.

Most intriguing is the kind of depiction found on the *Caleta* sim, with its polluted harbor. Fans of industrial grunge will likely not be particularly moved by its bleak, toxic feel, but—and this is significant—*Caleta* is also an 'Infohub', one of many newcomers' areas in *Second Life*. It also lies along the 'Great Second Life Railroad', a virtual railway that stretches across a large number of islands. Both characteristics increase the likelihood of its being accidentally discovered by users, and its unusually dystopian atmosphere is attention-getting. It may be that negative depictions in virtual worlds can serve the same image-rhetoric functions that DeLuca (1999) found to be served by the 'stunts' of Greenpeace, Earth First!, and other radical environmental groups in the 1990s, which called attention to environmental issues by enacting visual performances rather than through traditional verbal rhetorics. A dystopian presentation may cut through the noise and psychological defenses more effectively than an arcadian setting or an educational one.

The importance of our depictions of nature cannot be minimized. Consider O'Neill's (2001) observation that

> future generations and nonhuman beings pose particular problems of representing those who cannot speak and have in that sense no possibility of voice or presence in processes of environmental decision making.

The absence of such representation raises major problems concerning the ethical and political legitimacy of decisions made in the absence of their voice. At the same time it raises problems also for forms of environmental action and advocacy that are legitimised by appeal to the claim that protagonists are speaking and acting on behalf of those who are without voice. (483)

Yet speak we must. As O'Neill concludes, '[T]he articulation of any nonhuman interests or values here remains a human affair. The presence of nonhuman nature in deliberation about environmental choices requires human representation' (494). So it remains incumbent upon humans to make the best attempt to represent nonhuman nature as fully as possible, and it may be that, given the limitations of something like *Second Life*, many of its animals are honorable representations.

These depictions reflect and construct our views of real-world nature, with direct impact on policymaking. Orland, Budthimedhee, and Uusitalo (2001) warn that the utilization of virtual reality tools in land-management planning may result in the loss of healthy critiques of implausible projects (because the simulation looks and feels so authentic, even when—as with the biophysics of *Second Life*—it is impossible). Or the awareness that a land-use project *is* virtual may cause unwarranted skepticism about its feasibility. In either case, the authors stress the need to 'avoid situations where accidentally or deliberately misleading virtual environments are used to make significant environmental planning decisions' (Orland et al. 2001).

The point is brought home by Lange (2001), who found perceptions of the realism of various depictions of the landscape to be generally very strong, especially with views at middle and higher distances. One advantage of this realism is the ability to compress time and show subtle environmental effects not normally observable by most people. However,

[o]ne has to keep in mind that the image information only reflects one moment of one day of the whole year. The real landscape is a dynamic system undergoing continuous seasonal and daily change of atmospheric conditions. This diversity and variation cannot be captured in a simulated environment. Potential limitations become obvious when the real landscape is set against the virtual landscape. (Lange 2001, 180)

Thus even the most scientifically accurate of *Second Life*'s virtual nature can be problematic.

If virtual constructions of 'nature' can thus impact our perceptions of real-world spaces, it's also possible that the imaginative immersion that takes place for users can serve to, in a sense, import nature into highly artificial virtual spaces, making them more natural. Of course, the most literal form of this is the artificial ecosystem, which attempts to mirror real-world biophysical processes. But nature speaks in other ways in the virtual world; the seeming inevitability of natural objects (trees, animals, landforms) in most *Second Life* islands, as well as the presence of real-world physics, tells us that even in imagination, we cannot entirely remove humanity from the natural systems that sustain us.

Additionally, as more recent work in 'mixed reality' and 'augmented reality' demonstrates, the real/virtual divide continues to be effaced in new and challenging ways. Virtual forms can be layered over mediated views of the real environment, allowing us to see, for example, a depiction of historical structures superimposed on a live view of a cityscape viewed on an iPhone's built-in camera. The ability to experience the virtual as intimately connected to the real, in real time, could greatly magnify the impact of virtual natures in both positive and negative ways—allowing us to visualize, for example, the way a new building will fit into the landscape, or to 'see through' a reservoir to observe what was covered by impounded waters. Direct geospatial mapping between the real and the virtual will likely continue to blur the boundaries between what is ontologically real and that which is constructed by symbols and cultural processes.

There is much more to be learned. *Second Life*'s islands are as ephemeral as websites, making them difficult to catalog and requiring regular searches to identify newly emergent sites of interest—especially 'subversive' depictions such as *Caleta*. A more finely grained analysis could seek evidence of specific thematic elements and compare these across one or more demographic variables, such as nationality, region, gender, and others. *Second Life* is an international space, constituted from many cultural perspectives. Much might also be learned through structured interviews with Linden employees, the owners of simulations, and 'environmental builders' who create islands and the plants and animals to populate them. And we do not yet know how these islands are experienced by users except through conjecture. I hope to pursue several of these lines of inquiry in subsequent work, and given the rich history of literature on text-based virtual worlds, the visual rhetorics of 3-D worlds will be investigated by others as well.

The potential impact of virtual worlds is likely to increase as they become more commonplace, especially if they evolve into the pervasive interaction media envisioned by Linden Lab and others. They will likely construct and reflect our views of nature in new ways because of their phenomenological immersivity, the relative ease of creating content, and open distribution networks. And as the editors of *Enviropop: Studies in Environmental Rhetoric and Popular Culture* observed:

> [T]he languages and images of popular culture situate humans in relation to natural environments, create and maintain hierarchies of importance, reinforce extant values and beliefs, justify actions or

inactions, suggest heroes and villains, and create past contexts and future expectations. (Meister and Japp 2002: 4)

REFERENCES

Baudrillard, J (1981). *The precession of simulacra*, trans. SF Glasier. Online. Available HTTP: http://www.egs.edu/faculty/baudrillard/baudrillard-simulacra-and-simulation-01-the-precession-of-simulacra.html (accessed 17 April 2007).

Book, B (2003) Traveling through cyberspace: tourism and photography in virtual worlds. Paper presented at the conference *Tourism and Photography: Still Visions—Changing Lives*, Sheffield, UK, July 20–23.

Brady, D and A McConnon (2006) Booking a room in cyberspace. *Business Week* 4000 (September 11): 12.

Davis, SG (1997) *Spectacular nature*. Los Angeles: University of California Press.

DeLuca, KM (1998) The rhetorical force of landscape art. Paper presented at the *National Communication Association*, November 22.

———. (1999). *Image politics: The new rhetoric of environmental activism*. New York: Guilford Press.

Gartner Group (2008). Gartner says 90 per cent of corporate virtual world projects fail within 18 months (Press release, May 15). Online. Available HTTP: http://www.gartner.com/it/page.jsp?id=670507 (accessed 16 March 2009).

Hovardas, T and GP Stamou (2006) Structural and narrative reconstruction of rural residents' representations of 'nature', 'wildlife', and 'landscape'. *Biodiversity and Conservation* 15: 1745–70.

Jana, R and A McConnon (2006) Second life lessons. *Business Week Online*. October 31. Online. Available HTTP: http://www.businessweek.com.proxy.lib.fsu.edu/innovate/content/oct2006/id20061030_869611.htm (accessed 2 April 2007).

Jones, DE (2006) I, avatar: Constructions of self and place in Second Life and the technological imagination. *gnovis*, January 10. Online. Available HTTP: http://gnovis.georgetown.edu/article.cfm?articleID=50 (accessed 17 April 2007).

Kirkpatrick, D (2006) No, Second Life is not overhyped. *Fortune*, November 10. Online. Available HTTP: http://money.cnn.com/2006/11/09/technology/fastforward_secondlife.fortune/index.htm (accessed 2 April 2007).

Krug, C (n.d.) Virtual tourism: The consumption of natural and digital environments. In *Interactivity of Digital Texts*, ed. J Frenk and C Krug. Online. Available HTTP: http://www.uni-muenster.de/interact/publications/digital/environments.html (accessed 5 April 2007).

Lange, E (2001) The limits of realism: perceptions of virtual landscapes. *Landscape and Urban Planning* 54: 163–82.

Meister, M and PM Japp (eds) (2002) *Enviropop: Studies in environmental rhetoric and popular culture*. Westport, CT: Greenwood.

Mitman, C (1996) When nature is the zoo: Vision and power in the art and science of natural history. *Osiris*, 2nd Series, Science in the Field 11: 117–43.

O'Neill, J (2001) Representing people, representing nature, representing the world. *Environment and Planning C: Government and Policy* 19: 483–500.

Opel, A and J Smith (2004). ZooTycoon: Capitalism, nature, and the pursuit of happiness. *Ethics and the Environment* 9, no. 2: 103–20.

Orland, B, K Budthimedhee, and J Uusitalo (2001) Considering virtual worlds as representations of landscape realities and as tools for landscape planning. *Landscape and Urban Planning* 54, no. 1: 139–48.

Ottesen, K (2008) A rhetoric of trails: Trail design and our relationship to landscape. *Interdisciplinary Studies in Literature and Environment* 15, no. 2: 229–36.

Patin, T (1999) Exhibitions and empire: National parks and the performance of manifest destiny. *Journal of American Culture* 22, no. 1: 41–59.

Robertshaw, J (2006) Cephalopodcast April 23, 2006: The ecology of second life. Online. Available HTTP: http://cephalopodcast.com/blog/2006/04/23/the-ecology-of-second-life/ (accessed 24 March 2007).

Rymaszewski, M, WJ Au, M Wallace, C Winters, C Ondrejka, and B. Batstone-Cunningham (2006). *Second Life: The official guide.* Hoboken, NJ: Sybex.

Second Life. (2007b) Second Life: Knowledge base. Online. Available HTTP: http://secondlife.com/knowledgebase/ (accessed 10 April 2007 and identified by knowledgebase ID in the text).

Stewart, RS and R Nicholls (2002) Virtual worlds, travel, and the picturesque garden. *Philosophy and Geography* 5, no. 1: 83–99.

Stumpo, J (2008) E-cology: *EverQuest* and the environment(s). *Interdisciplinary Studies in Literature and Environment* 15, no. 2: 29–40.

Turkle, S (1995) *Life on the screen: Identity in the age of the Internet.* New York: Simon and Shuster.

Turnhout, E, M Hisschemoller, and H Eijsackers (2004) The role of views of nature in Dutch nature conservation: The case of the creation of a drift sand area in the Hoge Veluwe National Park. *Environmental Values* 13: 187–98.

Urry, J (2002). *The tourist gaze: Leisure and travel in contemporary societies.* London: Sage.

Utterson, A (2003) Destination digital: Documentary representation and the virtual travelogue. *Quarterly Review of Film and Video* 20: 193–202.

8 Avatar Needs and the Remediation of Architecture in *Second Life*™

Astrid Ensslin

INTRODUCTION: ARCHITECTURE AS SOCIAL SPACE

Architecture is a form of functional art that seeks to meet the physical requirements of any given environment—territorial or virtual—and, equally importantly, the basic physical, social, and emotional needs of the people inhabiting and interacting with it. In other words, built environments are 'textual' spaces that reflect both their physical embeddedness and their social functions. Thus, according to Bryan Lawson (2001), architectural spaces are 'containers to accommodate, separate, structure and organize, facilitate, heighten and even celebrate human spatial behavior' (4). Buildings structure human relationships and guide human behavior in terms of power, constraint, and creativity (cf. Proshansky et al. 1970; Markus 1993). They seek to satisfy human spatial needs, which Robert Ardrey (1967) first summarized in terms of stimulation (e.g., entertainment; aesthetic pleasure; amusement; sensory, cognitive, creative, and mnemonic inspiration), security (shelter, balance of temperature, stability, privacy, protection against intruders), and identity (expression of self and other, belonging), and which form the basis of human territorial behavior (Lawson 2001: 18).

Human beings tend to seek a well-balanced degree of stimulation in order not to get bored by under- or stressed by over-stimulation. They further require varying degrees of stability, continuity, and predictability, for which reason having a 'home' constitutes one of the most essential human needs. As a result, travelling and moving house tend to be among the most stressful activities for many people (Lawson 2001: 21). Finally, the expression of one's own identity (cf. Goffman 1959) is of prime importance and is performed in a variety of semiotic systems, among which are the acquisition, creation, and customization of spatial objects and environments.

The perceived freedom to interact with architectural space is ultimately delimited by the structural boundaries imposed by it. Thus,

> [o]n a social level, buildings have the purpose of constraining behaviour. In a very physical way, they direct our movement into certain trajectories or prevent us from going to certain places. They keep certain

spaces dry and warm, while leaving others cold and wet. They keep certain people out, or other people in. Further, buildings also have the potential to induce behaviour and influence our attitude. (Harry et al. 2008: 65)

Architecture seeks to direct people's movements, their interactions with each other, as well as their physically contingent sensations ('dry and warm' vs. 'cold and wet') and psychologically and aesthetically determined emotions. It indexes public as opposed to private spaces, and inspires communicative, communal, or indeed solitary, meditative uses.

As pointed out by Lawson (2001), human spatial needs are directly derived from 'fundamental internal needs' (17). Those needs are inextricably linked to the physical conditions of the actual world, which I shall henceforth refer to as 'First Life' (FL). Although, of course, virtual worlds and actual worlds cannot and should not be conceived of as two separate, independent phenomena, there are a number of essential differences which impact the needs and behaviors of avatars as re-embodiments of the player-user in the virtual world.

In what follows, I shall explore the main differences between First Life and *Second Life* architectural requirements by revisiting Abraham Maslow's (1943) basic human needs hierarchy in light of empirical evidence revealing the prepotent needs of *Second Life* avatars (Linden Lab 2003–09). Inspired by Michael O'Toole's (1994) and Maree Kristen Stenglin's (2009) applications of Michael Halliday's (1978) three communicative metafunctions to built spaces, I shall then go on to examine the social semiotics of *Second Life* architecture, in particular in the context of the physical and physiological idiosyncracies of virtual environments, and I shall adapt O'Toole's architectural approach to the three Hallidayan communicative metafunctions to the specificities of *Second Life*. Drawing on Bolter and Grusin (1999; cf. Heilesen 2009), I round off this chapter by showing that FL and SL architectures remediate each other despite their apparent geo-physical discrepancies. I conclude that, although offering a seemingly ideal experimentation platform for pioneering architects, *SL* developers are lagging behind the affordances yielded by contemporary digital technology and that the populist agenda exhibited by *SL* can be only of limited use to pioneering FL architects.[1]

HUMAN VS. AVATAR NEEDS

In this section, I shall revisit Abraham Maslow's (1943) hierarchy of human needs and reapply it to *Second Life* avatars. My motivation for doing so is based on the observation that, paradoxically, *Second Life* residents tend to emulate FL architectural designs in a virtual world which exhibits a radically different set of geo-physical, meteorological, and physiological rules.

Preliminary observations of what activities avatars tend to engage in leads to the hypothesis that their needs must be located near and/or beyond the peak of the Maslowian basic needs pyramid, and be related to issues of self-expression, identity, and communication.

In 1943, American psychologist Abraham Harold Maslow developed his theory of basic human needs, which is grounded in his ascertainment that 'man is a perpetually wanting animal' (395). As illustrated in Figure 8.1, Maslow distinguishes between five levels of needs, which build upon each other in the sense that lower level needs have to be fulfilled in order for higher level needs to arise in the first place. For instance, (most) human beings in a developed country will temporarily prioritize the satisfaction of hunger and thirst over their personal security and further needs higher up the scale, such as self-esteem and creativity.

At the bottom level, physiological needs such as breathing, food, water, (reproductive) sex, sleep, homeostasis, excretion, and shelter ensure survival.[2] Maslow (1943) refers to them as 'the most prepotent of all needs', for 'in the human being who is missing everything in life in an extreme fashion, it is most likely that the major motivation would be the physiological needs

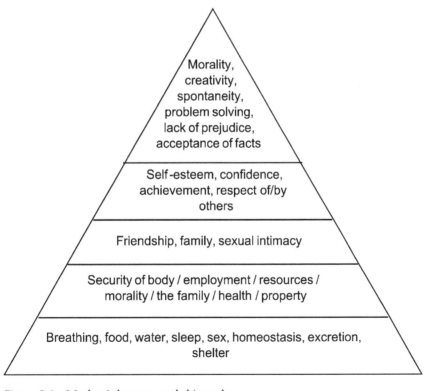

Figure 8.1 Maslow's human needs hierarchy.

rather than any others' (373). Likewise, once all physiological needs are satisfied, they disappear to make way for what Maslow calls safety needs. As pointed out in the previous section, safety needs are strongly related to spatial needs as they involve stability, permanence, and predictability across numerous aspects of human life (e.g., health, family, accommodation, income, and property). Importantly, the need for safety often manifests itself in 'the very common preference for familiar rather than unfamiliar things' (379), a point to which I shall return in the next section.

Provided that physiological and safety needs are met, the need for love, belonging, friendship, affection, and intimate (rather than reproductive) sex will arise. People need to feel part of a group, to communicate and relate to other members of society. By the same token, once the love needs complex is gratified, human beings will seek esteem in the sense of achievement, appreciation, and respect from others. Maslow subdivides these needs into two groups, (1) self-oriented confidence, independence, and freedom, and (2) other-oriented factors such as reputation, attention, recognition, and prestige. The need for self-actualization, finally, concerns individual human abilities, skills, and talents, which contribute significantly to identity formation and give rise to the urge to do what one is made to do—be that playing music, writing novels, or engineering cars.

Beyond the five human needs, Maslow (1943) assumes yet does not go into depth about a set of complementary 'desires' such as that for understanding and knowledge, aesthetic appreciation, and spiritual needs. As we shall see later, it is the latter two in particular that seem to prevail in *SL* avatars.

Fixed though his five-stage model may appear, Maslow himself emphasizes that it cannot be applied with absolute rigidity. He argues that 'the specific form that these needs will take will of course vary from person to person' (383), and that, depending on cultural and social circumstances, some people will intuitively reverse the order of some needs in the hierarchy and, for instance, prioritize self-esteem over love (386). Likewise, surely some higher level needs such as creativity and achievement can—in extreme situations of flow (cf. Csikszentmihalyi 1988)—lead to a (temporary) suspension of lower level needs such as hunger and thirst.

In order to establish what distinguishes avatar needs from human needs, I conducted a survey in *Second Life* in October 2008, which involved 41 short, semi-structured interviews with avatars across a wide range of sims. Most sims came under the categories shopping, hangout, adult, mature, arts and culture, and education, the vast majority being dedicated shopping sims. This distribution seems to reflect the dominant behavioral patterns of *SL* residents, as 'there is in Second Life no more popular activity than shopping' (Linden Lab 2006–08: 63, quoted in Schich and Krämer 2008: 42). I interviewed avatars in English, German, and Spanish, which are the three languages I can converse in. This gave rise to a predictable Anglo-European and American bias, and further studies into the needs of East

Asian, Persian, and Arab avatars, for instance, are needed to complement the findings presented here.

The interviews were loosely structured around my core question, 'what are the most important needs of a *SL* avatar?', and frequently led to follow-on questions such as 'what do they/you need to survive and be happy?'. Figure 8.2 shows the absolute numbers of the most frequently given answers.

According to the interviewees, the most important needs are those for clothes (n = 11), friendship (n = 9), skin (n = 8), looks/beauty/appearance (n = 8), and interaction with others (n = 7). These are followed by the needs for money (n = 5), a house or home (n = 5), physical shape (n = 4), hair (n =4), design and building skills (n = 4), shoes (n = 3), nice character and fair treatment (n = 3), self-customization and self-expression (n = 3), 'nothing' (n = 3), and, further down the line, equality, intelligence and learning skills, comfort, fun, work, and land (all n = 2). Answers given only once were not included in the figure.

Divided into more general needs areas, four prime avatar needs can be identified (see Figure 8.3): aesthetic (42% of all answers), communicative and interpersonal (24% of all answers), material (12% of all answers), and emotional (10% of all answers). Aesthetic needs comprise factors such as beauty and appearance—more generally, clothes, skin, shoes, hair, bags, glamour, fashion, and accessories. Communicative and interpersonal needs involve friendship, communication and interaction with others, nice

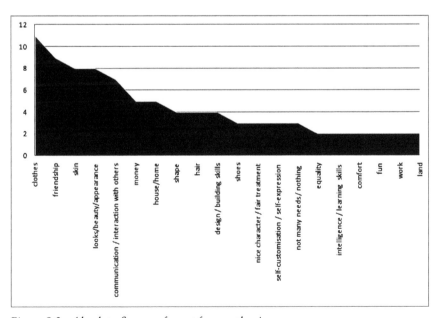

Figure 8.2   Absolute figures of most frequently given answers.

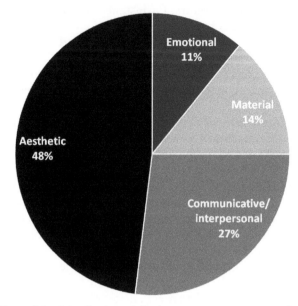

Figure 8.3   Distribution of the four prepotent avatar needs.

character and fair treatment, equality, respect, community, connection with lifetime companion, an *SL* partner, making others happy, and understanding other people's behaviors. Under material needs come proprietary matters such as money, a house or home, land, prims, and life-enhancing assets such as top technology. Emotional needs, finally, include comfort, fun, security and self-protection, spirituality, music, experimenting with others' behavior and feelings, privacy, diversity, realism, and mixing reality with fantasy.

Compared to Maslow's basic needs hierarchy, aesthetic needs, which he considers a higher level desire that goes beyond the five basic needs, seem to be prepotent with *Second Life* avatars. The second basic avatar need, communication and interpersonal exchange, can be compared to Maslow's third level: love and belonging, although some aspects, such as respect and equality, overlap with the esteem level. Material needs may be subsumed under Maslow's second level ('material' safety), and emotional needs combine aspects from levels two ('emotional' safety) and, again, a range of higher level desires such as spirituality, aesthetic (acoustic) pleasure, and entertainment (both benevolent and sadistic, in the case of 'experimenting with others' behaviors and feelings').

Strikingly, the need for emotional safety and privacy may be directly linked to another emotional need occurring in the data, which is that for taking pleasure in exploiting other avatars' emotions. The fact that a number of interviewees emphasized the importance of protecting themselves against abuse by others suggests that an environment that invites experimentation and creativity at numerous levels leads not only to peaceful, aesthetically, and emotionally pleasing artifacts and behaviors but to exploitative, abusive behavior as well.

Given the results of this study,[3] combined with additional observations and logical reasoning, let me now revisit Maslow's hierarchy of basic needs and adapt it to *SL* avatars. Figure 8.4 illustrates this radically transformed pyramid.

At the lowest level, Maslow's physiological needs have been adjusted to meet the requirements of the cybernetic feedback loop, i.e., the circuit integrating the user, the hard and the software, which ultimately enables human-machine interaction. I have called these needs 'cyber-physical' as they involve the physical requirements of having a human 'body'—the player—interacting with the computer. Without these parameters, avatars cannot come into existence in the first place, and they apply in every single instance of entering the virtual environment. In other words, avatar needs are ultimately contingent upon the basic needs and higher level desires of the player in question, which gives rise to a complex dual logic underlying avatar behavior.

Provided all cyber-physical needs are fulfilled, avatars need to be able to navigate the virtual environment successfully. Needs of this second layer can be subsumed under the label creative/heuristic as they involve

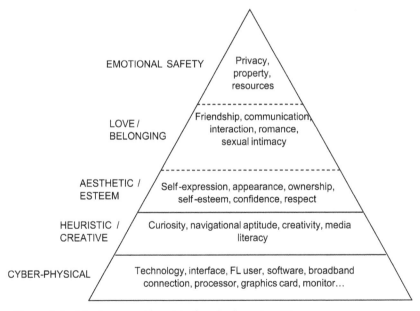

Figure 8.4 Needs pyramid revisited and adapted to *SL* avatars.

activities that help avatars to find their bearings in *SL*. Avatars have to be able to apply a variety of creative heuristic processes in order to learn, for instance, how to move about, to meet and communicate with other avatars, to conduct successful searches, and to obtain, purchase, design, and build objects that will help form their *SL* identities. Furthermore, they have to be sufficiently media-savvy to indulge willingly and proactively in such activities.

Levels one and two of the revisited needs hierarchy were not mentioned explicitly by interviewees, which leads me to assume two things: (1) These needs, as well as their gratification, are taken for granted—much in the same way that most human beings living in developed countries consider the availability of food, drink, and accommodation as a given; and (2) these needs mainly concern the user behind the avatar rather than the avatar itself, although, of course, the same can be said to a certain extent about the remaining three layers as without those needs users would not actually be tempted to embark on any *SL* activities in the first place. Let us therefore assume that the degree of overlap between user and avatar needs is considerably skewed towards the user in the first two needs levels, whereas the needs of the avatar in the sense of the physical re-embodiment of the user in the virtual world are mostly situated within the top three layers of the pyramid.[4]

Level three concerns aesthetic and esteem needs, which came across as closely interrelated in the avatar interviews. In *SL*, physical beauty is an asset that leads to self-confidence and admiration expressed by others explicitly, by means of verbal communication, or implicitly, by signaling respect, interest, and admiration through body language or the mere willingness to interact. An important aspect here is, of course, the fact that the virtual disembodiment and re-embodiment vis-à-vis FL corporeality enables users that are unhappy with their FL physical appearance to design 'perfect' virtual bodies and explore social processes without the perceived lack of attractiveness. Similarly, anecdotal evidence suggests that users spend a significant part of their time in *SL* customizing their avatars' bodies and attire, as avatars 'need' to be physically attractive or salient in other, imaginative ways in order to 'fit in with the crowd'. The psychological implications of material ownership and the ability to 'purchase' the ideal body come into play at this level as well.

The fourth level involves needs related to love and belonging. It is therefore the only category of avatar needs that overlaps almost entirely with one of Maslow's: that for love and belonging. As opposed to FL, family ties in *SL* play a relatively insignificant role although, of course, many an FL couple or family regularly engage in joint *SL* activities. Nevertheless, as revealed in the interviews, making and meeting friends, casual chat and gossip, romance, flirtation, and sexual intimacy constitute far more sought-after activities than cherishing family bonds.

The highest basic needs complex concerns emotional safety, which again is interrelated with the need for love and belonging and, less directly, with esteem needs. (Interpermeability between the three top layers in the pyramid is indicated by dotted lines.) The need for emotional rather than physical safety prevails because avatars are not exposed to the same physical dangers facing human beings. By contrast, integrity of character and fair treatment appear to be of prime importance, as the building of mutual trust is impeded by the scarcity of social cues characteristic of online communication (Walther 1996). Thus, the need for property and related resources directly feeds into the need for privacy and emotional security, for which reasons some (experienced) *SL* residents build fortress-like edifices surrounded with privacy walls to protect themselves from intruders.

The four prepotent needs established in this study translate into *SL* spatial needs as follows. The predominance of aesthetic needs, with a strong focus on 'personal' beauty, allows the assumption that *SL* architecture is strongly inclined towards the facilitation of appearance-related behavior. Indeed, *SL* buildings tend to be commercially oriented in that they offer vast open spaces for the exhibition and acquisition of commercially available objects such as clothes, skin, hair, and accessories. The preponderance of 'adult' sims, in which erotic and/or pornographic artifacts are on offer, underscores this observation. Similarly, a mixture of architectural and horticultural aesthetics can be observed in numerous places, where creative spirits experiment with spatial arrangements appealing to a combination of avatars' aesthetic, emotional, and spiritual needs.

The need for communication and interpersonal exchange is cogently inscribed in the *SL* user interface, which offers a variety of communication channels including instant messaging, voice, and text-based chat. The system sends a visual signal once a 'friend' has either entered or left *SL*, and there are a number of further, paratextual online services, such as mailing lists and blogs, that enable metacommunication at various thematic levels. Furthermore, as I shall elaborate later, seating facilities are crucial, and the ways in which cushions, benches, chairs, as well as the hard- and softscape of landscaping (Tapley 2008: 159) visibly invite communal activities, especially conversation, discussion, and debate, forms one of the most important aspects of *SL* interpersonal architecture.

Material needs are strongly linked to aesthetic needs, and in fact, *Second Life* is first and foremost a platform for buying and selling clothes and other fashion products, as well as for trading and renting land and other property. The *Second Life* website, www.secondlife.com, contains a separate site called 'Land', where regular updates on purchasing and renting land are available, and having an *SL* account 'privileges' residents in terms of enabling them to make commercial transactions of various kinds.

Finally, emotional needs are the most challenging of all four needs complexes highlighted here, not least because they are highly individualized and often difficult to 'guess'. The spatial openness of the *SL* environment makes residents prone to abuse, as it is virtually impossible to avoid or prevent contact with potentially abusive avatars. Privacy restrictions can be employed on privately owned property only, and it is at the discretion of each individual user to intuitively trust or distrust new acquaintances.

Clearly, in relating avatar needs to spatial and, more specifically, architectural phenomena in *SL*, one inadvertently faces the hen-or-egg question: Are those needs created by the affordances of the virtual environment, or are they inherent? As avatars, like their human counterparts, tend to adapt to any given 'liveable' environment, it can be assumed that the former is the case. However, as with the controversy surrounding technical determinism vs. social determinism (the McLuhan-Williams debate, see Lister et al. 2009), I am inclined to think that a mixture of both is indeed happening: that, on the one hand, basic (spatial) needs are both transferred from First Life as quasi-inherent parameters, and, on the other hand, that those transferred expectations are mixed with needs emerging as a result of interacting with the mechanics and affordances of *Second Life*. This ultimately results in a dual semiotic mechanism, which remediates First and Second Life architectural structures in mutually referential processes. I shall return to and elaborate on this issue in the section *Second Life* Architecture and Its Metacommunicative Functions.

ARCHITECTURE IN *SECOND LIFE*: A SOCIAL SEMIOTIC APPROACH

Architecture as Social Semiotic

In this section I adopt a social semiotic approach to *SL* architecture, which is based on Michael O'Toole's (1994, 2004; cf. also Pang 2004 and Alias 2004) application of Michael Halliday's systemic functional grammar to three-dimensional objects. This will inform my discussion of selected *SL* and FL architectural phenomena in light of the aforementioned mixture of First Life and *Second Life* avatar needs.

In his systemic-functional semiotic model of architecture, O'Toole draws on the three metacommunicative functions of language outlined by Michael Halliday (1978): ideational (or 'experiential', which is O'Toole's preferred term), interpersonal, and textual. The ideational function of language lies in its referentiality and relation to extralinguistic objects—its 'lexical content', as it were (O'Halloran 2004: 2). Extended to architecture, this function involves the ways in which buildings are designed to embody and activate certain experiences. According to O'Toole (1994: 86), experiential functions of architecture can be looked at in terms of the building as a whole as well as its diverse sub-units (e.g., floor, room, and smaller elements forming the interior design). They concern the practical functions of a building (e.g., public vs. private, industrial, commercial, agricultural, educational, residential) as well its orientation to light, wind, earth, and service (water, sewage, and power). When applied to the floor level, the experiential function involves matters of access as well as what individual floors are used for, such as labor, trade, administration, storage, parking, waking, or sleeping. At room level, functional uses are even more diverse, as they can range from domestic uses such as cooking, laundry, bathing, playing, and retreat to commercial and administrative uses like restaurants and bars, store departments, and departmental offices. Elements of architectural spaces again relate to the elements in that, for instance, lamps, shades, and curtains control lighting; windows, fans, and conditioning regulate air circulation; central heating, fireplaces, and stoves balance temperatures; carpets, rugs, and partitions muffle sound and noise. Seating furniture offers both comfort and communicative functionality, and tables provide surfaces for eating, drinking, work, and leisure activities.

The interpersonal function of architecture relates to the communicative possibilities and restrictions it offers to its users, as well as the emotions and sensations created in the user whilst interacting with a building. On a macro level, buildings operate interpersonally by their size, verticality, chthonicity, façades, cladding, and color, as well as their orientation to neighbors, the road, and the entrant. At floor level, rooms 'communicate' with their users through ceiling height, spaciousness, accessibility, openness, views, and color. Thus, they express power relations, as well as separation and/or integration of diverse groups of people. Depending on their interior design, rooms may appear comfortable or sterile, modern or traditional, opulent or bare; they come in a variety of designs, such as rustic, pioneer, colonial, suburban, working class, or slum, and may either foreground or background their various functions. Emotive messages are further enhanced by individual elements, which are either relevant or redundant, conventional or surprising, rough or smooth in texture, decorative or plain, stylistically coherent or incoherent, and, in the case of TV sets, radios, and stereo systems, may mediate and project further levels and means of communication.

Finally, the textual function of architecture brings its various systems and units in relation to each other and to surrounding buildings and objects. At building level, architecture is positioned in the context of the surrounding urban, suburban, or rural environment as a whole, which includes adjacent buildings, transport, and road systems, as well as internal aspects such as 'rhythms' (contrasting shapes and angles), surface textures, roof-wall relations, reflectivity, and opacity. Floors have to be seen both in parallel with and in opposition to other floors, as well as surrounding and adjacent rooms, and connecting structures such as corridors, stairs, lifts, and escalators. They contain varying degrees of partitioning, in terms of both amount and permanence of dividing elements. At room level, the design of lighting and sound has a texturing effect, and relations between rooms as well as between 'inside' and 'outside' are indexed by connecting devices such as doors, windows, and hatches. Finally, focal points such as desks, altars, and hearths lend individual rooms a sense orientation, power, and centeredness. The texture of individual elements finally surfaces in furniture finishes and fabrics, as well as their relative positioning to light, heat, ground/floor, and ceiling.

In a recent article, Maree Kristen Stenglin (2009) provides a social semiotic analysis of the Hyde Park Barracks Museum in Sydney. She claims that her approach is ultimately applicable to virtual as well as physical spaces (35), yet she fails to provide any examples to underscore her point. The following section aims to address this lacuna by exploring the extent to which the experiential, interpersonal, and textual functions of architecture can be applied to built spaces in *Second Life*.

Second Life Architecture and Its Metacommunicative Functions

SL territory is structured in terms of a grid system. Every section of this grid, called 'sim' (short for 'simulation'), is hosted by one server and covers 256 m² (Schich and Krämer 2008: 33). Sims can be purchased, rented, sold, and auctioned, thus forming one of the major income sources in *SL*. Sims are there to be developed and built upon, and depending on population figures the number and variety of physical objects to be found in individual sims can be considerable. There is no such thing as town-planning or building restrictions: within the technological restrictions of *SL* (max. 15,000 prims per sim, see Schich and Krämer 2008: 33), architectural and other design ideas may unfold virtually without limits.

SL architecture includes both built and natural environments. As a result, natural spaces—in the sense of pristine wildernesses—do not exist. Untouched land is rendered in terms of flat, barren surfaces, and the generally thin population of *SL* further indexes the creative appeal communicated by them. The absence of nature as an independent, dynamic, and potentially destructive force entails that every sensory object in *SL* has a function bestowed upon it by one or many of its millions of residents. In other words, every perceivable object in *SL* underlies the ideological agendas of its maker, which renders *SL* a uniquely rich social semiotic environment.

Both natural and built environments are created from 'prims', which are primitive three-dimensional geometric shapes, such as (half) boxes, (half) cylinders, (half) prisms, (half) cones, (half) spheres, toruses, tubes, and rings. The 'metaverse' (cf. Stephenson 1992) that is created through them is mostly urban, although a multitude of dedicated horticultural spaces exist, which are mixed with, embedded in, and laid out around 'built' structures (see Joseph Clark's chapter in this volume). As a matter of fact, the ontological and interactional make-up of *SL* does not necessitate a division between open and closed, natural and human-made environments. In other words, the absence of meteorological and geo-physical factors, of (extreme) weather conditions, temperatures, and climate zones, as well as life-threatening geological processes such as earthquakes, tsunamis, avalanches, and rock slides leaves avatar-built architecture categorically unexposed to earthly erosion and damage.[5]

Turning back to O'Toole's social semiotic approach to analyzing architecture, the following comparisons can be drawn between FL and *SL* built spaces. The interpersonal and textual functions of architecture remain largely the same, whereas the experiential function shows considerable differences. As outlined previously, the experiential function of architecture puts buildings and their sub-systems in relation to the elements (light, wind, earth, heat, water) and the natural resources required by developed societies (power, water supplies, sewage, oil and gas). The parameters given by Linden Lab are radically different. There is indeed a day cycle, which consists of Sunrise, Noon, Sunset, and Midnight (Tapley 2008: 167). But the Terrain tab in the World > Region/Estate menu allows users to 'Fix the Sun' at any point during the four sun phases, thus abandoning the 'natural' day cycle. This allows users to modify lightness levels permanently and to create a variety of emotive effects, such as the eerie atmosphere of a gothic castle (Tapley 2008: 167–69).

As pointed out previously, temperatures and aggregate states are non-existent, and gravity exists at a reduced level, which allows objects to float in mid-air and avatars to fly like birds. There is sufficient gravitation to maintain the 'top' and 'bottom' of buildings and avatars although, clearly, the sense of chthonicity perceived in FL is significantly reduced in *SL*. Power and water supplies, including indicators of excretion and sewage, are therefore of a mostly cosmetic rather than vital quality, and toilets in particular cannot be read in any other way than satirically.

Leaving aside those experiential functions that are aligned to the elements, *SL* buildings do of course have 'practical' (O'Toole 1994) experiential functions, such as public/private, educational, entertainment, and commercial. These functions, albeit not always immediately obvious from the visible design, are commonly reflected in the category labels assigned by land and property owners. That said, category labels (e.g., educational, shopping, hangout, mature) are hardly fluid or comprehensive enough to capture the full range of uses *SL* buildings tend to be designed for and put to, and interior and exterior designs often change with the avatars interacting with them.

Due to the fact that otherwise essential experiential architectural functions are suspended in *SL*, particular semiotic, creative, and artistic emphasis can be placed on interpersonal and textual functions. The need for emotional safety, for instance, is reflected in *SL* architectural idiosyncrasies such as air-born Skyboxes, underground dungeons, and underwater dwellings (cf. Tapley 2008: 130). The observation that '"Oceanfront" property is always in demand' (Tapley 2008: 146) again suggests the need for privacy, but equally that for aesthetic appearance and a romantic atmosphere. In terms of architectural textuality, Rebecca Tapley (2008: 164) distinguishes between 'IC' ('in character'), meaning consistent in style, and 'OOC' ('out of character'), meaning a mix of styles, the choice between which lies with the individual *SL* resident. She advocates, however, 'neighborly consideration' as '[r]esidents of Second Life who gravitate toward themed areas really want to lose themselves in whatever the particular, fantastical time, place, or situation may be' (Tapley 2008: 164). Similarly, users are well advised to keep adjoining areas as non-interruptive as possible, which reflects both interpersonal and textual concerns.

Although there exists no agency or institution in *SL* that regulates urban planning and design, certain unwritten rules, or norms, apply within the *SL* community. These norms, or 'expectations' (Tapley 2008: 176), are partly rooted in users' FL experiences of urban, suburban, and rural areas and have a normative impact on the creative possibilities offered by *SL*. Thus, FL textual norms recur in *SL* in terms of the way in which buildings relate to each other functional and visual design (Tapley 2008: 176), as well as orientation to road (cf. O'Toole 1994). FL interpersonal norms recur in aspects of accessibility, wayfinding, and navigability (Tapley 2008: 176), or orientation to entrant (O'Toole 1994); and in terms of the ways in and frequency at which buildings invite certain types of interaction and participation. Finally, the way *SL* buildings are designed often signals their intended practical-experiential functions (O'Toole 1994). The most salient examples of how 'predictable' (Tapley 2008: 177) activities are semiotically inscribed in *SL* interiors are shopping precincts and fashion stores as they foreground the objects of their intended user interaction and provide views unrestricted by roofs and walls. Other sims and *SL* buildings allow for more 'spontaneous' (Tapley 2008: 177) participation, inviting users to explore their contents via their context-sensitive pie menus.

To conclude this section, every 'built space' is a translation of its individual designer-creator's inherent aesthetic, communicative, and functional agenda. As my following analysis will show, such agendas are not simply derivations of avatar needs but representations of a more complex semiotic system that works as an extension of First Life in the virtual world (cf. Tapley 2008: 176, Rosca 2008: 113) but also combines a variety of creative, *SL*-needs-based approaches to virtual architecture.

Remediating First Life Architecture: Mediating between Physical and Virtual Spaces

In video games, which include both offline, single-player, and online, multiplayer environments, spatial phenomena usually work in a mimetic way. They are 'hybrid' (Gerosa 2008: 51), 'scripted spaces' (Klein 2004, quoted in Harry et al. 2008: 65), i.e., narrative devices which are 'almost always more or less concealed references to the aesthetics of the real world [. . .] [and] not yet liberated from references to the history of architecture'

(Gerosa 2008: 51). This makes perfect sense in pre-scripted rule-governed ludic environments, which limit player agency and creativity so as to make them act within the given spatio-temporal boundaries. Players do not normally get involved in designing spatial objects; even in so-called 'creative games' (e.g., The Game Creators' 2001 *3D Gamemaker*) they are merely given choices between ready-made characters, objects, and environments. It is part of video games' immersive quality that players delve into artificial worlds emulating the physical world, as the willing suspension of disbelief causes them to believe that the symbolic nature of spatio-temporality in the game stands for the actual. Notably, this happens in environments 'where none of the utilitarian functions—protection from the elements, air circulation, seating, etc.—have any relevance. [Those] symbolic functions bring legibility to what could otherwise be an incomprehensible abstract space' (Harry et al. 2008: 65).

Second Life, on the other hand, is not a video game but an inherently open-ended virtual community that invites users to design and create new structures, practices, and environments, as well as to make their own rules about how to interact with one another in particular socially determined situations and locations. For instance, in Luskwood, a furry-themed sim,[6] any non-furry avatar is likely to feel like an outsider although, interestingly, Luskwood residents do not tend to actively discriminate against non-furries but indeed invite non-furry residents to attend special events held on the island (Carr and Pond 2007: 85).

In the open, creative environment offered by *Second Life*, spaces serve as 'projection surfaces for spatial ideas that are not realizable in the physical world' (von Borries and Böttger 2008: 59). In fact, it may seem peculiar that, given avatar needs as discussed in the section Human vs. Avatar Needs, distinctly 'First Life' architectural phenomena such as sloping roofs or bridges spanning crevices are ubiquitous. After all, the physical quality, i.e., the wetness, of rainfall, which makes it 'run off' uneven surfaces or otherwise form potentially dangerous puddles on people's rooftops, is suspended in virtual worlds. By the same token, *Second Life* avatars do not physically require 'paths' of any kind leading from, to, and between locations—flying is considerably quicker and provides a better spatial overview over the territory at hand.

Indeed, what *SL* architectural practice shows is 'a new form of ideal architecture', which combines forms reminiscent of the material world with an innovative, experimental style inspired by the parameters of virtual worlds (Gerosa 2008: 53; see Doesinger 2008 for a discussion of the First Annual Architecture and Design Competition in *Second Life*). From the vantage point of media history, this dual process of indexing traditional forms and, simultaneously, creating new structures can be described in terms of remediation (cf. Heilesen 2009). According to Bolter and Grusin (1999), remediation is a common semiotic and functional process that works both ways whenever a new technology is introduced:

'Old media' structures are adopted and partly adjusted, or 'refashioned', and it is only gradually that medium-specific, new forms begin to evolve and replace 'old' forms. Simultaneously, 'old media' 'refashion themselves' (Bolter and Grusin 1999: 15) by beginning to exhibit structures borrowed from 'new media', thus adapting to newly emerging needs and merging with new technologies. This mutual refashioning process surfaces in contemporary physical and virtual architecture. Indeed, I would argue that specific SL affordances such as the ability to fly and the defiance of gravity more generally have been part of pioneering architectural agendas for a long time—predating by far the popularization of virtual environments in the first decade of the 21st century.

As discussed previously, examples of remediating physical architecture in SL abound. The predominance of chairs and other seating furniture, combined with the ubiquitous 'sit' button, is just one example. Clearly, avatars are not subjected to the human physiological need to sit in order to rest or to avoid exertion by standing up over long periods of time. That said, chairs are 'rich social objects' (Harry et al. 2008: 70) which have a number of communicative, interpersonal functions. In contrast to the 'transient' (Harry et al. 2008: 70) impression given by standing up, sitting on a chair indexes commitment to the location and any habitual or temporary social practices associated with it. Chairs further signal certain types of social order, communicative situations, and power hierarchies—through the ways in which they are arranged, for instance in a circle, in rows, or in rectangular form, with two 'heads'. According to Harry et al. (2008: 70), '[t]his [communicative] richness makes chairs one of the most socially successful objects in Second Life'.

A second example are buildings that seem to be exact replica of First Life residential homes, with sloping roofs, stairs leading up to entrances, outdoor lighting to prevent tripping, and (smoking) chimneys. Figure 8.5 exhibits some such characteristics—including a traditional half-timbered cladding—yet combines them with a distinct SL location. Built on a steep hillside, it ridicules the laws of FL nature, as a house built in a similar FL environment would never receive planning permission. The meteorological impossibility of a nocturnal rainbow further enhances the surrealism of this particular location.

As the physical constraints that FL architecture is subjected to categorically prevent the transfer of many virtual mechanisms, locations, and structures into physical ones (such as reduced gravitational forces), it is less straightforward to find examples of FL architecture 'refashioning itself' (cf. Bolter and Grusin 1999). That said, the dream of defying gravity, of abandoning chthonic constraints, and of simulating natural processes has preoccupied architects around the world for a long time. American architect Lebbeus Woods's Aerial Paris (1989), for instance, incorporates its creator's radically experimental philosophy, which seeks to innovate spatial thinking within the confines of the laws of nature.

Figure 8.5   FL characteristics in *SL* residential architecture but distinct *SL* location.

Aerial Paris is a speculative 'creation of a community in the air of France [. . .] [in which] [r]esidential areas levitate due to opposing magnetic forces in Earth's electromagnetic field' (Smith 2004), and the fact that Woods uses earth-bound building materials such as wood, metals, and fabric enhances the paradoxical effect it has on the onlooker. To provide another 'historical' example, American architect Buckminster Fuller's idea of 'cloud nines', or floating geodesic spheres (cf. for instance the Eden Project), is based on the speculation that given a considerable diameter and a certain amount of warm air inside such a sphere, the construction will start to float.[7]

In view of climate change and rising sea levels, a group of Dutch architects have recently started designing 'amphibious' buildings, which can float on water (Palca 2008). Some of these houses, which are built on poles to keep the buildings on an even level as water levels rise, already exist in Maasbommel, Holland, and further projects, which increasingly resemble *SL* floating houses, are in planning.

A similarly water-bound yet ecologically negligent project is 'The World', which is currently being constructed off the coast of Dubai. The visionary insular layout resembles *SL* sims, and 'The World', in combination with textually related terraforming projects developed by Nakheel in the Arabian Gulf (e.g., Palm Jumeirah), further enhances the luxurious, quasi-synthetical, seemingly spotless atmosphere communicated by Dubai's ambitious architectural projects of the past two decades.

Finally, the winning proposal for the Guggenheim Hermitage Museum at Vilnius by Zaha Hadid Architects shows a yet unforeseen degree of aerodynamic design that embodies Hadid's preferred concepts of velocity, fluidity, and lightness. The dynamic effect communicated by the design renders the building virtually weightless, like a 'mystical object floating above the extensive artificial landscape strip, seemingly defying gravity by exposing dramatic undercuts towards the surrounding entrance plazas. Large activated green fields flow around the museums sculptural mass, underlining its enigmatic presence with curvilinear lines echoing the elongated contours of the building' (archiCentral 2009).

As the preceding examples have demonstrated, the remediation of FL and *SL* architecture takes place bi-directionally. Numerous examples can be found that demonstrate that *SL* is used as an extension of FL concepts, as architectural concepts that are demanded by FL natural laws are swiftly copied and pasted into *SL* sims in seemingly unreflected ways. The redundancies created by this phenomenon render *SL* as a hybrid architectural environment, which in some instances appears almost reluctant to relinquish FL concepts in favor of a more creative, exploratory *SL* dynamic. By the same token, *SL* affordances such as gravity defiance and the dissociation of architecture from its chthonic constraints began to be reflected in FL architectural visions and practices far earlier than the popularization of *SL* and other virtual worlds commenced, and architects continue to design forward-thinking projects, particularly in view of climate change and, paradoxically or not, of the contemporaneous increase in aesthetic-luxurious ambitions occurring in select areas around the globe.

CONCLUSION

This chapter has shown how the results of a survey into the needs of *SL* avatars compare with observable architectural phenomena in *SL*. Based on the insights delivered by a series of semi-structured interviews, I have revisited Maslow's basic needs hierarchy and established that, in addition to vital cyber-physical and heuristic-creative needs, *SL* avatar needs tend to be situated either at the top of or indeed beyond Maslow's basic needs. Respondents mostly mentioned aesthetic and esteem needs, followed by love and belonging and emotional safety.

The second part of this study introduced a social semiotic approach to *SL* architecture. Addressing a lacuna indicated by Stenglin (2009), I examined the extent to which O'Toole's (1994) three metacommunicative architectural functions translate into a virtual environment where 'earthly' phenomena such as the elements, aggregate states, physical illness, and gravitation are either suspended or significantly reduced. My conclusion was that, whereas the interpersonal and textual functions readily apply to *SL* structures, the experiential function needs to be qualified.

Lastly, I explored Bolter and Grusin's concept of remediation in the context of *SL* architecture and demonstrated, on the one hand, how *SL* architecture refashions FL architecture. On the other, I mentioned a number of past and present FL architectural projects to demonstrate that attempts at defying 'earthly' limits such as gravity and chthonicity are not necessarily inspired by the recent popularization of virtual worlds but indeed date back far longer.

In view of the empirical results of this study, the question arises as to why comparatively little architectural advantage has been taken of the innovative, experimental potential offered by *Second Life*. As award-winning German architect Stephan Schütt argues,

> the developers of Second Life are running behind the possibilities [warranted by contemporary digital technologies]. After all, they have to construct something that doesn't overstretch First Life users' abilities or imaginative powers; something users can comprehend and doesn't entirely wear out their habitual ways of seeing. *Second Life* imitates First Life and adds a few pretty accessories. [...] In my view, *Second Life* phenomena fall significantly behind the possibilities afforded by the digital medium. They ultimately serve the ancient dreams of humankind: the ability to fly and eternal youth. Today's architects' virtual thinking reaches far beyond what *Second Life* can offer.[8]

In view of these expert remarks, it remains to be seen whether *SL* can indeed serve as a breeding ground for new architectural ideas (cf. Doesinger 2008), or whether the 3D systems specifically developed by and for pioneering architects will indeed circumvent, replace, and ultimately outlive popular virtual worlds and their apparent creative affordances.

NOTES

1. For a poster discussing selected aspects of this chapter, see Ensslin and Muse (2009).
2. According to Maslow, '[h]omeostasis refers to the body's automatic efforts to maintain a constant, normal state of the blood stream' (1943: 372).
3. As hinted previously, more empirical research is needed to further qualify, quantify, and diversify the results obtained in this study.
4. Needless to say that, as re-embodiment of the user, the avatar ultimately carries aspects of though not the totality of the user's overall cognitive, emotional, and spiritual disposition.
5. It has to be noted that all these meteorological and geological processes can indeed be programmed and enacted in *SL*. They do not, however, have any life-threatening impact and therefore serve as mere performances of natural spectacles. In fact, a wide range of natural disasters are deliberately staged

by *SL* residents to draw attention to FL environmental problems (cf. Clark's chapter in this volume).
6. Furries are 'anthropomorphic animal character[s]' (Carr and Pond 2007:52) in *SL*.
7. I would like to thank Stephan Schütt for his helpful comments and suggestions regarding this section.
8. Personal email correspondence between Schütt and the author, 29 June 2009 (translation mine). Stephan Schütt's award-winning Microsoft Rheinau Art-Office building along the River Rhine at Cologne can be viewed at http://www.nemetschek.co.uk/de/pdf.nsf/unternehmen/microsoft_rheinauartoffice_koeln_d.pdf/$file/microsoft_rheinauartoffice_koeln_d.pdf (accessed 29 June 2009).

REFERENCES

Alias, S (2004) A semiotic study of Singapore's Orchard Road and Marriott Hotel. In *Multimodal discourse analysis: Systemic-functional perspectives*, ed. KL O'Halloran, 55–79. London: Continuum.
archiCentral (2009) Guggenheim Hermitage Museum // Vilnius // Lithuania // Zaha Hadid Architects, archicentral.com, 9 June 2009. Online. Available HTTP: http://www.archicentral.com/guggenheim-hermitage-museum-vilnius-lithuania-zaha-hadid-architects-10705/ (accessed 2 July 2009).
Ardrey, R (1967) *The territorial imperative: A personal inquiry into the animal origins of property and nations*. London: Collins.
Bolter, JD and R Grusin (1999) *Remediation: Understanding new media*. Cambridge, MA: MIT Press.
Carr, P and G Pond (2007) *The unofficial tourists' guide to Second Life*. London: Boxtree.
Csikszentmihalyi, M (1988) *Optimal experience: Psychological studies of flow in consciousness*. Cambridge and New York: Cambridge University Press.
Doesinger, S (2008) Exploring a new concept of inside and outside and what it means to be virtually home! In *Space between people: How the virtual changes physical architecture*, ed. S Doesinger, 12–23. Munich: Prestel.
Ensslin, A and E Muse (2009) Creating spaces for virtual communities: The role of architecture in Second Life. Poster given at *MeCCSA 2009*, Bradford, 14–16 January 2009. Online. Available HTTP: http://www.bangor.ac.uk/creative_industries/documents/slposter.pdf (accessed 2July 2009).
The Game Creators (2001) *3D Gamemaker*. PC DVD. Rugeley: Focus Multimedia Ltd.
Gerosa, M (2008) Degrees of virtualization. In *Space between people: How the virtual changes physical architecture*, ed. S Doesinger, 46–55. Munich: Prestel.
Goffman, E (1959) *The presentation of self in everyday life*. London: Penguin.
Halliday, MAK (1978) *Language as a social semiotic: The social interpretation of language and meaning*. London: Edward Arnold.
Harry, D, D Offenhuber, and J Donath (2008) The social role of virtual architecture. In *Space between people: How the virtual changes physical architecture*, ed. S Doesinger, 64–70. Munich: Prestel.
Heilesen, S (2009) Teleporting the library? *Journal of Gaming and Virtual Worlds* 1, no. 2.
Klein, N (2004) *The Vatican to Vegas: The history of special effects*. New York: The New Press.
Lawson, B (2001) *The language of space*. Amsterdam: Architectural Press.

Linden Lab (2003–09) *Second Life.* Online. Available HTTP: http://secondlife.
com (accessed 2 June 2009).
———. (2006–08) *SLHandbook.* Online. Available HTTP: http://www.slhand-
book.com (accessed 29 June 2009).
Lister, M, J Dovey, S Giddings, I Grant, and K Kelly (2009) *New media: A critical
introduction,* 2nd ed. London: Routledge.
Markus, T (1993) *Buildings and power: Freedom and control in the origin of modern building.* London: Routledge.
Maslow, A (1943) A theory of human motivation. *Psychological Review* 50, no.
4: 370–96.
O'Halloran, KL (2004) Introduction. In *Multimodal discourse analysis: Systemic-
functional perspectives,* ed. KL O'Halloran, 1–7. London: Continuum.
O'Toole, M (1994) *The language of displayed art.* London: Leicester University
Press.
———. (2004) Opera ludentes: The Sydney Opera House at work and play. In
Multimodal discourse analysis: Systemic-functional perspectives, ed. KL
O'Halloran, 11–27. London: Continuum.
Palca, J (2008) Dutch architects plan for a floating future. npr.org, 28 January
2008. Online. Available HTTP: http://www.npr.org/templates/story/story.
php?storyId=18480769&ps=bb1 (accessed 2 July 2009).
Pang, KMA (2004) Making history in *From Colony to Nation*: A multimodal
analysis of a museum exhibition in Singapore. In *Multimodal discourse analy-
sis: Systemic-functional perspectives,* ed. KL O'Halloran, 28–54. London:
Continuum.
Proshansky, HM, WH Ittleson, and LG Rivlin (eds) (1970) *Environmental psychology: Man and his physical setting.* New York: Holt Rinehart Winston.
Rosca, A (2008) Immaginaria. In *Space between people: How the virtual changes
physical architecture,* ed. S Doesinger, 113. Munich: Prestel.
Schich, M and S Krämer (2008) How simple life deconstructs utopia. In *Space
between people: How the virtual changes physical architecture,* ed. S Doesinger,
30–45. Munich: Prestel.
Smith, K (2004) Lebbeus Woods's fascinating work at the Carnegie. *The Carnegie Pulse,* 23 September 2004. Online. Available HTTP: http://www.tcpulse.
com/2004/09/23/ac/ledduswoods/ (accessed 2 July 2009).
Stenglin, MK (2009) Space odyssey: Towards a social semiotic model of three-
dimensional space. *Visual Communication* 8, no. 1: 35–64.
Stephenson, N (1992) *Snow crash.* New York: Bantam Books.
Tapley, R (2008) *Designing your second life: Techniques and inspiration for you to
design your ideal parallel universe within the online community, Second Life.*
Berkeley, CA: New Riders.
von Borries, F and M Böttger (2008) Seduction and false promises in Ludic City.
In *Space between people: How the virtual changes physical architecture,* ed. S
Doesinger, 56–63. Munich: Prestel.
Walther, JB (1996) Computer-mediated communication: Impersonal, interper-
sonal, and hyperpersonal interaction. *Communication Research* 23: 3–43.

9 The Event of Space
Defining Place in a Virtual Landscape

Eben Muse

INTRODUCTION: SPACE AND PLACE

> But what is special about place is precisely that throwntogetherness, the unavoidable challenge of negotiating a here-and-now (itself drawing on a history and a geography of thens and theres); and a negotiation which must take place within and between both human and nonhuman. This in no way denies a sense of wonder . . .
>
> Doreen Massey (2005: 140)

Space and place are fundamental to the experience of interactive fiction, virtual realities, and computer games. In casual speech, both these terms are used almost interchangeably. Yet, as Yi-Fu Tuan points out, they connote distinct experiences.

> 'Space' and 'place' are familiar words denoting common experiences. We live in space. There is no space for another building on the lot. The Great Plains look spacious. Place is security, space is freedom: we are attached to the one and long for the other. There is no place like home. What is home? It is the old homestead, the old neighbourhood, hometown or motherland. Geographers study places. Planners would like to evoke 'a sense of place'. (Tuan 1977: 3)

Tuan seems to suggest that space is the larger material within which place can exist. An architect creates place out of space by using walls to create a void where none existed before his borders. A child creates a place out of space by hiding behind the sofa and reading a book. Anita Leirfall takes the point further, arguing that place can never exist independently of its spatial origin (quoted in Aarseth 2007: 44). Place, she argues, is fundamentally spatial and visual; it is described as though it were carved out of space.

Landscape artists working with paint and canvas use the space of the frame to compose a landscape: effectively creating an ideological 'place' out of 'space'. The painter or architect of a virtual world, on the other hand, has no frame to work with when creating a place. The audience for virtual worlds (in games or other environments) effectively crawls through the frame and explores the world in any manner they see fit, from any perspective and to any purpose. The term 'effectively' is used with caution here, because the viewer of these virtual landscapes is always the subject of an illusion of dimensionality, of deep space which does not exist.

It is this effect of space and place which this chapter will try to explore. The assumptions within traditional discourse in visual art regarding perspective, frame, fore-, middle-, and background no longer work as they once did, because the viewer can move through the landscape. The logic and effect of this experience may be discussed in terms of the graphic technology behind it, but this provides a limited source of debate that is constantly pushed out of date as graphic technology develops. This chapter considers a spatial-temporal model that builds space and place out of experience and design. It explores the possibility that, like the physical space described by Massey earlier, space of a virtual world is created by events, rather than being merely a location where events occur.

AURAL SPACE

One way to avoid the issue of the spatialisation of space and place is to shut our eyes and listen, following the lead of R. Murray Schafer in his study of aural landscapes, *The Soundscape*. Schafer attempts to classify the parts of the environment created by sound and identifies three aspects of what he refers to as the 'soundscape': keynote sounds, soundmarks, and sound signals. He adapts the concept of the keynote from musical composition:

> Keynote is a musical term; it is the note that identifies the key or tonality of a particular composition. It is the anchor or fundamental tone and although the material may modulate around it, often obscuring its importance, it is in reference to this point that everything else takes on its special meaning. (Schafer 1994: 9)

Sound mark and sound signal are categories of sound which demarcate places. Schafer describes a soundmark (a reference to the more traditional, and typically visual, landmark) as a sound that gives a place its unique identity. The sound may be unique to that place, but is more likely to be unique in its relation to other sounds and to the listener. The sound of a village bell ringing out the hour might be a soundmark, indicating for some traveler that he or she has arrived home.

The second demarcation sound is the sound signal; less emotive than the soundmark, sound signal has a specific message to convey—a police whistle, for instance, or a teacher's instruction. Clearly these two categories are defined only indistinctly. The ringing bell signals time; the teacher's instruction denotes a location. Schafer further distinguishes them by stressing that a soundmark is a 'community sound & specially regarded or noticed by the people in that community' (274); it is essentially emotive in character. Sound signals, in contrast, are 'listened to consciously' (275) and have a strong cognitive element. However he continues to group them together in opposition to keynote. He relates the terms to the visual equivalents of figure and background, defining figure as the soundmark or sound signal, background as the keynote. The same sound may be a keynote, a soundmark or a sound signal, depending on the context and the listener.

> Whether a sound is figure or ground has partly to do with acculturation . . . , partly with the individual's state of mind . . . , and partly with the individual's relation to the field. . . . It has nothing to do with the physical dimensions of the sound. (Schafer 1994: 152)

In the acoustic environment, sounds shift between soundmarks and sound signals as their cognitive and emotive loads shift. Soundmarks are more highly emotive, while sound signals are cognitive. This subjective aspect means they must also shift according to the listener (the walker, the kayaker, and so on). It is the relation between sounds and listeners that define the marks and signals. For the purpose of this chapter, and to account for this mutability, both marks and signals will be subsumed into a category of placemark. This will also expand its use beyond the aural. A placemark may be a sound, but it may as likely be a visible landmark, such as a tree, a cliff, or a no trespassing sign.

A PLACE: RIVER WALK

> As I walk down a riverbank, I identify a number of places—sunlit spots, places with a rock to sit on, and a place with a view of the rapids. They are spatially delimited and defined by the borders that arise along the river. When I close my eyes and listen, the change is subtle (apart from the increased danger of walking into the river). The sound of running water is a constant (a keynote). At some points the sound becomes stronger as the rapids rise to denote sections of the river (soundmarks). For paddlers (who also create soundmarks as they paddle or shout), the sound of rapids is more likely to be a sound signal, warning of faster or rockier water ahead. Other sounds are even more highly cognitively loaded, as in a sudden whistle or a call of 'watch out!' as I nearly step off the bank and into the water.

In a soundscape the distinction between space and place quickly dissolves into 'ghostlier demarcations' (to borrow a phrase from Wallace Stevens's poem 'The Ideal of Order at Key West' (1990: 128)). Sounds are rarely cut off the way visuals are, so moving from place to place is a gradual change.

As I walk down the riverbank, I do not cross clearly demarcated aural borders; sound fades away gradually instead of stopping suddenly. I cannot cross a wall of sound. Visually, in contrast, I constantly move from one visibly demarcated location to another; I literally cross from one side of a wall to another, and the visual landmark marks out the territory.

If I view my riverbank from the vantage of a moving car or a local hillside, these visible demarcations of place may blur and blend together. The visible distinctions dissolve as did the aural ones. I continue, however, to note the clear demarcation of visible place: Instead of places along a riverbank I perceive a riverbank in a landscape, visibly marked out by the ribbon of moving water or the lush growth that rises beside rivers. The riverbank place has subsumed the places along the riverbank. De Certeau describes a similar effect as he looks down on New York City from the top of the World Trade Center; it is what he describes as 'the imaginary totalizations produced by the eye' (1984: 93).

Aural distinctions dissolve because sound is intrinsically temporal. Every sound has properties of amplitude, frequency, and duration, the latter two making sense only temporally. Although digital sound is recorded in slices (the numerical value of the sound's amplitude is recorded at regular intervals, typically 44,000 times per second for music), none of those slices has any qualitative value on its own. The amplitude must be played back at the correct frequency over a period of time before the sound comes into being as a recognizable artifact.

Visuals are also sliced (see Figure 9.1). Unlike a sound slice, the visual slice continues to be a cohesive, meaningful artifact that exists outside of the temporal. Visual representations do not require time in order to be understood.

Figure 9.1   Visuals are also sliced: E. Muybridge, 'The Horse in Motion', c. 1878.

When Eadweard Muybridge produced his first sequential images of a running horse in 1878, his achievement was to be the first to capture slices of the visible world. At the time, he was described as having found a way to make 'time stand still' (Solnit 2004: 196). The frames in a film strip can be viewed individually laid out in sequence on a page and still tell their story; frames can be dropped at random and the story remains the same. A screenshot of a location or event in a game is used to illustrate the game at a moment in the gameplay; screenshots, in fact, are commonly used to advertise games. To claim the ability to slice space is to assume that space is in some sense immutable; that a photo can indeed capture a moment encourages the viewer to define the moment as primarily visual and spatial. The photograph defines place as moment and moment as place, both of them expressible by the visible referent. Social geographer Doreen Massey, calling for a 'reimagination of things as processes' (20), argues that such a conflation inherently misrepresents what it attempts to illustrate.

> Space conquers time by being set up as the representation of history/ life/the real world. On this reading space is an order imposed upon the inherent life of the real. (Spatial) order obliterates (temporal) dislocation. Spatial immobility quietens temporal becoming. It is, though, the most dismal of pyrrhic victories. For in the very moment of its conquering triumph 'space' is reduced to stasis. The very life, and certainly the politics, is taken out of it. (Massey 1994: 30)

Such an argument leads back to sound as a potential model for avoiding this spatio-temporal conflict. Although sound is spatial (sound changes as it moves through the physical world; we can identify the location of sounds), it is also bound in and by time.

A PLACE: *PRINCE OF PERSIA*

> In the virtual world experienced through *Prince of Persia* (Ubisoft 2008), the Prince emerges from the canyons into a desert landscape. A sudden release from the claustrophobic canyon walls, the spacious desert extends to distant mountains on one side and to a crumbling temple on another. The colour palette of the landscape is muted but the detail is sharply textured as though drawn in pastel pencils; the visual quality of this desert is very similar to that of the canyon. Although the temple in which the princess disappeared dominates the horizon, the desert itself is largely defined by its spatial emptiness—a large, sandy void. Nothing happens here; the prince meets no one here.

Prince of Persia (Ubisoft 2008) uses a specific and identifiable visual style which distinguishes it from other games, although it retains a noticeable similarity to those which also use the Scimitar game engine, such as *Assassin's Creed* (Ubisoft 2007). It is a style defined by colour palette, use of texture and paint technique, and by style of drawing for characters and locations. This visual style remains consistent throughout the game, although the colour palette and lighting effects may change in different sections. In Schafer's soundscape model, the background sound, the one that is not always noticed because it is fundamental to the experience, is the keynote.

> Even though the keynote sounds may not always be heard consciously, the fact that they are ubiquitously there suggests the possibility of a deep and pervasive influence on our behavior and moods. The keynote sounds of a given place are important because they help to outline the character of men living among them. (Schafer 1994: 9)

In a virtual world like *Prince of Persia*, the keynote partly equates with the game engine (in the case of *Prince of Persia* that engine is Scimitar), the technological background to game design which controls the visuals, functions, and logic of the game world.

The keynote also includes the game's rule set, created partly by the game engine but also by the game designers who create a set of social rules and physical rules that regulate the background space of this world. The Prince, for instance, is physically unable to dig; therefore the sand of this desert, which in another virtual space might encourage a player to explore beneath, here remains decorative, signifying little and not affecting play beyond creating a space to pass through. The social rules of the game mean that the Prince must remain with the Princess (she has by now disappeared into the entrance of the temple); the intrinsic interest of this place is therefore reduced again (and that of the temple increased). A player may choose to explore the area, but by this point in the gameplay he or she will know that they should be heading for the temple; those distant mountains are most likely illusions (within this computer-illusion of a world).

The social rules which dictate personalities also add to the keynote. The way the game defines the gender of Prince and Princess and the nature of their relationship sets a tone for much of the experience of this world. Part of what differentiates the sense of this place from the physical world beyond the game machine is that, in this reality, a certain type of stereotype (in this case a gender stereotype) is proven true. This, again, is part of the un-noticed background that defines all else.

Espen Aarseth argues that these 'background' rules (which he terms 'automatic rules') are the defining element of computer game worlds because they make virtual space different from real space:

> Drawing on both Leirfall and Lefebvre, I will posit spatial representation of space that is not in itself spatial, but symbolic and rule-based.

The nature of space is not revealed in this separation, and the resulting product, while fabricating a spatial representation, in fact uses the reduction as a means to achieve the object of gameplay, since the difference between the spatial representation and real space is what makes gameplay-by-automatic-rule possible. In real space, there would be no automatic rules, only social rules and physical laws. (Aarseth 2001: 45)

It may be worth querying this definition of space (both real and virtual). Aarseth uses the already classic game *Myst* (Miller and Miller 1993) to posit that the utilitarian basis for game space means it cannot be a real place.

The landscape in Myth, for all its initial beauty, and as all computer game landscapes, merely looks like a landscape, but is really a three-dimensional scheme carefully designed to offer a balanced challenge to the player. (Aarseth 2007: 168)

I would argue that both the form of the landscape and its origin are of less significance than our mediated experience of it. Presence is frequently described as the experience of 'being there' (Goffman 1974; Pinchbeck and Stevens 2005; Lombard and Ditton 1997; Heeter 1992; Jacobson 2002; Rettie 2004, Seegert 2009). Following Rettie's lead, we can use Goffman's (1974) theory of framing to refine this definition further:

If presence is 'being there', involvement relates to 'being' and the frame explains what is meant by 'there', it defines the situation or environment. The term 'involvement' is not used in the sense of interest in the content of an experience, but to describe the allocation of attention. For example, the experience of presence in a theatrical performance means that one is focused on an experience that is framed as being a play. When someone is engrossed in a situation or experience they feel present; frames define the nature of this presence. (Rettie 2004)

Presence thus becomes a process in which thought and feeling act together to create a sense of place (assuming Massey's [2005] spatio-temporal definition of place). This sense of presence or place may arise when listening to a stereo ('just like being in a concert'), watching a big-screen television ('just like being in the movies'), or reading a book ('just like being in the character's shoes'). It arises when the divisions between first order and second order mediations are merged in the audience's mind (although there is no reason to expect that the audience does not recognize the difference). Daniel Pinchbeck points out that presence 'creates a disposition towards a particular set of stimuli/response couplings within the dominant frame of spatial consciousness' (2005). When a sense of presence is high, the player is more willing to obey the social rules and physical laws of the virtual environment.

A PLACE: ZEN GARDEN

My *Second Life*™ avatar sits on the riverbank (actually he seems to be sitting in the riverbank). The grass is green and smooth, the fauna familiar though smoothly drawn with *Second Life* prims. I am acutely aware that I am staring at a computer screen, one in which very little is happening. If this were a scene in a film it would be barely watchable. But I am, in fact and to my surprise, feeling content and comfortable here. I am happy to stay a while, sitting in this river and watching the cherry blossom leaves fall and disappear.

Yordie Sans's Zen Garden is a 'three-dimensional scheme carefully designed' (Aarseth) to create an experience. That experience is not bound by automatic rules any more than the experience of the riverbank place—which is as much as to say that both are and that experience of both depends on my attitude to, my reaction towards, those rules. Separating frame from experience is the equivalent of taking a photo to be a slice of space.

A reading of virtual place that prioritizes rules is useful for both ludic and narrative understanding of game space. However, if the 'defining element in computer games is spatiality' (Aarseth 2001: 44), then it is reasonable to begin prioritizing the experience of that space as an aesthetic in itself, separately from the story or game with which it coexists. The social geographer's use of a spatio-temporal definition of place moves us towards this, as does the non-dimensional nature of the Schafer's soundscape which encapsulates visuals, rules and laws. Ultimately what is required is a way of discussing virtual space that includes rule-bound worlds such as found in many games (e.g., *Prince of Persia* and *Myst* [Miller and Miller 1993]) and virtual worlds in which the rules are commonly made up by the inhabitants (*Second Life* [Linden 2003–09], *World of Warcraft* [Blizzard 2004–10]) or even where gameplay often consists of confounding the rules (*The Sims* [Wright 2000]). Before moving forward it may be worth a review of how the problem of creating space and place has been managed in other visual art traditions.

MOVING THROUGH ALBERTI'S WINDOW

The art of perspective painting in Western culture extends back at least to Pompeii in the first century BC. Geometric rules for dimensional effects are evident in frescoes found in the ruins of that city and in earlier paintings dating from the reign of Alexander the Great (Russo 2004: 58). However, it was in the 15th century that the science became an established aspect of painting, used by such artists as Michelangelo, da Vinci, Masaccio, Piero della Francesca, and Andrea Mantegna. In Western art tradition, the delineation of landscape has been dependent on perspective technologies ever since.

Perspective is a mathematical method for creating a three-dimensional space on a two-dimensional canvas. At its simplest, perspective is the art of making objects in a painting become smaller as they move away from the viewer. As can be seen in Figure 9.2, geometric perspective is created by locating a 'vanishing point' on a horizon line. The horizon line is the limit of our sight; when looking at an ocean it is where the sky meets the sea. The vanishing point is where objects disappear on the horizon; when travelling on a road across the American West, it is where the road disappears. The lines that mark the roadsides are 'orthogonal' lines which converge on a single point before they vanish.

Perspective creates an illusion of depth in an image. When it is more obvious, the depth seems greater. The road across the American west draws the eye along the lines of perspective to the vanishing point, forcing the viewer to notice the change in the road's width as it recedes into the distance. This road image has become synonymous with wide open spaces because of the strength of its perspective geometry. Without the road in the picture, the eye would lack one of the necessary clues to judge the distance to the horizon and the image becomes flatter. Without the road, the viewer would have no way to judge the distance to the mountains.

Perspective works as a painting technology because it enforces a control over the viewer of the scene. It creates a frame (represented physically by the picture frame or canvas edge) and positions the viewer in relation to that frame. The perspective lines that generate outwardly from the vanishing point or points shift as the imagined position of the viewer shifts. If the

Figure 9.2   The road draws the eye to create depth.

viewer is looking down on the ocean, the horizon is lower; if the horizon line is across the top of the frame, the viewer is looking upward. Returning to the western road, the effect is dependent on whether the viewer is positioned standing on the road (as it is imagined to extend beyond the picture frame) or to the left or right of that road. The composition of the image, especially through perspective, depends on the artists establishing where his or her imagined viewer is located outside the frame. As Julian Thomas points out, this means the artist is in control of the viewer, not simply spatially but also temporally.

> Perspective art represents a form of visual control, which freezes time and presents things as they empirically appear to be. At the same time, perspective establishes not merely a set of spatial relations on the canvas, but a fixed relationship between object and subject, locating the viewer outside of the picture, and outside of the relationships being depicted. The viewer is thereby rendered transcendental, outside of history. (Thomas 1993: 20)

The metaphor par excellence for perspective, and the first written explication of geometric perspective, is Alberti's window. In 1435 Leon Battista Alberti composed the treatise *Della Pittura*, which codified the technique which was already starting to be used, as well as providing a guide on how to implement that technique. His volume included step-by-step rules as well as a diagram of 'an open frame gridded by perpendicular threads through which the artist should view the scene to be painted, and then transfer the coordinate details in scale onto his similarly gridded picture' (Edgerton 2006). The threads on the window provided a set of coordinates in a rectangular frame. By copying the contents of those coordinates to a page, the image observed could be accurately reproduced. The system required only that the coordinate systems of the window frame and the page remain consistent, and that (equally importantly) the viewer/artist maintained his or her own position relative to the window frame. The view from the window became fixed in time and space as did the position of the viewer.

Despite its origins in mathematical and geometric sciences, perspective has always been an illusionist's trick. The surface of the canvas or paper is two-dimensional. No one can enter the canvas and walk around. If viewers move slightly to the left, they will not be able to see behind a tree or other object in the scene; there is no behind the tree to see. Artists and painters have been aware of this aspect of perspective from very early on. Although M. C. Escher's woodcuts are probably the best known examples of a modern artist playing with the paradox of perspective, medieval painters were also showing an aptitude for exploring this side of its nature (Lister et al. 2008: 118).

Whereas Renaissance painting had traditionally emphasized the sacred dimension when depicting the world, so that space and the objects in it were valued for their symbolic value, Alberti's window separated human-ity from the world, allowing the painter to be a technician as much as an artist. 'In essence, even if inadvertent, it shifted the purpose of perspective painting not as a depiction of divine mystery revealed by geometry, but as worldly perfection framed by geometry' (Edgerton 2006). It also created a power relationship between the object and the viewer. The view seen through the window was reduced to an image that could be accurately reproduced and thereby controlled. The 16th century artist Albrecht Dürer caught the nature of this new relationship in his wood cut 'Draftsman Making a Perspective Drawing of a Woman' (Figure 9.3), which imagines the artist-as-technologist, separated from the supine subject of his gaze by a wire mesh like a one-sided cage.

Virtual worlds reveal these power relations in a moment of reverse remediation: when a user takes a screen-shot image, the screen shot con-verts three-dimensional space into a three-dimensional illustration 'which freezes time and presents things as they empirically appear to be' (Thomas 1993: 21). The viewer steps out the window and abandons responsibility for events within the world. Suddenly the space of the screen ceases to be an interactive space; the avatar and any other characters become fixed objects in the landscape. The spaces behind the visible fronts of objects cease to exist except in the viewer's memory or imagination. The landscape and its inhabitants are frozen in time like one of Muybridge's horses; but when viewing a virtual world, the snap-shot and the viewed world fill the same canvas (computer screen) and the alteration is instantaneous, making the shock of the change more immediate.

Perspective does more than order space; it also creates a temporal order. Western culture often defines time in spatial terms: 'that's behind us' is another way of saying that an event is 'in the past'. As objects approach the foreground of an image, they move from the past into the present or the present into the future. Lakoff and Johnson (1980) suggest that (in English

Figure 9.3   Albrecht Dürer (1471–1528) 'Draughtsman Making a Perspective Draw-ing of a Woman', 1525. Etching. The Metropolitan Museum of Art, New York.

culture at least) this is because 'time in English is structured in terms of the time is a moving object metaphor' (42). 'Distance implies time' according to geographer Yi-Fu Tuan (1977: 119). In Masaccio's painting 'Peter heals the lepers with his shadow', St Peter is portrayed as moving forward through the deep space of the painting, his shadow healing as he passes. Peter is in the middle ground of the image; in the foreground is a leper and in the background is a healed leper. In the middle ground with the saint stands a leper being healed (Lister et al. 2008: 118). The depth of space allows the painter to portray the entire process within a single moment of time. It is as though, by expanding the depth of the canvas the artist is able to flatten the depth of time.

The landscape of virtual worlds differs from the traditional still landscape because the viewer does not remain in a fixed position. One of the key elements of perspective geometry is a fixed point-of-view, and when viewers stand before a painting or photograph from anything other than the assumed viewpoint, their perspective appears incorrect, and they can easily locate the position where the painter/viewer should be. A step in the right direction might be to look at cinematic space, because camera movement clearly mirrors the movement of a spectator. However, the fundamental move required by digital landscapes in virtual environments is the independence of the camera. The creator of the virtual environment has no more control over how it is viewed (in what order or from what perspective points) than does an architect for a building or a garden landscape. In effect, the virtual landscape allows the viewer to step through Alberti's window into the represented world. This is, of course, only another illusion. The computer screen, like the painter's canvas or the photographic negative, remains two-dimensional.

This apparent conflict of dimensionality is apparent in the 'photo tourism' technology recently developed by Snavely, Seitz, and Szelinski in research undertaken for the University of Washington and Microsoft Research. Their imaging technology 'takes unstructured collections of photographs such as those from online image searches and reconstructs 3D points and viewpoints to enable novel ways of browsing the photos' (Snavely et al. 2006: 835). Available as a photo sharing website, Photosynth.net, the technology locates points of similarity between photographs and creates a three-dimensional montage which the viewer may browse through, zooming in and out of the virtual landscape and moving about different points-of-view, different perspectives. Because the movement between images is instantaneous, and because the images overlap in space and also in time, the effect can be a powerful reconstruction not just of a location but equally of a period of time, an event at that location. So 'Islington Town Hall—Our Wedding' (Figure 9.4) brings together a collection of 80 photographs into a dynamic montage or *photosynth*. The viewer can watch the ceremony in slices; the temporal path through the event controlled by the visual path through the space. Zooming into the

Figure 9.4   Islington town hall—our wedding (ron_edwards 2008).

picture is as likely to move the viewer backward in time as it is to move them forward.

ARCHITECTURAL SPACE

While perspective is about creating space, architecture strives to break that space up and organize it into places. Form and space are presented not as ends in themselves but as means to solve a problem in response to conditions of function, purpose and context—that is, architecturally (Ching 2007: ix). Architecture (not only the architecture of buildings but also of landscape) apportions volumes of space within planes (wall, floor, ceiling) made of various materials (wood, concrete, sky, trees, grass); or it displaces space by a volume (a building, a hill, a clump of trees, a wall) (Ching 2007: 29). The challenge of architectural design is to create space, structures and enclosures which will be experienced through movement in space-time (Ching 2007: ix), to 'embody the human effort to structure space in meaningful and useful ways' (Werner and Long 2002: 20).[1]

If virtual worlds bring the viewer in through Alberti's window, architecture does away with the window and the wall altogether as it attempts to organize lived experience within space. To stand still and admire a building is to misunderstand it. Lived spaces must be experienced temporally and spatially. S. E. Rasmussen (1964) illustrates this in his description of a viewing of a church in the town of Nordlingen.

Instead of a street picture you get an impression of a whole town and its atmosphere. Nordlingen is a medieval town surrounded by a circular wall. Your first glimpse of it, after passing through the town gate, gives you the conception of a town consisting of identical houses with pointed gables facing the street and dominated by a large church. And as you penetrate further into the town your first impression is confirmed. Nowhere do you stop and say 'it should be seen from here. . . . You are now in the middle of the picture itself. This means that you not only see the houses directly in front of you but at the same time, and without actually seeing them, you are aware of those on either side and remember the ones you have already passed. (Rasmussen 1964: 40)

Architecture becomes an art of placement and relationships; it begins with the basic design elements (point, line, place, and volume), creating each in turn by extending its predecessor (a dot extended becomes a line, a line extended a plane, a plane extended a volume). A volume must have shape, however, and that is created by adding or removing one shape from another, the resulting shape resulting from the relationship. This object's properties create what may be termed the keynote of the structure or landscape. Each plane and volume has qualities of color, texture, scale, and proportion. These set the tone for the result (Ching 2007).

The way the objects relate to one another (their sequence, relative qualities, and construction) creates potential placemarks—potential because these foreground figures are processes not products. They require a viewer to embed them with cognitive and emotive content. Architects therefore do not create place; they create its potential.

Space is not merely a container around us, and buildings are not just geometrical orderings of planes and solids that surround us. Rather, we dwell through these places, we abide alongside them. Heidegger's term 'dwelling' succinctly describes the way that people are on earth; it is a verb which conveys a sense of a continuous being which unites the human subjects with their 'environment'. (Thomas 1993: 28)

A PLACE: LOST WORLDS GROTTO MARBLE LOUNGE

I usually fly in to this part of *Second Life* from Quan Li, the surfing island next door. I'm not sure what the connection between the two places is. They seem to be part of an archipelago of Pacific islands, luxuriant green with palm trees rising to impossible heights from their slopes. The other islands have camp-fires burning and wooden shacks to display posters. This space is created from slabs of boulder set on top of a waterfall. Ionic columns stand about or lie collapsed on the floor (blocking my movement). A lounge and cushions offer seating by the side of a large pool of water fed by two waterfalls. Labels appear everywhere ('sit by pool', 'shower-M', and 'shower-F', 'cuddle-M' and 'cuddle-F') attached to small, floating marbles. I sit my avatar by the pool, my feet dangling in the water. My avatar faces the back wall of the grotto, which appears to recede into the distance. If I walk the avatar across the water to the back, however, it turns out to be an illusion; an image done in perspective to make the space appear deeper than it was.

The grotto is a void on a hilltop, created by the placement of slabs of rock and made deeper by perspective illusion. The grotto from within provides a sense of comfort; the tone (particularly at sunrise) is calm, with natural textures, subdued colors, and slowly moving elements of water and fire. The space is protected by the large boulders, but the depth of the space (the perspective painting makes it larger inside than outside) stops it from being oppressive. The chaise lounge and the pillows mark it out as a place of relaxation, but also of conversation. Labels like 'cuddle', 'conversation', and 'listen' all suggest community and conversation.

The planes and solids of the grotto function like automatic rules in a game. The slabs of rock forming roof and walls create a confined, intimate space by limiting movement across the hill top. The fallen Doric columns limit movement within, enforcing a social rule that divides the grotto into separate social areas: lounge, cushions, pool. These architectural objects define my avatar's activity and movement and, in consequence, my experience of the place. The water discourages me from noting the perspective illusion painting because I have to jump in (fully clothed) to cross over and examine the wall. The labels encourage me to abide by the rules of the place: lounge, chat, and take a shower with a friend. The affordances provided by the architectural design are the rule set.

A SPACE: *SECOND LIFE* CHICHEN ITZA

While travelling in *Second Life* I visit the Mayan ruins of Chichen Itza. I sit on a giant blue butterfly and float around a heritage park, listening to jungle sounds. Someone named Didi is below me, possibly wondering where to get a butterfly for her/him self. I'm wondering how I get off this insect. The butterfly takes me to various views of the park, taking me up and around the Castillo of Chichen Itza, which dominates the park space because of its large size. Other visitors fly around the Castillo without the butterfly. I risk clicking the 'stand' button while in flight with the result that I am able to dismount the butterfly. I can now walk about. A wooden bridge crosses a stream and a stone walkway provides smooth walking around the site, but neither I nor anyone else here use them; we simply walk or fly. I can walk up the steps of the Castillo, but the experience is the same as flying. Looking down, other people wander or fly about. Posters are on many walls and a large sign tells me this is Mexico. One person is trying on a Mayan princess outfit.

The place is full of details (trees, ruins, shops, posters, streams) which frequently get in the way of viewing or moving. Few have any practical function; they are virtual imitations of practical resources one might find in a tourist park. The keynote of this place could be the moving water, or the ancient monuments, or the shops; but each competes with the other to create a cacophony. The Castillo could be a tremendous placemark, but it feels reproduced, a copy of a real thing. The entire place has an air of reproduction, of tourist shop. There are few cognitive placemarks here, apart from guides for climbing on the butterfly. None of the features of the place invite activity. The functional elements such as bridges and walkways are redundant and ignored.

Being on the butterfly is a bit like watching a movie; the avatar is moved around to the correctly composed perspectives of the parts of the site deemed of interest by the programmer of the insect. I recognize the keynote of this place: reproduction, display, and commodity; this is a virtual tourist trap. Space reproduced, represented, and controlled. An effort has been made to reduce the potential for individual experience of this place in its (mostly useless) walkways, bridges, and butterfly rides.

In *The Practice of Everyday Life*, Michel de Certeau describes three 'operations' of the city: 'the *own* space (un espace propre)', the 'nowhen' of the city as system, and the city as concept/subject (95). The space 'propre' is the city of practice, of 'physical, mental and political' activity that pollutes the city as system. He compares the nowhen of cities to city maps, which 'only refer . . . to the absence of what has passed by'. His description of these referential tracings suggests what has happened in this *Second Life* Chichen Itza.

> The trace left behind is substituted for the practice. It exhibits the (voracious) property that the geographical system has of being able to transform action into legibility, but in doing so it causes a way of being in the world to be forgotten. (de Certeau: 97)

TOWARDS A DEFINITION OF SPACE

Attempts at creating presence, the sense of being in a virtual place, typically focus around creating a cohesive set of sensory inputs that simulate a real environment (Jacobson 2002; Lombard and Ditton 1997; Pinchbeck and Stevens 2005; Slater 2003), or else create a world of affordances and rules that reflect the disposition of its users (Pinchbeck 2005; Rettie 2004; Riva et al. 2004; Waterworth and Waterworth 2003; Lombard and Ditton 1997), so that the inhabitant of the virtual world is a part of that world, almost like a programmed extension.

For a player to feel present in a game reality, therefore, implies particular perceptual methodologies and behavioral responses. . . . One could argue that a present player's perception is operating according to the rules of the game environment, rather than according to the limitations of the interface. The dominant schema, in other words, are linked to the affordances of the landscape, rather than the action of manipulating mouse, joystick or keyboard. Presence creates a disposition towards a particular set of stimuli/response couplings within the dominant frame of spatial consciousness. (Pinchbeck 2005: 4)

These models of presence are bound by technology, but presence itself is part of a continuum of space and of lived experience.

Presence is a process that creates a sense of place; place therefore is constantly being defined by experience. A particular place may share a common tonality or keynote with other places, making it part of a larger, identifiable landscape. Those other places may not be contingent within the space; they may be linked more tightly by keynote than geography. The place itself is distinguished from other places in the same landscape less by borders than by placemarkers holding both cognitive and emotive content. The placemarkers may be unique to a place, but they are more likely to be unique in their relationship to other elements of the place or to the observer. These relationships occur both spatially and temporally and are defined through experience of the process of that space.

In virtual environments, space can be created only through movement. Until the avatar or camera moves, virtual environments are as flat as a painting, possessing only the illusion of depth created through depth cues and perspective. If my avatar stands on the edge of a *Second Life* island and stares out to sea, the ocean appears to spread out to the horizon; if he attempts to fly to that horizon, however, he is stopped by an invisible plane. The depth is there, but not the space. Likewise in the Marble Grotto, if my avatar tries to ascend the stair in the back of the cave, he is stopped because it is a painting used to create an illusion of space. The depth is there, the space is not.

To create space in a virtual environment therefore requires movement. Space is fundamentally spatio-temporal, whether in the physical or virtual world. It is dynamic, created by the experience of movement. Physical space requires movement through objects (volumes, planes, organic, and non-organic) which allows us to experience the relationships between them and with ourselves. Social space requires movement among social objects (people, customs, and histories) which, again, allow us to experience the relationships between them and with ourselves (Lechte 1995; Massey 1994, 2005; Tschumi 1996; Tuan 1977). As Tuan and others (Heeter 1992; Jacobson 2002; Lombard and Ditton 1997; Pinchbeck and Stevens 2005; Riva et al. 2004; Waterworth and Waterworth 2003) point out, this space (fundamental to both forms of presence) is fundamentally tied to the body.

Movements such as the simple ability to kick one's legs and stretch one's arms are basic to the awareness of space. Space is experienced directly as having room in which to move. Moreover, by shifting from one place to another, a person acquires a sense of direction. Forward, backward, and sideways are experientially differentiated, that is, known subconsciously in the act of motion. Space assumes a rough coordinate frame centered on the mobile and purposive self. (Tuan 1977: 12)

Discussing virtual environments in terms merely of dimensional illusion is, therefore, to make a categorical mistake. It is as though we described thought in terms of grammar; grammar allows us to describe thought, but only by distorting it into syntagmatic and paradigmatic dimensions. Likewise a virtual environment may follow dimensional rules to express itself, but it remains possible to separate the representation from the referent. Following Lefebvre, the rules of perspective and the elements of architectural design belong to the 'conceived space' of planners (Lefebvre 1992). Recalling the Dürer woodcut in Figure 9.4, we should also remember the power relation it illustrates as the subject is quantified and recorded. Representation alters how we conceive of presentation.

> What is at issue, in the production of representations, is not the spatialisation of time (understood as the rendering of time as space), but the representation of time-space. What we conceptualize (divide up into organs, put it how you will) is not just time but space-time. In the arguments of Berson and de Certeau too the issue is formulated as though the lively world which is there to be represented (conceptualized/written down) is only temporal. It certainly is temporal; but it is spatial too. And 'representation' is an attempt to capture both aspects of that world. (Massey 2005: 27)

A map, for instance, is not just a reduction of information, a simplification of the three-dimensional space onto a two-dimensional screen or page. (Space, I repeat, is not dimensional, only its representation is.) It is a change of perspective. If I revisit the Mexican island in *Second Life*, I can move my camera from eye (or butterfly) level to that of the stars, staring straight down on the landscape. From there the items on the screen lose their third-dimension and become two-dimensional drawings. On the fringes of the screen the software reconstitutes some dimensionality, but that disappears as I move my camera to hover over other sections of this landscape. The landscape becomes a map without ceasing to be the landscape. Despite Korzybski's semantic arguments to the contrary (Falconar 2007: 8), the map in *Second Life* is the territory. The representation, the map, seems to replace the experience in virtual worlds; instead of movement creating space, we move through dimensional (representational) space. We traverse the map instead of the map representing our traverse.

SPACE OF CHANCE

If movement creates space, then it follows that a designer who controls movement controls the creation of that space. Architecture 'initiates, directs and organizes behavior and movement' (Pallasmaa 2005: 62), thereby controlling the spatial experience of a building. In similar fashion mapmakers control the journey through their representation of roads and landmarks on the way. When the mapmaker is also the maker of the landscape, when the map becomes the landscape, the space of the map becomes clearly defined and understandable, possibly even designed so as to prepare a better experience; the designer can, for example, put the mountain where it does not block the sunset.

What the designer cannot do (neither the architect nor the map maker nor even the virtual world builder), is create the space, because they are not in control of the subject who moves in and experiences that world. Space, even in the rules-based virtual world, is re-created every time the landscape is experienced.

Design involves creating working relationships between aspects of the object(s) created. For instance, architectural design is about 'organizational pattern, relationships, clarity, hierarchy' (Ching 2007: 6). Likewise a well-designed landscape painting requires the castle on the hill to fit on the hill (unless the artist has another purpose in mind), a holistic design process usually created through perspective geometry. Doreen Massey, while valuing this aspect of design, warns about the limits of this holistic thinking:

> 'Everything is connected to everything else' can be a salutary political reminder that whatever we do has wider implications than perhaps we commonly recognize. But it is unhelpful if it leads to a vision of an always already constituted holism. The 'always' is rather that there are always connections yet to be made, juxtapositions yet to flower into interaction, or not, potential links which may never be established. Loose ends and ongoing stories. (Massey 2005: 107)

Massey, a little facetiously perhaps, calls for the 'space of chance' which 'lies within the constant formation of spatial configurations, those complex mixtures of pre-planned spatiality and happenstance positionings-in-relation-to-each-other' (Massey 2005: 116). This is a space in which it is possible to meet the unexpected. Returning for a moment to the church in Nordlingen described by Rasmussen, we find a design of a city in which the visitor is encouraged to encounter the space from many angles and perspectives. The city has been designed to create the potential for unexpected spaces to be created as the visitor travels the streets. Many of us who have been lost in cities that appear to have no plan have had a similar experience; we create places which, although they may be located on the map, are not recognizable to us there. When we look at the map, the plan of the city may become immediately recognizable (or perhaps not). Through movement and experience, we could not see that plan; now that we do, the city as a place changes again.

Massey describes similar phenomena in the experience of social spaces. She contrasts our sense of street markets as 'humming with spontaneity', although in fact it is regulated by an 'intricate construction of multiple routines' (Massey 2005: 112). It is through the experience of those routines that the visitor creates their market space. The rules are the background, the keynote of the place they have created by experiencing the market, which allows them to recognize the space they move through as a market—as their market.

It is in this light of hidden rules and laws which govern a visual or social environment (as well as many other environments), that we can re-assess the idea that it is programmed rules which make a virtual space or game space different from the physical. These rules are the environment which the visitor or player will work within and which neither the visitor nor, in fact, the game designer can fully recognize. If space is created through movement, and space is the defining feature of virtual lands like *Second Life*, than it is worth studying the potential for movement within worlds as a way of understanding not how they are created (because that is to freeze them into an unreal snapshot, out of space and out of time), but how they provide the potential for the creation of spaces, for the space of chance.

NOTES

1. A fuller discussion of the purpose and methods of architecture taken from an alternative perspective is provided by Astrid Ensslin (this volume).

REFERENCES

Aarseth, E (2001) Allegories of space: The question of spatiality in computer games. In *CyberText yearbook 2000*. Finland: Research Centre for Contemporary Culture.
———. 2007. Allegories of space. In *Space time play: Computer games, architecture and urbanism: the next level*, ed. F Borries, SP Walz, and M Böttger. Basel: Birkhäuser. Online. Available HTTP: http://dx.doi.org/10.1007/978-3-7643-8415-9_13 (accessed 10 March 2010).
Blizzard Entertainment (2004–10). *World of Warcraft*. Online. Available HTTP: http://www.worldofwarcraft.com/ (accessed 10 December 2009).
de Certeau, M (1984) *The practice of everyday life*. Berkeley: University of California Press.
Ching, F (2007) *Architecture—form, space and order*, 3rd ed. Hoboken, NJ: Wiley.
Edgerton, SY (1975) *The renaissance rediscovery of linear perspective*. New York: Basic Books.
———. (2006) Brunelleschi's mirror, Alberti's window, and Galileo's 'perspective tube'. *História, Ciências, Saúde-Manguinhos* 13, no. 10: 151–79.

Falconar, T (2007) *Creative intelligence and self-liberation: Korzybski non-Aristotelian thinking and enlightenmen*, rev. ed. Carmarthen: Crown House Publishing.

Goffman, E (1974) *Frame analysis: An essay on the organisation of experience.* New York: Harper and Row.

Heeter, C (1992) Being there: The subjective experience of presence. *Presence: Teleoperators and Virtual Environments* 1, no. 2, spring 1992, MIT Press): 262–71.

Jacobson, D (2002) On theorizing presence. *Journal of Virtual Environments* 6, no. 1. Online. Available HTTP: http://www.brandeis.edu/pubs/jove/HTML/V6/presence.html (accessed 4 April 2010).

Lakoff, G and M Johnson (1980) *Metaphors we live by.* Chicago: University of Chicago Press.

Lechte, J (1995). (Not) belonging in postmodern space. In *Postmodern cities and spaces*, ed. S Watson and K Gibson, 99–111. Oxford: Blackwell.

Lefebvre, H (1992) *The production of space.* Oxford: Blackwell.

Linden Lab (2003–09). *Second Life.* Online. Available HTTP: http://secondlife.com (accessed 2 June 2009).

Lister, M, J Dovey, S Giddings, I Grant, and K Kelly (2008) *NewmMedia: A critical introduction*, 2nd ed. London: Routledge.

Lombard, M and T Ditton (1997) At the heart of it all: The concept of presence. *Journal of Computer Mediate Communication* 3 (2). Online. Available HTTP: http://jcmc.indiana.edu/vol3/issue2/lombard.html (accessed 6 May 2009).

Massey, DB (1994) *Space, place and gender.* Minneapolis: University of Minnesota Press.

———. (2005) *For space.* London: Sage.

Miller, R and R Miller (1993) *Myst.* CD-ROM. Spokane, WA: Cyan Worlds

Muybridge, E (c. 1887) The horse in motion. 'Sallie Gardner,' owned by Leland Stanford; running at a 1:40 gait over the Palo Alto track, 19 June 1878 Photograph. Library of Congress Prints and Photographs Division.

Pallasmaa, J (2005) *The eyes of the skin: Architecture and the senses*, 2nd ed. Chichester: Wiley.

Pinchbeck, D (2005) Is presence a relevant or useful construct in designing game environments? In *Proceedings of The Third Annual International Conference in Computer Game Design and Technology.* John Moores University, Liverpool, November 8. Online Available HTTP: http://thechineseroom.co.uk/GDTWpresence.pdf (accessed 6 June 2009).

Pinchbeck, DM and B Stevens (2005) Presence, narrative and schemata in *Proceedings of Presence 2005: 8th Annual International Workshop on Presence.* London, September 21–23, 2005. London: University College, London, 221–26. Online. Available HTTP: http://www.temple.edu/ispr/prev_conferences/proceedings/2005/Pinchbeck%20and%20Stevens.pdf (accessed 4 April 2010).

Rasmussen, SE (1964) *Experiencing architecture*, 2nd ed. Cambridge: MIT Press.

Rettie, R (2004) Using Goffman's frameworks to explain presence and reality. In *7th Annual International Workshop on Presence, Presence 2004 Conference Proceedings* (Valencia, October 2004). Online. Available HTTP: http://www.temple.edu/ispr/prev_conferences/proceedings/2004/Rettie.pdf (accessed 5 June 2009).

Riva, G, J Waterworth, and EL Waterworth (2004) The layers of presence: A biocultural approach to understanding presence in natural and mediated environments. *CyberPsychology and Behavior* 7, no. 4: 405–19.

ron_edwards (2008) Photosynth—Islington Town Hall—Our Wedding. Photosynth.net. Online. Available HTTP: <http://photosynth.net/view.aspx?cid=05ba60f7-906e-44f7-a358-04f244e2d431> (accessed 4 October 2009).

Russo, L (2004) *The forgotten revolution: How science was born in 300 BC and why it had to be reborn*, trans. S Levy. London: Springer.

Schafer, RM (1994) *Soundscape: Our sonic environment and the tuning of the world*. Rochester, VT: Destiny Books.

Seegert, A (2009) "Doing there" vs. "being there": Performing presence in interactive fiction. *Journal of Gaming and Virtual Worlds* 1, no. 1: 23–27. Online. Available HTTP: http://www.atypon-link.com/INT/doi/abs/10.1386/jgvw.1.1.23_1 (accessed 5 March 2010).

Slater, M (2003) A note on presence terminology. *Presence-Connect* 3 (January). Online. Available HTTP: http://www.cs.ucl.ac.uk/research/vr/Projects/Presencia/ConsortiumPublications/ucl_cs_papers/presence-terminology.htm (accessed 5 May 2009).

Snavely, N, SM Seitz, and R Szeliski (2006) Photo tourism: Exploring photo collections in 3D. *ACM Transactions on Graphics (Proceedings of International Conference on Computer Graphics and Interactive Techniques)* 25, no. 3: 835–46.

Solnit, R (2004) *Motion studies: Time, space and Eadweard Muybridge*. London: Bloomsbury.

Stevens, W (1990) *The collected poems of Wallace Stevens*. New York: Vintage.

Thomas, J (1993) The politics of vision and the archaeologies of landscape. In *Landscape: politics and perspectives*, ed. B Bender, 19–49. Providence/Oxford: Berg Publishers.

Tschumi, B (1996) *Architecture and disjunction*. Cambridge, MA: MIT Press.

Tuan, Y (1977) *Space and place: The perspective of experience*. London: University of Minnesota Press.

Ubisoft (2007) *Assassin's Creed*. DVD. Montreal: Ubisoft.

———. (2008) *Prince of Persia*. DVD. Montreal: Ubisoft.

Waterworth, JA and EL Waterworth (2003) The core of presence: Presence as perceptual illusion. *Presence-Connect* 3. Online. Available HTTP: http://presence.cs.ucl.ac.uk/presenceconnect/articles/Jul2003/jwworthJul11200314441/jwworthJul11200314441.html (accessed 5 May 2009).

Werner, S and P Long (2003) Cognition meets le Courbusier—cognitive principles of architectural design. In *Spatial cognition III: Routes and navigation, human memory and learning, spatial representation and spatial learning*, ed. C Freksa, W Brauer, C Habel and KF Wender, 112–26. Berlin: Springer.

Wright, W (2000) *The Sims*. CD-ROM. Emeryville, CA: Maxis.

Afterword
Virtual Worlds and the Research Question

Tom Boellstorff

INTRODUCTION

At the beginning of the 21st century's second decade, the study of virtual worlds stands at a fascinating crossroads. Not only are the number of virtual worlds expanding at a dizzying pace; 'genres' of virtual worlds continue to expand as well. This runs the gamut from those organized as games to those set up for training or education (including those combining all these domains); from those aimed at children to those aimed at adults or the whole lifespan; from those aimed at specific languages or world regions to those global in membership; and from those designed for greater photorealism and immersion to those designed with increasing simplicity so as to be accessible via social networking sites (like Facebook) and mobile devices.

For researchers, the upshot of these continuing transformations is that we face substantial challenges in tracking how virtual worlds come into being and alternately grow, stabilize, shrink, or go out of existence. One source of the difficulty lies in the fact that these shifts can be due to combinations of in-world developments, interactions with other virtual worlds and online technologies, and effects of physical-world socialites local, national, regional, and global in scale. There is thus a pressing need for further research from a range of methodological and theoretical approaches—including the fields of media and communications studies, as the contributions to this volume demonstrate. Whereas understandable concerns with design, social impact, and politics often direct conversations about virtual worlds into a quest for conclusions and definitive pronouncements, it is crucial to linger in spaces of inquiry. The greatest barrier to a more informed, contextual, and relevant understanding of virtual worlds is not that we have failed to obtain the right answers, but that we too often fail to pose the right questions, thereby steering our research programs into wild goose chases for solutions that will never come.

What makes crafting effective research questions trickier than it might at first seem is that like most forms of contemporary technology linked to the Internet, virtual worlds often fall prey to a 'hype cycle' that alternately heralds them as nascent agents of total social transformation, or dismisses them as faddish contrivances with but ephemeral significance. Both caricatures are obviously false; as is usually the case, the truth lies between or even beyond such polarizing extremes. It is in a less dogmatic middle ground that we can forge new paradigms for virtual worlds research, and even hazard some future trajectories. Yes, virtual worlds are here to stay and will play significant roles in human sociality worldwide. No, we are not at the cusp of some Matrix-like future in which virtual worlds displace actual-world socialities. As the number of virtual worlds grows, we will find not a unilinear evolution but a broadening range of sociotechnical forms. Some persons will spend time in virtual worlds as a means to escape some aspect of their actual-world lives; others will spend time in virtual worlds in ways that augment, extend, or collaboratively interact with the actual-world lives of themselves and others; but most persons will probably do both in some fashion, because fantasy and continuity need not preclude each other. Beyond such broad observations, it will prove most productive to set hype cycles aside and turn from both evangelists and naysayers, so as to reflect on promising questions for virtual worlds research in the future.

VIRTUAL, ACTUAL, AND REAL: IMBRICATION AND DISTINCTION

Perhaps the most crucial area for continuing virtual worlds research involves forms of imbrication and distinction between virtual worlds and the physical world. (As in my other writings on virtual worlds, I distinguish virtual worlds from the 'physical' or 'actual' world; I do not use the phrase 'real world' analytically, because virtual worlds and other online technologies are decidedly real technological formations with real socialities and social effects.) This issue of imbrication and distinction—pivotal because it highlights the novel contribution of virtual worlds—continues to be one of the greatest sources of misunderstanding and needless posturing in debates over the significance of virtual worlds for human life. Too often, terms like 'blurring' or 'convergence' are used to construct a teleological narrative in which ostensibly separated virtual and actual worlds tend inexorably towards unification.

This narrative is doubly wrong. First, virtual worlds and the actual world do not begin from a position of separation. Of course, the selfhoods and socialites that form within any virtual world can be distinctive to that virtual world. For instance, two people can meet in a virtual world and have meaningful social interaction (from falling in love or starting an in-world business to playing a game of checkers) without any need for those two persons to have met in the actual world beforehand, or any need for those two persons to meet in the actual world alongside their virtual-world interaction. But whereas virtual-world sociality can thus be distinct from actual-world sociality—exhibiting cultural logics that have taken form in-world and are thus not directly derived from any particular actual-world culture—this distinction does not mean utter separation. At a fundamental level, virtual worlds are predicated on actual-world bodies, computers, and electricity for their existence. More directly, as in cases of culture change elsewhere, virtual world cultures do not appear out of whole cloth: every time persons enter virtual worlds they bring beliefs, practices, and subjectivities from the actual world. From assumptions about gravity and gender to practices of commerce and altruism, virtual worlds are profoundly shaped by actual-world cultures. Because persons in virtual worlds come from myriad actual-world cultures and then create and are affected by emergent cultural logics taking form in-world, virtual-world sociality can never be reduced to actual-world sociality. But a narrative of originary separation ending in blurring or convergence elides the fundamental and ongoing influence of actual-world cultures on virtual worlds (not to mention influences of virtual-world cultures on the actual world).

Alongside the mistaken presumption of an originary separation, a second flaw in teleological narratives of convergence is that there is no endpoint in which actual and virtual worlds 'blur' into an indistinguishable morass. Without necessarily displacing computers, mobile devices like cell phones and tablet computers will increasingly represent key modalities for engaging with virtual worlds. Yet even when using such mobile technologies, people will remain quite clear as to when they are online and offline. Indeed, the whole point of online worlds in the first place is that they bring something to the table, so to speak; if they overlap completely with the actual world, why bother with them at all? Instead of blurring, what we find are increasingly complex and multifaceted forms of indexicality and communication between virtual worlds and the actual world (and also between various virtual worlds, as well as between virtual worlds and other online technologies like social networking websites and blogs). The imbrication and even overlay of virtual worlds and the actual world does represent to some degree a departure from earlier virtual-world technologies. Even in such earlier cases, however, separation between virtual and actual worlds was less a function of technological capability than linked to elements of role-playing or gaming that used a 'magic circle' of rules to create a sense of distinct sociality (Carillo Masso; Huizinga 1950: 57).

Virtual world researchers can ask productive and relevant questions in regard to contextual imbrication (rather than complete amalgamation) if they deploy paradigms for analysis and design not beholden to this teleological narrative of purportedly discrete virtual and actual worlds moving towards total fusion. Forms of artistic practice can play an important role in framing these questions (Sermon and Gould). In turn, such research contributes to ongoing efforts to better understand what constitutes the 'virtual' itself. This includes the vital question of what aspects of virtuality are unique to virtual worlds, versus what aspects draw upon longstanding notions and experiences of virtuality in the actual world (Sherman).

CREATION, COLLABORATION, CONTROL

The foundational feature of virtual worlds is that they are places. Because a place can in theory be inhabited by a single person, there is no definitional barrier to the existence of virtual worlds with a sole inhabitant. But just as few actual-world places have only one resident for very long, so virtual worlds are almost always places of sociality, interaction, and intersubjectivity. The fact that virtual worlds are places means that they can be construed not just in terms of globalized online networks, but in terms of localities and even partially as nation-states (Sherman). Another set of crucial research questions, then, involve asking after what new forms of culture and society might be in formation in virtual worlds, how such forms of culture and society differ within virtual worlds (at a subcultural level) and between virtual worlds, and what differences and continuities exist between forms of culture and society in virtual worlds and in the physical world.

Although the notion of creation obviously has a long history, researchers continue to point to distinctive forms and consequences of creation and creativity in virtual worlds, not least because of their fundamental role in the forging of virtual world spaces themselves (Boellstorff 2008: 205–11; Muse). Indeed, the very title *Creating Second Lives* flags this centrality of creation to virtual-world subjectivities and socialities. Drawing upon cultural domains ranging from religion to capitalism and the figure of the artist, notions of creativity have strong consequences for selfhood in virtual worlds. In addition, creation is rarely a completely solitary endeavor, online or offline. As a result, a promising avenue for future virtual-world research addresses questions of collaboration and participation (Sermon and Gould). Because virtual worlds (like other places of sociality) are never wholly egalitarian, questions regarding how forms of virtual-world governance and social control are constituted and implemented, and often in ways that trouble easy divisions between owner and user, are of great importance (Burgess; Malaby 2006).

TEXTUAL AND GRAPHICAL SOCIALITIES

As I have noted elsewhere, one common misunderstanding of virtual worlds involves the assumption that they must be graphical, as the misnomer '3D web' indicates (Boellstorff 2008: 91–92, 2010: 127). However, whereas purely textual virtual worlds exist—as could virtual worlds based entirely on sound, smell, or some other sensory input—vision continues to dominate virtual-world socialities. This means, for instance, that notions of the landscape and control over a naturalized visual field will pose a continuing set of important questions for virtual-world research (Boellstorff 2008: 89–96; Clark; Muse).

The dominance of visuality in virtual worlds has important consequences for embodiment, which plays a vital role in forms of cultural difference like sexuality, race, and gender (Boellstorff 2008: 134–38, 2011; Carrillo Masso; Doyle; Fizek and Wasilewska; Gee 2008; Nakamura 2007; Sundén 2003; Taylor 2002; Yee and Bailenson 2007). Because the procedures to create avatar bodies and virtual-world objects are often linked or nearly identical, a crucial area for continuing research involves questions like the imbrication of body-fashioning and architecture (Ensslin). Such research can help us better frame notions of 'social constructionism' in the actual world; virtual-world socialities make apparent the cultural work that 'constructs' actual-world human landscapes in contexts of political and socioeconomic inequality.

Whereas visuality is thus clearly central to virtual worlds—and likely to become even more so, given the growing power of graphics cards and growing bandwidth of Internet connectivities—it will be crucial to develop research foci beyond questions of visuality itself. For instance, an attention to the role of text and narrative in forms of presence, immersion, and belonging can helpfully reframe the effects of visuality (Sermon and Gould), and contribute as well to questions of gender and other aspects of selfhood (Carrillo Masso).

CONCLUSION: THEORY AND METHOD

No domain of human life is exhaustively understood or researched to completion, and culture is always a historical fact, changing over time. In the case of virtual worlds, however, we encounter a novel modality of human sociality for which the maxim '"cultures" do not hold still for their portraits' (Clifford 1986: 10) is particularly opportune. So often it seems like our object of study is running ahead of our tools to comprehend it.

In such contexts of rapid change and exciting but oftentimes bewildering conceptual upheaval, crafting the right theoretical toolkit for the research questions at hand can be challenging indeed. It is precisely in such circumstances that a turn to method can be useful. A turn to method is not a turn away from theory; it is a turn to the core substantive issues that animate theory. Because theory is by definition an abstracted explanation for something, gaining a better understanding of that 'something' is crucial for effective theory, and it is through our methodologies that such better understandings emerge. I have found attending to questions of method crucial for developing research questions and theoretical insights (Boellstorff 2008, chapter 3; Boellstorff et al. forthcoming). With regard to virtual worlds, the fields of media and communications studies are, in turn, valuable not just for the answers they provide and the questions they pose, but for the methods they contribute. It is precisely through such kinds of engagements that a robustly interdisciplinary virtual worlds research community has taken form, holding the promise of a responsive and powerfully insightful set of insights that will help illuminate the emergent cultures of virtual worlds and their social consequences—online and offline.

REFERENCES

Note: Works cited without a date are chapters in this volume, and are not listed in the following.

Boellstorff, T (2008) *Coming of age in Second Life: An anthropologist explores the virtually human.* Princeton: Princeton University Press.
———. (2010) A typology of ethnographic scales for virtual worlds. In *Online worlds: Convergence of the real and the virtual*, ed. WS Bainbridge, 123–34. London: Springer.
———. (forthcoming) Placing the virtual body: Avatar, chora, cypherg. In *A companion to the anthropology of bodies/embodiments*, ed F Mascia-Lees. London: Blackwell.
Boellstorff, T, B Nardi, C Pearce, and TL Taylor (forthcoming) *A handbook of ethnographic methods for virtual worlds.* Princeton: Princeton University Press.
Clifford, J (1986) Introduction: Partial truths. In *Writing culture: The poetics and politics of ethnography*, ed J Clifford and G Marcus, 1–26. Berkeley: University of California Press.
Gee, JP (2008) Video games and embodiment. *Games and Culture* 3, no. 3/4: 253–63.
Huizinga, J (1950) *Homo ludens: A study of the play-element in culture.* Boston: Beacon Press. Originally published 1938.
Malaby, TM (2006) Coding control: Governance and contingency in the production of online worlds. *First Monday*, Special Issue number 7. Online. Available HTTP: http://firstmonday.org/issues/special11_9/malaby/index.html#m2 (accessed 15 December 2006).
Nakamura, L (2007) *Digitizing race: Visual Cultures of the Internet.* Minneapolis: University of Minnesota Press.
Sundén, J (2003) *Material virtualities: Approaching online textual embodiment.* New York: Peter Lang.
Taylor, TL (2002) Living digitally: Embodiment in virtual worlds. In *The social life of avatars: Presence and interaction in shared virtual environments*, ed. R Schroeder, 40–62. London: Springer-Verlag.
Yee, N and J Bailenson (2007) The Proteus effect: The effect of transformed self-representation on behavior. *Human Communication Research* 33: 271–90.

Contributors

Tom Boellstorff is Professor in the Department of Anthropology at the University of California, Irvine, and Editor-in-Chief of *American Anthropologist*, the flagship journal of the American Anthropological Association. He is the author of *The Gay Archipelago: Sexuality and Nation in Indonesia* (Princeton University Press, 2005); *A Coincidence of Desires: Anthropology, Queer Studies, Indonesia* (Duke University Press, 2007); and *Coming of Age in Second Life: An Anthropologist Explores the Virtually Human* (Princeton University Press, 2008).

Elizabeth Burgess is based in the School of Arts, Histories and Cultures at the University of Manchester, where she teaches in the department of English and American Studies. She holds degrees in English, from the University of Liverpool, and in Post-1900 Literature, Theory and Culture, from the University of Manchester. Elizabeth's research interests are centred on post-1950s texts, with a specific focus on reading, play, and interactivity in printed and digital media.

Isamar Carrillo Masso is an Assistant Lecturer in Visual Culture and New Media at the School of Creative Studies and Media, Bangor University. Her current research interests include (critical) discourse analysis, (gender, race, religious) representations in (new) media, video games, and multimodal corpora. Ms Carrillo Masso graduated with distinction in 2008 from University of Reading, and is currently reading for a Ph.D. in New Media at the Bangor University under the supervision of Dr Astrid Ensslin.

Joseph S. Clark is a faculty consultant in instructional technology and design at Florida State University, where he also teaches a course in New Communication Technologies and Contemporary Society. He is pursuing a doctorate in Environmental Communication and his dissertation critically explores cultural conceptions of the "natural" environment as reproduced in multiuser virtual environments. His research interests also include environmental education, ecojustice, gender, new media, and augmented reality.

Denise Doyle, with a background in Fine Art Painting and Digital Media, is an Artist Researcher, Writer, and Senior Lecturer in Digital Media at the University of Wolverhampton. Denise's research investigates the Artist's experience of the Imaginary in Virtual Worlds, and is developing a framework for a new theory of the Imagination that incorporates experiences of mediated spaces created through interdisciplinary research in Art and Technology. Denise has recently guest co-edited, with Dr MacCallum-Stewart, a Special Issue on the Imagination and Virtual Worlds for the *Journal of Gaming and Virtual Worlds*, where she also sits as an editorial board member. Her research interests include: virtual worlds, interactive film, database cinema, philosophies of the imagination, practice-based research methods, critical theory and media arts practice, phenomenological and ethnographic research methods, digital narratives, and multiplayer games and virtual learning environments.

Astrid Ensslin is Senior Lecturer in Digital Humanities at the School of Creative Studies and Media, Bangor University. Her main research interests are in the areas of digital media (especially digital literature, video games, and virtual worlds), semiotics and discourse analysis, and language in the (new) media. She is founding editor of *Journal of Gaming and Virtual Worlds*. Her main publications include *The Language of Gaming* (Palgrave Macmillan 2011), *Canonizing Hypertext: Explorations and Constructions* (Continuum 2007), *Language in the Media: Representations, Identities, Ideologies* (co-edited with Sally Johnson, Continuum 2007), and articles in *Language and Literature*, *Corpora*, *Journal of Literature and Aesthetics*, *Language Learning Journal*, *Gender and Language*, and *Sprache und Datenverarbeitung*.

Sonia Fizek is a final year research student and a part-time tutor in the School of Creative Studies and Media, Bangor University. Her doctoral work focuses on developing a methodological toolkit for player character analysis in offline computer Role-Playing Games (cRPGs). She is a member of PALA (Poetics and Linguistics Association), the Polish Association for Game Research), ISSN (The International Society for the Study of Narrative), and DiGRA (Digital Games Research Association). Her Master's dissertation, entitled 'Literature of Transition—Critical Evaluation of Cyberliterature and Its Innovative and Traditional Elements', was completed with distinction in 2007 at Lodz University, Poland. She has published in *the Journal of Gaming and Virtual Worlds* and in *Dekada Literacka*, a Polish literary magazine. She is also writing about video games culture for the Internet issue of *Polityka*, a Polish news magazine.

Charlotte Gould is Senior Lecturer in Digital Media at the University of Salford, School of Art & Design and has developed a number of interactive environments for urban big screens that explore user identity and the notion of a floating narrative. Through this work she encourages creative urban play and looks at the way the audience can experience the urban space through telepresent technology. Through her research she explores the creative and cultural potential that urban screens have to offer in the digital media age and how these emerging technologies and the digital infrastructure impact on the way that the public interacts within the urban environment. She has developed a series of projects which allow the public to complete the work through the creation of their unique narrative and has undertaken a number of interactive installations and projects with key industrial partners, which include an interactive installation for Moves09 at the BBC Big Screen in Liverpool and for the BBC Big Screen at the Glastonbury Festival. She also produced an interactive installation for ISEA09 at the Waterfront Hall Belfast and for Moves10 at the Bluecoat Gallery Liverpool. She is principal investigator of Hub, an innovation space and pop up gallery which aims to support the regeneration of the City of Salford and further create links between the university, its local community, and the creative industries that surround it with a series of exhibitions which engage with the community through interactive exhibitions and workshops.

Eben Muse lectures on digital and interactive media at the School of Creative Studies and Media, Bangor University. He comes into the digital field through a research background in folklore, mythology, and film which he studied at SUNY Buffalo. He is associate editor of the *Journal of Gaming and Virtual Worlds*. He is currently developing papers on the roles of spatiality and temporality in interactive fiction, 3-D worlds, and social landscapes.

Paul Sermon is Professor of Creative Technology and Associate Head for Research and Innovation at the School of Art & Design, University of Salford. He has developed a series of celebrated interactive telematic art installations that have received international acclaim. Through a sustained research funding income he has continued to produce, exhibit, and discuss his work extensively at an international level. Paul Sermon graduated with a BA Hon's Fine Art degree under Professor Roy Ascott at the University of Wales in 1988 and received an MFA degree from the University of Reading, England, in 1991. He was awarded the Prix Ars Electronica 'Golden Nica', in the category of interactive art for the hyper media installation 'Think about the People now' in Linz, Austria, in 1991. He produced the ISDN videoconference installation 'Telematic Vision' as an Artist in Residence at the Center for Art and Media (ZKM) in Karlsruhe, Germany, in 1993 and received the 'Sparkey Award' from the Interactive Media Festival in Los Angeles, for the telepresent video installation 'Telematic Dreaming' in 1994. Paul Sermon was a nominee at the World Technology Awards 2005 and holds a number of external appointments that influence research policy. Since 2004 he has been an AHRC Peer Review College member, member of the NWDA funded North West Art & Design Research Group, Chair of Media Arts Network Northwest [ma-net], and advises on various international journal and conference editorials. External collaborations include the AHRC funded REACT (Research Engine for Art and Creative Technology).

Kevin Miguel Sherman is a Ph.D. candidate at Auckland University of Technology. He also works as a researcher on the New Zealand component of the World Internet Project under the auspices of the Institute of Culture, Discourse and Communication which is headed by Professor Allan Bell. Mr. Sherman's research interests include the study of virtual worlds in situ, virtual world attachment, political activism on the Web, and more general Internet-related research.

Monika Wasilewska is a second year Ph.D. student and a part-time tutor at the School of Drama and Theater at Lodz University (Poland). Her academic research focuses on gender studies and queer theory as reference points in the study of modern culture, particularly theater and drama. Her Master's dissertation, entitled '(Re)constructions of Femininity and Masculinity in New Polish Drama,' was awarded by the Theater Institute in Warsaw and was singled out as one of the best dissertations completed at the Faculty of Philology (Lodz University) in the academic year 2007/2008. As an undergraduate, in 2007 and 2008 respectively, she received a prestigious Scholarship funded by the Ministry of Science and Higher Education. Apart from several academic articles published in conference proceedings, as a theater critic for *Gazeta Wyborcza*, the biggest Polish daily newspaper, she has written hundreds of reviews and articles. In 2008 she also received an annual prize for the best junior cultural critic.

Index